THE POLITICAL PHILOSOPHY OF ANTONIO GRAMSCI

The Political Philosophy of Antonio Gramsci

ADITI MISRA

Commonwealth Publishers
NEW DELHI-110002
(INDIA)

Published by

COMMONWEALTH PUBLISHERS
4378/4B, GALI MURARI LAL
ANSARI ROAD, NEW DELHI-110002
INDIA

First Published, 1991

ISBN 81-7169-126-9

THE POLITICAL PHILOSOPHY OF
ANTONIO GRAMSCI

Printed at

Gaurav Printers
Maujpur
Delhi-110053

Preface

Antonio Gramsci is the most prominent Marxist thinker after Marx and Lenin. He come into prominence in Western English speaking world during late fifties and early sixties. His views on state, hegemony intellectuals and his philosophical ventures into the fundamentals of Marxism were considered highly relevant for Western world where objective conditions pointed towards a revolution yet it failed to materialise. The countries of the Third World were enthralled by Gramsci's sharp analysis of peasantry. Still most of the works on Gramsci take up specific themes and very little work has been done to present the political philosophy of Gramsci incorporating his active political experience and analysing his theoretical formulations. Agianst this backdrop, the present study strives to attain precisely this objective.

In fact, the Gramsci studies gained momentum in English speaking world during the seventies. This was due to the advent of Eurocommunism. In Italy itself, Gramsci's writings were initially published in 1956-57 in parts, that may also be, as suggested by White in his article "Gramsci and the Italian Communist Party" to facilitate Togliatti's stances. With the establishment of Gramsci Institute in Rome, almost all his prison writings were published. Thus, when the English writings started they had the advantage of having access to all his writings in Italian. Despite all this, complete translations are still not available in English. The fragmented and scattered nature of the prison writings—mostly in the forms of notes and letters, and the polemical, pamphleteer's style of his writings before imprisonment and to the difficulties in undertaking a study on Gramsci.

In this perspective, the works done so far cover only partial aspects of Grasmscian political ideas and philosophy. Anderson in his artical "The antinomies of Antonio Gramsci" (1976-77) has criticised Gramsci's concept of hegemony and war of position on a more or less 'literal' reading. Boggs in his book, *Gramsci's Marxism* (1976) has presented a simplistic concept of hegemony without conprehending Leninist views. Buci-Glucksmann, in her book *Gramsci and the State* (1980), has analysed the concept of state in Gramsci against the reductionist concept of orthodox Marxism as well as structuralism. Cammett in *Gramsci and Origins of Italian Communism* (1967) has presented Gramscian ideas in the light of labour movement. Clark, in *Antonio Gramsci and The Revolution that failed* (1977) has also dwelt on Factory Council movement. Davidson in *Antonio Gramsci An Intellectual Biography* (1977), Fiori in *Antonio Gramsci* (1970) and Spriano in *Gramsci and the Party : the Prison Years* (1979) have dealt very extensively with biographical aspects of Gramsci. In David (Ed.) *Gramsci and Italy's Passive Revolution* (1979), passive revolution is discussed with reference to nineteenth century Italian history. Entwistle in *Antonio Gramsci—Conservative Schooling for Radical Politics* (1979) has for the first time in English analysed Gramsci's theory of education. Femia in *Gramsci's Political thought* (1981) has highlighted his concept of hegemony its prove his social-democrat leanings. Salamini, in *Sociology of Political Praxis* (1981) forcefully argues that Gramsci's Marxism is a sociological praxis. Admson in *Hegemony and Revolution* (1980) has stressed the cultural aspects of hegemony. Joll in *Gramsci* has presented a—succinct account of main idias of Gramsci. Sassoon in *Gramsci's Politics* (1980) has given a valuable account of his political ideas. Togliatti's *On Gramsci* (1979) deals with formation of Italian Communist Party. Urry in *The Anatomy of Capitalist Societies* (1981) has, for the first time, discussed civil society in great details. Nemeth's *Political Philosophy* (1980) has presented the idealist mooring of Gramsci's philosophy. This survey of literature reveals overemphasis on certain of his concepts—e.g. hegemony, passive revolution, gross neglect of certain aspects—his worldview, philosophy and politics in philosophical perspective. In India, apart from two M. Phil. theses in J.N.U., New Delhi by Miss. Madhu Prasad (1975) and Mr. L. Srinivas (1984), there has been no doctoral studies on Gramsci. A number of articles are found, the most recent being *Economic and Political Weekly*. (Details of all references here are given in bibliography).

In view of such paucity of work, the present study covering all aspects of Gramscian philosophy which is praxis—unity of theory and practice—strives to isolate the cardinal points of his philosophy and evaluate them in the light of his practice. Admittedly there are certain aspects that are not touched or discussed in detail due to the philosophical nature of the study. The writings on culture, education, literature and folklore, linguistics are discussed only in so far as they concern his philosophy as most of these issues deal with speific Italian developments. The universal points impinging on his political philosophy are discussed in the following way.

In the first chapter, the topic is discussed. As philosophy is the pursuit of knowledge especially that which deals with 'ultimate' reality; 'Reality', for Gramsci, does not exist in and for itself, but only in historical relationship with the men who modify it. Moreover, philosophy of each man is contained in his actions, and, therefore, philosophy is also politics. It is in this sense that we have taken the study of 'political philosophy' of Gramsci. In order to place evolution of Gramsci's politics in historical perspective, a socio-political account is given. A brief biographical sketch is presented to identify the 'permanent' elements of his philosophy that are explained in subsequent chapters. The burden of second chapter is to present the ideational background which shaped Gramsci's political philosophy. The third chapter analyses marxism as the worldview, the critical conception of the world. This *weltanschauung* of proletariat is based on philosophy of praxis and historical materialism. 'Historicism' precludes 'absolute' truths and 'truth' is a knowledge of reality as well as a tool to change this reality. The fourth chapter presents Gramsci's concept of intellectuals who articulate a worldview. Identified on the basis of their role in production processes, there are two categories of intellectuals—organic and traditional They operate essentially at the level of superstructure even though rooted in the structure. The study takes up the relationship between base and superstructure. The fifth chapter studies politics as an autonomous science. The proletariat organised in party, strikes to control the state. The sixth chapter studies various forms of state, its element of coercion and hegemony and strikes to discuss strategies suitable for different socio-economic conditions. The goal is the end of exploitation and ultimate absorption of political society into civil society. In the concluding chapter, after a critical appraisal of Gramscian political philosophy, a resume of conclusions as deduced in earlier chapters is presented. The key-note of the resume is—"The creation of Marxist state is the establishment of its worldveiw and its supercession is the end of the philosophy of praxis. It would be superceded by "the reabsorption of political society into civil society."

The methodology followed is historical—analytical.

A word about foot-notes. When a book is referred in the foot note for the first time, all the details name of the author, name of the book, publisher's name, place of publication and page number are given uniformly; but, in the subsequent references only the name of the author, name of the book and page number is given. Again, in the case of Antonio Gramsci, a few important quotations are repeated, but foot notes for such quotations are given only once when quoted for the first time. We have consulted two different editions of Gramsci's *Quaderni del Carcere* from Italian sources and therefore in one edition only note book number and fragment is given, otherwise general rule is followed.

I must express my deepest gratitude to Dr. (Miss) N. Pant who had to guide and encourage me to complete this work when the providence had deprived me of the able guidance of Prof. M. Jha under whom the work was started. Steering from midcourse is definitely much more difficult than from the start.

I find no words to acknowledge the guidance given by late Prof. Manoranjan Jha who persuaded me to take up the challenging work and prompted me to go adead.

My sincere thanks are due to Prof. H.N. Tripathi, Head, Department of Political Science, whose helpful advices have suitably improved the work.

I am thankful to the Indian Council of Social Science Research (ICSSR) for the assistance in the form of one year fellowship as well as travel grants. My thanks are also due to National Library, Calcutta, Ajay Bhawan Library, New Delhi, The Council of World Affairs, New Delhi, JNU Library, Delhi and Delhi University Library, New Delhi for their co-operation in collecting the material.

I express my sincer gratitude to Dr. Stefano De Santis, Lecturer of Italian, Dept. of Foreign Languages, B.H.U., for helping me in consulting the Italian sources of Gramsci's writings and other Italian literature on Gramsci.

ADITI MISRA

Contents

1

Introduction

The analysis of Gramsci's political philosophy presupposes an understanding of the term 'political philosophy'; and this in turn involves the knowledge of the term 'philosophy'.

'Philosophy is essentially a contraction of two Greek words meaning 'love of wisdom'. Literally, it may suggest the unfolding wisdom; but technically it may be defined as 'the critical evaluation of all the facts of experience'. The key term is 'evaluation'; since only philosophers evaluate while scientists describe facts. And, by way of evaluation the philosophers either give value-judgements or invest value into the 'fact' evaluated.

For Plato, philosophy originates with critical discussion; as such dialectical method is inherent in it. For him, this world is the world of 'daily change, or of mere appearances; it is the dialectics that enables 'philosophy' to probe through the shadow world and have a direct access to the 'ultimate reality'.

According to *The Oxford Dictionary*, philosophy is "love, study or pursuit of wisdom or knowledge, especially that which deals with ultimate reality or with the most general causes and principles of things".[1] For Thomson: "Philosophy arises out of intellectual curiosity from the need to understand ourselves and our world. Philosophy is not a substitute for action but an essential preparation for self-directed action which is undertaken with some assurances, that the course to be followed is wise and sound".[2] In fact, philosophy is "neither pure speculation nor pure criticism, *it is speculation controlled by criticism*".[3] It is "the science of general laws of being (i.e. of nature and society) and human thinking, the process of cognition.'[4]

And, if philosophy is the science of laws of being, political philosophy becomes "application of philosophy (mainly ethics) to questions relating to individuals as organized in a state"[5] According to *Encyclopaedia of Religion and Ethics,* political philosophy is but a part of political theory, the other part of political theory is political science or analysis of facts. Political philosophy implies "a criticism and moral evaluation of political society."[6]

Both the above viewpoints reveal two important concerns of political philosophy—the empirical study of men and their organizations and the philosophical reasons behind their behaviour. It follows that one can "look upon political philosophy as in some sense systematic, proceeding from a view of reality and knowledge (ontology and epistemology) to a view of the individual (psychology) and a view of the social bond (sociology) and so to a general ethic, a political ethic

---

1. J. Coulson, C.T. Carr, L. Hutchinson and D. Eagle (Ed.), *The Oxford Illustrated Dictionary*, Clarendon Press, Oxford, 1984, p. 634.
2. S.M. Thompson, *The Nature of Philosophy—An Introduction*, Holt, Rinehart & Winston, New York, 1961, p. 26.
3. P. Edwards (Ed.), *The Encyclopaedia of Philosophy*, Collier MacMillan Ltd., London, 1967, Vol. 6., p. 218. (Emphasis added).
4. I. Frilov (Ed.), *Dictionary of Philosophy* Progress Publishers, Moscow, 1980, p. 318.
5. A.C. Ewing, *The Fundamental Question of Philosophy*, Allied Publishers Pvt. Ltd., New Delhi, 1982, p. 16.
6. J. Hastings (Ed.), *Encyclopaedia of Religion and*, Ethics, Vol. X. T & T Clark Edinburg, 1963, p. 98.

and finally to a set of recommendations about the form of state and about political conduct".[1]

Gramsci emphatically denies the esoteric nature attributed to philosophy and declares; "It is essential to destroy the wide spread prejudice that philosophy is a strange and difficult thing just because it is the specific intellectual activity of a particular category of specialists or of professional and systematic philosophers."[2] Gramsci finds that, there are two categories of philosophy "spontaneous philosophy' which is proper to everybody,"[3] and a critical conception of the world. The term "philosophy" is often used to denote the latter category. However, there is an essential relationship between the two. As a matter of fact, critical philosophy carries a criticism of the spontaneous philosophy in order to attain a coherent view of the world. The critical conception of the world postulates a criticism of the past philosophies "in so far as this has left stratified deposits in popular philosophy."[4] Highlighting the differences between various philosophies, Gramsci perceived that until "classical German philosophy, philosophy was conceived as a receptive, or at the most an ordering activity, i.e. as knowledge of a mechanism that functioned objectively outside man. Classical German philosophy introduced the concept of 'creativity' of though, but in an idealistic and speculative senso."[5] It is manifest that Gramsci takes 'creative' in a relative sense. For him, "reality does not exist on its own, in and for itself, but only in an historical relationship with the men who modify it. etc."[6] Philosophy in this sense, is the history of an epoch which it represents. Since there are broadly two categories of philosophy—viz. incoherent view of masses and critical

---

1. Paul Edwards, *Encylcopaedia of Philosophy*, Vol. 6, p. 370.
2. Antonio Gramsci, *Selections From Prison Notebooks*, (translated by O. Hoare and G.N. Smith), Lawrence and Wishart, London, 1978, p. 323.
3. *Ibid.*
4. *Ibid.*, p. 324
5. *Ibid.*, p. 346.
6. *Ibid.*, p. 346.

philosophy—it is clear that "Philosophy in general does not in fact exist. Various philosophies or conceptions of the world exist, and one always makes a choice between them."[1]

It, thus, follows that in order to make philosophy 'critical', a conscious choice has to be made in an "'historicist' fashion, and at the same time to put the 'will' (which in the last analysis equals practical or political activity) at the base of philosophy. But it must be rational, not an arbitrary, will, which is realized in so far as it corresponds to objective historical necessities, or in so far as it is universal history itself in the moment of its progressive actualisation."[2] The practical viability and effectiveness are therefore the essential requirements along with its theoretical tenets. Thought and action are, thus, inherent components of philosophy. As such, a contradiction between professed goal and action reveals an incoherent view of the world.

It is against this backdrop that Gramsci queries: "And since all action is political, *can one not say that the real philosophy of each man is contained in its entirety in his political action*?"[3] and exhorts "*every, philosophy is a 'politics.'*"[4]

This viewpoint postulates a wider meaning and scope of 'political philosophy.' To make it a historical reality, the study of philosophy requires a study of the cultural setting in which political activity takes place. And, to make the philosophy acceptable to the masses a "'cultural-social' unity through which a multiplicity of dispersed wills, with hetrogeneous aims, are welded together with a single aim,"[5] is required. "In this sense," according to Gramsci, "the real philosopher is, and cannot be other than, the politician, the active man who modifies the environment, understanding by

1. *Ibid.*, p. 326.
2. *Ibid.*, p. 345.
3. *Ibid*, p. 326 (Emphasis added).
4. *Ibid.*, p. 372 (Emphasis added.)
5. *Ibid.*, p. 349.

environment the *ensemble* of relations which each of us enters to take part in."[1]

In order to undertake a study of political philosophy of Antonio Gramsci, it, thus, becomes imperative to understand the ensemble of relations—to be exact, the historical, the socio-cultural and political setting—that gave shape to his ideas.

II

The political climate in which Gramsci was born in 1891 and acquired his roots, was laid up by the settlement of 1871. It had redrawn the map of Europe, as a result of which six big powers had emerged on the international scene—England, Russia, France, Germany, Austria-Hungary and Italy—Italy being the weakest among the big powers. The settlement had left intact the three sprawling dynastic empires of Eastern Europe—Austria-Hungary, Russia and Turkey: it had endorsed the emergence of Germany and Italy as unified nations and had put its seal of approval on the Third Republic of France. The subsequent settlement of the Balkans in 1878 by the Congress of Berlin had brought Russia back into the fold of European diplomacy in so far as it then became an integral factor in the international balance of power.[2]

Henceforth, diplomacy involved all the six powers in a system of alliances which ultimately divided Europe into two power blocs,[3] culmination of which was the sad advent of the

1. *Ibid.*, p 352.
2. In fact, among the six big powers that emerged as a result of 1871 settlement, Britain was the biggest sea and colonial power. Her interest was paramount in non-European politics ; Russia was the biggest territorial power and in this capacity her primary interest lay in Eastern and far Eastern politics. But the Near Eastern question and the Berlin Settlement of 1978 threw doors open for her to get involved in European politics.
3. The two power blocs were *Entente* bloc and the Triple Alliance bloc. *Entente* powers were Britain, France and Russia. Triple Alliance bloc was formed by Germany, Austria Hungary and Italy.

First World War in 1914. The tragic alliance system was manipulated in the beginning by Bismarck, the German Chancellor, in search of his nation's security against France. It ended by embroiling all the powers in War. Italy, the weakest of the big powers, joined the Alliance system in the hope of improving her position in the international politics; and to attain her aim she played 'the jackal policy'. She entered into Triple Alliance with Germany and Austria-Hungary in 1882. However, without formally renouncing the Triple Alliance, she joined the War in 1915 against her Triple Alliance partners and in favour of Triple *Entente* powers (England, France and Russia) by signing the secret Treaty of London.

The significant feature of the period of forty year after the settlement of 1871 is that it was a period of internal tension between forces seeking to consolidate the political and social order that had been established by it (the settlement of 1871), and rival forces seeking to transform society by new forms of organizational reforms. These were also the years of peace in the sense that hardly any conflict between nations culminated in an open war despite the prevailing atmosphere of distrust and hatred. In fact, it was, as has rightly been termed, an 'era of armed peace'.

Two elements made the situation complicated. First, the restless nationalist aspirations of the people of the Balkans; and second, the overseas rivalries of the great powers themselves for possession of colonial lands. Behind these political and diplomatic entanglements lay the socio-economic realities of increasing population and the problems of industrialization, investment, trade, etc., in shifting ratios.

The forces of continuity and change both were active in the period of an uneasy peace (1871-1914). The forces of continuity were those liberal-conservative constitutions, classes and creeds who were trying to find stability through wider electorate and parliamentary representative institutions and central authority. The forces of change and revolution were those socialist, anarchist and communist movements who were demanding more complete democracy and economic reorganization of the social system.

In almost the whole of Western and Central Europe, parliamentary institutions developed between 1871 and 1974—although they varied widely in form and effectiveness. France was ahead of all in having effective universal male suffrage. The electoral laws of 1848, that were revived in 1871, and again in 1875, gave the vote to some ten million people. The electorate of United Kingdom after the Act of 1884 consisted of about five million (roughly 1/6 of the population). Switzerland had universal male suffrage after 1874. In Belgium until 1893, property-qualification restricted the electorate to less than five per cent, but a reform of that year brought universal male suffrage. In the Netherlands, reforms of 1887 and 1896, extended the electorate from 2% to 14% of the population; universal suffrage in 1890; Norway pioneered female suffrage in 1907. In Portugal and Sweden electorate remained comparatively restricted until after 1900.

The two new states—Germany and Italy—were quite different in that respect. Bismarck had permitted universal male sufferage for the election of the members of *Reichstag*; but the real power was wielded by the *Bundestat* (Upper House), and still more by the Emperor and the Chancellor. In Italy the constitutional monarchy retained its mid-nineteenth century restrictions. Even the electoral reforms of 1882 widened the electorate to only about two million or 7% of population. Most Italian men gained voting rights in 1912. The age for voting rights was twenty-one in the United Kingdom, France and in most of the other countries. In Germany it was 25, and in Italy it was as high as 30 even in 1914.[1]

It is a common knowledge that the vote of the masses could successfully be utilized to favour a strong government with nationalist policies as well as to favour revolutionary forces. In France it was used to a type of moderate

---

1. All these figures are taken from D. Thompson, *Europe Since Napoleon*, Hazall Watson and Viney Ltd., Penguin Books, Harmondsworth, Middlesex, 1966, pp. 351-353.

republicanism. The crushing of Paris Commune[1] in 1871 is a case in point. Same is true with Bismarck's manipulations of German *Reichstag* and Crispi's domination of the Italian Parliament.[2]

The growth of population and the comparative enlargement of the electorate made the masses conscious of their rights. With the success of Industrial Revolution, there was a shift in population from rural areas to industrial towns; and in consequence this 'flight to towns' opened various problems to be tackled by the state, such as arrangements for the dwelling and better working conditions of the wage-earning class, etc. However, this demand for an active State function came into conflict with the then established liberal philosophy of *laissez faire*. The formation of determined public opinion made possible because of the growth/emergence of education, popular association and press[3]—intensified the demand for a positive state.

And, this 'Cry of the Times' paved the way for articulating such new and scientific doctrines as realism, positivism, secularism, nationalism, etc., along with consolidating socialist and Marxist doctrines of having either 'maximum' and 'minimum' aims. The choice before the socialists was one of basic method and stratagy. Should they try to get political power by working within the framework of parliamentary democracy or should they preserve intact their revolutionary impulse and strive to crush capitalism *in toto* through socialist revolution?

---

1. Pair Commune (March 1 71-May 1871) was set up after elections were held in Paris under the leadership of miscellaneous group of revolutionaries. This popularly elected govt. ol Paris was crushed by regular troops after bitter fighting.
2. In 1894, Italian premier Crispi launched an attack on the socialists, dissolving their associations, suppressing their newspapers and arresting many people.
3. In France *L'Humanite* edited by socialist Jean Jaures, in Germany the Social-Democrats' *Vorwarts* ; in Britain *The Daily Herald*, and in Italy *Avanti* (to which Gramsci also contributed), have a central importance in the history of socialism.

The failure of the Paris Commune resulted in the development first in Germany and then in nearly every other country of 'Social-Democratic' parties-these manifested the former type of socialist method and strategy; whereas Syndicalist and Anarchist Movements in France and Russia represented the latter strategy. However, socialist thinkers of all kinds whether backing revolutionary or democratic programmes had this common point that they were more interested in the social-economic restructuring of the society rather than on such short-term gain as immediate increase in pay, shortening of working hours, etc. As such the socialist programmes were primarily the initiative of the intellectuals and political agitators rather than of masses. Social democratic norms were spread by German Social Democratic Party (formed in 1875), the British Democratic Federation (formed in 1881), Fabian Society (1884) and Independent Labour Party (1893).

In Italy the socialist party was founded by Turati (1857-1932) in 1892 and a Marxist ideology was supplied to it by Antonio Labriola (1843-1904), a Roman professor. However, the economic backwardness of the country kept it relatively unimportant.

In Russia, Plekhanov (1857-1918) founded the first Russian Marxist Party in 1883. In the beginning, the Social Democratic Party was modelled upon the Social Democrats of Germany. But in 1903 its course was altogether changed due to the advent of Lenin (1870-1924) on the scene. Lenin was convinced that the future lay only with a highly organized movement and a disciplined revolutionary party. Such a chasm was bound to lead to a break in the party that occurred in the same year. As a result two groups emerged—Mensheviks (minority men) under Martov (1873-1923) and Bolsheviks (the majority men) under Lenin. Trotsky (1877-1940) supported Mensheviks, who yielded a party comparable to German Social Democrats. Bolsheviks, under Lenin, were those who were in favour of controlling the party by means of a small elite, the fanatical and organized experts who would be ruthless in their revolutionary policy. So was born modern Bolshevism, the nucleus of Russian Communist State of today. The aim of this party was to capture complete political power by the total overthrow of the existing regime.

Thus, socialist parties before 1914 had two forms-first, the parliamentary democratic form as manifested in the British and Scandinavian Labour parties and the parliamentary socialist groups of France and Italy; and second, socialist revolutionary parties as manifested by the Russian Democratic party after 1903 under Lenin. The nomeclature 'socialism' to the former and 'communism' to the latter was given as late as in 1918.

The history of International Working Men's Association[1] makes the connections and conflicts between the tow forms of socialism more manifest. If the First International was destroyed because of the tension between 'Marxists' and 'Anarchists', the Second International[2] was divided on two issues—first, whether the socialists should accept ministerial offices along with the non-socialists in the government; and second, in the event of a war, whether the socialists should join it to defend the nation. These issues were the touchstone of the choice between socialism and nationalism. The Western social-democrats like Jaures (1856-1914) and Babel (1840-1913)

---

1. International Working Men's Association (The First International) was founded in 1864 in London. The Paris Commune (1871) was hailed by International as its own influence. It had internal squabbles over its aim and split in 1872. Proudhon, Bakunin and Lassalle too were members of the First International ; and Bakunin and Marx had sharp differences over organizational issues—the former advocating a loose association of independent groups as in a federation with practically no central authority and the latter stressing the need for a disciplined political party working towards conquest of State. International was dissolved in 1876.
2. In 1889 a new Socialist International (Second International) was founded. Engels played on active role in it. From the very beginning it was confronted by differences between anarchists and socialists. It stressed on political actions thereby successfully excluding anarchists who distrusted political action. It could not solve doctrinaire differences of the two factions of Russian Socialist Party. It could not give a satisfactory answer to the question of participation in nationalist wars. Lenin denounced its bankruptcy in not turning the war into struggle for revolution.

believed that workers' interest lay in ending the war by whatever means it may be possible even by general strike and sabotage. Lenin and Rosa Luxemburg (1870-1919) held that a European War would so weaken the machinery of the capitalist state that Socialist Revolution would become possible. Against this backdrop, it was not a surprise that in 1914 socialist parties in almost every country backed their national governments in the War.

Such was the socio-political scenario and international climate in which Gramsci was born and grew as a boy. In his youth, which came to a tragic end in 1937, he saw the devastation wrought by the First World War, emergence of the Soviet State and an uneasy peace settlement which gave birth to Fascism, Nazism and the world economic crisis. All this ultimately led to the Second World War in 1939.

The International situation, emerging out of the Great War, in 1920s was a temporary redistribution of the balance of power. The simultaneous military and political collapse of old Russian, Turkish, Austro-Hungarian and German empires and the victoro of Allied powers brought a new constellation of big powers. Along with three European powers—Britain, France and Italy—two non-European powers—the USA and Japan—emerged on the international scene as big powers. The map of Central and Eastern Europe was redrawn in a way that replaced the old dynastic frontiers by new frontiers based on realities of national grouping, economic viability and of military security; thus, Poland was revived, Yugoslavian territories extended and Czechoslovakia created.

If one consequence of the War was to translate nationalist enthusiasms into reality—though this principle was also violated at places to suit the demands of the victors—the second was to bring democratic ideals and institutions to people who had not known them before. Accordingly, in one defeated country after another, new democratic constitutions were set-up—Germany set the pace with the establishment of Weimer Republic. Social Democrats supported the new assembly; independent socialists and the Marxian Spartacits led by Karl Liebknecht (1871-1919) and Rosa Luxemburg echoing Lenin's cry 'all power to the Soviets' opposed it. An attempted communist revolution in 1919 failed and both Liebknecht and Luxemburg were killed. The same year saw the creation of German workers party. It attracted demoralized soldiers, political intrigues, etc. The next year Adolf Hitler (1889-1945), an unknown Austrian ex-corporal, joined the party and it was renamed the National Socialist German Workers' Party. In spirit the party was anti-democratic, anti-liberal and anti-communist. In November 1923, the party attemped a putsch in Munich and Hitler was imprisoned for five years. In fact, he prepared the first volume of his autobiography—*Mein Kampf*. Here were all the ingredients of the party that overthrew Weimer Republic ten years later and established the Nazi rule.

In Italy the constitutional monarchy of king Victor Emmanuel III survived the World War; but political and social conditions for democracy there were no better than in Germany. Although, Italy was among the victors, the Peace Settlement could not fulfil her ambitions (guaranteed by Allies by secret treaties); and the remained ever dissatisfied. By 1919 the Fascists (fasces being the symbol of authority) had formed a strong arm-fighters group under the leadership of Mussolini (1883-1945), the former socialist journalist. In the elections of 1921, the fascists gained thirty five seats and in October 1922, after a successful 'March On Rome', they captured political power and formed the government. Democracy on the defensive after 1918, was completely overthrown by 1924.

In Austria, Hungary, Poland, Greece, Yugoslavia and Bulgaria democracy was equally short-lived. However, in Baltic borderland, ceded by Russia in 1918, and recognized as the independent states of Finland, Estonia, Latvia, Lithuania and in Czechoslovakia democratic institutions were somewhat more durable. In most of the Eastern European countries the fragile democratic institutions that came up after the First World War culminated in people's democracies after 1945.

In resume, it can be said that the uncertainty and instability caused by the First World War had far reaching consequences. First in time, occurred the triumph of

Bolshevism under the leadership of Lenin in 1917; then came the victory of fascism in 1922, followed by the World Economic Crisis between 1929-34, and the resurgence of Japan and Germany as aggressive powers. The period also saw civil wars either in the latent form of a clash between communism and fascism (as in Spain). By this time, Gramsci was lying seriously ill in his death bed in the fascist prison; and the fascist powers—Berlin, Rome and Tokyo—had already formed their axis.

The Second World War was not far away.

III

Born in Ales, Sardinia, Gramsci became hunchback at the age of four as a result of an accident and suffered severe internal bleedings that contributed to a fragile physique and wounded emotions of abnormality. He was good at studies in liceo, but due to economic hardships had to discontinue studies for a couple of years that gave birth to an envy and hatred for the rich. Form 1908 to 1911, he went to study at Caglieri in senior liceo. His introduction to politics began here. The protests in 1906 in Sardinia against mainland too effected his formulations. He advocated a Sardinian nationalism and became aware of the peasants problems as well as of the regional issues.

Italian society was largely agricultural; however the process of industrialization in the North had aleady brought changes in the social structure in that region. Moreover, as Davidson says : "The breking-up of feudal estates during the Napoleanic wars had created a middle class in the North but the equivalent process in the South had merely resulted in a reconcentration of land as private property in the hands of former feudal magnates".[1] The appalling conditions in South gave birth to brigandry. The frequent uprisings in the 1890s had led to a period of repression and in its midst the Socialist

---

1. A. Davidson, *The Theory And Practice of Italian Communism*, Vol. I, Merlin Press, London, 1982, pp. 23-24.

Party (PSI) gained ground but only to fight for bourgeois liberties. It had as yet no redical programme. The South and the peasant masses, who were the followers of Bakumin[1] and opposed PSI's collaboration with other bourgeois classes, had to accept PSI support in the face of severe government repression to crush peasant uprising during 1892-1894 (where PSI heroically decided to take the blame for these). By 1900, the PSI also adopted policies favouring North and diluting its revolutionary content. There was a tendency in the North to blame South's poor development to its feudal forces and peasantry; and this tendency also influenced government policies. The South, in turn, blamed the North as an exploiter and accused it of acting as an imperialist power towards South.

In this social, political and economic milieu, Gramsci's ideas took shape. He came to realize the importance of social perception and its relationship with dailect. He also came to understand the way these (social perceptions) are perceived from a global or eclectic point of view. This largely depended on exposure to other languages (besides dialect which widened the horizon. As a matter of fact, the dialect gave one a basic approach to social conditions. He identified the ills of society and came to the conclusion that those were the outcome of division of society into the oppressors and the oppressed. He was also convinced that this class division had to be cured by the society itself. Gramsci, thus, had already begun to confront the problems of Italian socialism—but only as a Southerner.

In 1911, Gramsci won a scholarship to study in the University of Turin, politically one of the most active centres in Italy. His contact with the intellectuals of his time began here. His ideational background was also nurtured here as he

---

1. M.A Bakunin (1814-1876), Russian anarchist, whose conflict with Marx during 1869-71 broke up the First International. Bakunin advocated violent struggle or individual acts of terrorism in order to bring about revolutionary change. Marx and Engels criticised him for petty-bourgeois revolutionary ideas.

studied in detail the Italian masters; viz. Croce (1866-1952), Labriola (1893-1964) et al. Togliatti (1893-1964), a future friend and fellow communist also joined the University at the same time. Gramsci was exposed to the condition of a large industrial working class here. The doctrines of liberalism, catholicism, socialism were in the air. In fact, the inadequacies of liberalism led to a discussion of the socialist doctrines as an alternative for Italy; and many professors entered into this debate and made contacts with the socialist movement.

Gramsci also joined the fray and came in contact with the Italian variety of Marxism characterized as 'the philosophy of praxis'. The chief proponent of the term, Antonio Labriola (1843-1904), had advocated a unity of theory and practic while stressing on the primacy of concrete relations over consciousness. But unfortunately attempts were made to subsume him as an idealist and anti-materialist by the adherentof Rodolfo Mondolfo and Giovanni Gentilc (1875-1944). Gentile, had in the beginning toyed with the ideas of Marx but later on had turned to fascism, Mondolfo had tried to show the hiatus between Marx and Engels and carried an idealist interpretation. Labriola, Gentile and Mondolfo, gave it (plaxis) atleast three meanings;[1] and without tracing the

---

1. For Gentile, 'praxis' is a 'mediation' between man and nature. "Praxis is absorbed in the reality of the Spirit, which is Action". As Thought is real and absolute, Idea is object of Thought, Praxis is unity of thought and action. So philosophy of praxis is "the concept of knowing understood as doing". It is an "autopraxis". See Gentile, *La Reforma della Dialettica hegeliana*, quoted in Christine Buci-Glucksmann, *Gramsci and the State*, (Trans. by D. Fernbach) Lawrence and Wishart, London, 1980, p. 299.
   For Labriola, historical materialism was a method of research and not a design for change since "the sole given from which flowed all other particular practical social form, through determinate links". To understand given facts, the need is to start from highest development of thought which is a product of specific practice. This Marxism or philosophy of praxis postulated clear knowledge of objective world and past practice to understand history. See Labriola, "In Memory Communist Manifesto" *Essays on the Materialistic Conception of History*, Charles H. Kerr & Co., Chicago, 1908, p. 106.

roots of Gramscian usage, he may also be interpreted as an idealist.[1] A close scrutiny, however, reveals that Gramsci is deeply critical of Mondolfo and tried to restore the Marxian ideas of Labriola.

The influence of the most prominent neo-Hegelian, Benedetto Croce,[2] on the other hand, is undeniably great on Gramsci. Croce was for a time, pupil of Labriola but later on became a strong critic of Marxism. He exercised a great influence among the youths, including those of the left, on account of his anti-positivist stance. Gramsci was one who was greatly influenced by Croce. He himself later on referred to his approach as being "tendentially Crocean"[3] in his youth. But, gradually he outgrew this phase in the process of analysing the tenets of Marxism and carried out a critique of Croce.

The political climate of Turin, the 'petrograd of Italy, as Gramsci referred it, was very conducive for the grooming of a Marxist. Turin had advanced industries, notable FIAI, and a large number of worker including women. The heavy industry along with the cotton and wool industries had made much headway during the 1911 Libyan War,[4] and favoured neutrality in order to maintain their supplies to belligerent countries. This gave birth to the phenomenon of Taylorism[5] to raise

---

For Mondolfo, Marxism is "Voluntarism of praxis" where Conscious Will is an integral part of history. The effect of conscious action becomes cause of the subsequent action, even when it is the consciousness of lack which stimulates man to action. The 'critical-practical' theory of Marxism regards "consciousness and will" at the base of historical process. For Modnolfo, future action is the key to praxis. See Mondolfo, *Unanismo di Marx studi filosofic 1908-1966*, quoted in Davidson, *The Theory and Practice of Italian Communism*, Vol. I, pp. 66-68.

1. See Chap. II for a detailed discussion of idealist influence on Gramsci.
2. See Chap. II for detailed ideas of Croce.
3. Quoted in G.N Smith and Q. Hoare (edited and translated), 'Introduction' to Gramsci, *Selections From Prison Notebooks.*
4. In their search for a North African empire, Italians conquered Tripolitania and Libya from the Turks in 1911.
5. See Chapters II & VI.

productivity. (Gramsci, later on analysed its genesis when he was in the fascist prison). The workers were militant, although only few were organized in trade unions. There were strikes in 1907, 1912 and later on in 1913. Gramsci had first hand experience of workers struggle then (1912-1913). He had already joined the Socialist Youth Federation (SYF) in 1912-1913, butwas not very active.

In Turin, Salvemini, (a southerner) and Mussolini were two different types of heroes of socialist youth. The former, championing the cause of peasants had opposed the 1911 Libyan war through the columns of *L'Unita*, an organ for advocating a genuine unity of North and South Italy. Mussolini too opposed Libyan was in 1912. Parliamentary elections on the basis of universal suffrage in 1913 enthused Gramsci and he became interested in campaign sponsored by the Turinese section of the Socialist Party to elect a representative who could fight for 'more democracy in the South'. He started teaching workers enrolled in Youth Federation (F.G.S.I.) of the PSI. All these incidents led him away from his 'Southernism' in so far as he began to confront the problems of Italian socialism. He now realized that peasants and workers were natural allies in the struggle against Northern capitalists and feudal leaders. Gramsci's definite entry into the Italian socialist movement took place when he joined the Turin section of the Italian Socialist Party (PSI) along with Palmiro Togliatti in 1913. He started writing for the paper of Turinese socialist section, *Il Grido del popolo* (*The Cry of the People*).

The PSI at this juncture was dominated by left leaders; but its over-riding concern was to maintain unit between all factions of the party at any cost. The phenomenon of maximalism[1] was a product of this conflict between left and unita-

---

1. Maximalism, for Gramsci, is "to govern without having direct responsibility for government ; to compel the bourgeois government —through terror and through the strength of the unions and the parliamentary group—to implement that *limited degree of socialism which can be implemented in Italy, given the country's economic* (*Contd.*)

rist interests. The outbreak of the First World War saw the emergence of many leaders who later on had decisive role to play in the Italian politics. The Turin branch of PSI gave rise to Angelo Tasca who later on became the leader of the right wing of the PCI. Gramsci and Togliatti took an intransigent attitude against class collaborationism and passivity. Bordiga (1889-1970), a Neapolitan and Prominent Youth Federation leader favoured intransigence in order to make possible a return to Marxist orthodoxy and purity of class struggle. It is surprising that Mussolini, who later became the Fascist leader, was the first socialist to demand a change in the policy of neutrality in 1914 and Gramsci had supported him. Both abhorved the possivity of the party and advocated 'active neutrality'.[1] When Mussolini changed to interventionism, Gramsci[2] withdrew his support. But this mistake forever posed for Gramsci a problem of credibility in factional struggles of the party. Bordiga regarded the war as between different groups of capitalists fighting for shares in the world market. By 1915-16 he came to accet PSI's stance of neutrality. With worsening condition he wanted to engineer a revolution on class lines. He denounced the old methods of PSI as

---

condition and the danger of a blockade". See Gramsci, "Caporetto And Vittorio Veneto", *Selections from Political Writings*, Vol. II (translated and edited by Quintin Hoare) Lawrence and Wishart, London, 1978, p. 4.

1. The official line of PSI towards war was one of neutrality and it advocated 'neither support, nor sabotage'. Mussolini favoured 'active neutrality' stressing the combativity of masses. Gramsci, too, wanted to change to active, operative neutrality to prepare for revolution. That the perspective of Mussolini was different, became clear to Gramsci only later when Mussolini advocated interventionism. Despite Gramsci's opposition to imperialist war, this association with Mussolini tained his record.
2. Among the Interventionists, there were three sections—(1) nationalist and war-mongering factions (absorbed afterwards by fascists); (2) Southern Socialists who considered War as an opportunity to uphold the rights of peasantry; and (3) Social-Democrats and radicals of Risorgimento derivation who saw in the War a chance to defeat autocratic forces.

bourgeoisie and advocated new methods and stressed the need for a new International.

After his political initiative of supporting Mussolini's stance certainly a wrong one as st proved when Mussolini changed position, Gramsci joined PSI weekly, *Il Grido del Popolo* in 1915 and became a full-time journalist. His writings ranged from political commentary to international events. From 1916, he became theatre critic of *Avanzil* and wrote execlusively on cultural issues. He spent war years studying Marxist texts. The Russian Revolution decisived turned Gramsci away from idealist tendency and he was no longer "tendentially Crocean". He welcomed the Revolution in an article "The Revolution Against Das Capital" and stressed that the revolution had gone against a literal application of the text of Capital. As against a whole line of thought which regarded that socialism can be brought about only after undergoing the various stages of capitalist development, Gramsci welcomed the fact of Russian revolution as being truly Marxist. Despite Russia being a backward country, the Bolsheviks grasped the crup of Marx's philosophy that provided for active role of men in the process of history. In this context Gramsci said : "We... are convinced that the Russian Revolution is more than a proletarian event, it is a prolatarian act which must naturally lead to a socialist regime."[1] He further claimed : "The Bolshevik revolution consists more of ideologies than of events. This is the revolution against Karl Marx's *Capital.* In Russia, the *Capital* was more of a book of bourgeoisie than of the proletariat. It stood as a critical demonstration of how events should follow a predetermined course, how in Russia a bourgeoisie had to develop—before the proletariat could even thing in term of its revolt—The Bolsheviks are not 'Marxists'...They live Marxist thought—Thsi thought sees as the dominant factor in history not raw economics but men in society..."[2] Turin, too,

---

1. Gramsci, "Notes on Russian Revolution", *Selections From Political Writings* Vol. 1 (trnns. by J. Mathews,ed. by Q. Hoare), Lawrence and Wishart, London, 1977, p. 29.
2. Gramsci "The Revolution Against *Das Capital*" *Ibid.* pp. 34-35.

responded to Russian Revolution and the discontent with War, food crisis etc. spurred the proletariat to emulate the Russian example.

A spontaneous insurrection caught the PSI off guard in which anarchists were in the forefront. After four days of disorder, this insurrection was quelled and almost all the prominent socialist leaders were arrested. By then, Gramsci had become the editor of the *Il Grido del Popolo*—one of the few legally existing organs of the PSI, as others were banned by the government. He also occupied high post in the clandestine committee supervising the PSI activities. At a special conference of the PSI held in Florence in November 1917, Bordiga called for revolution and Gramsci supported him. But the PSI continued with 'neither support nor sabotage of war' policy and did not take action to turn the tide in favour of revolution.

By the time the war ended, Italy was in the grip of severe economic crisis. The situation for revolution seemed ripe. Bordiga was the first to grasp the importance of a disciplined vanguard party to lead a revolution, as was evident from Soviet example, and advocated the formation of PCI. For Gramsci the Soviet experience, the setting up of bodies of workers outside government was vital; and he tried to emulate this new apparatus of proletarian power in the process of revolution for Italy. In the next few years he became the advocate of Soviet model of Workers' Council for Italy. This preoccupation with workers' bodies took him to the heart of workers' struggle and helped him in formulating his orientations.

In fect, Italy at the end of the war, witnessed severe economic as well as socio-political problems. The agriculture was so badly effected that large number of peasants were ruined and petit-bourgeoisie got reduced to proletriat. But industry was thriving and government successfully tried to promoted reformist trade union leaders in order to diffuse worker's uprisings The defeat in 1917 of Italy at Caparetto[1]

---

1. Italian force facing Austrians were demoralised and were deserting the war. At the behest of General Cadorna, a confrontation at

had shwoed the hollowness of the War and leaders' resposibility for it. People, therefore, turned to PSI. In March 1919 the PSI welcomed the formation of the Third International.[1] The party also voted for working for the establishment of Soviet in Italy.

In 1919 elections PSI got 156 out of the total of 508 deputies in the parliament and received two million votes. Its membership multiplied and revolutionary rhetoric accentuated. It sent chills down the hrart of capitalists. Yet no concurrent planning, organization of its ranks was done; no allies were sought among peasantry and agriculture labourer. The Catholic Popular Party[2] fully utilized peasant discontest and origanized them. hhe discontented soldiers, too, received no succour from PSI and turned to fascists. In 1919, Gramsci Tasca, Toliatti and Terracini started *L'Ordine Nuovo* (The New Order) weekly to propagate their understanding of Leninisms Bordiga's *Il Soviet* and Serrati's *II Communismo* also helped in the understanding of Leninism. The important point to note is that Gramsci earlier wanted an educational movement to carry out a critique of the old civilization and from a new culture in order to destroy the old ideas and create new ones; but now he whole-heartedly devoted himself to the establishment of Factory Councils on the model of the Soviets. The existing Internal Commissions developed during the War into Factory Councils were to be used for the new conciliar system.

In fact, Gramsci's concept of worker's Council took place against the backdrop of practical experience in

---

Caparetto took place resulting in mass kilings and defeat of Italians.

1. Third International (1919-43) was formed in order to get rid of reformist tendencies of the *Second International* and to formulate tactics to deal with chnnging socio-political scene. The main architect of Third International was Lenin.

2. Catholic Popular Party, as its name suggests was supported by the Vatican and founded in 1919. It tried to provide a focus for the demands of peasants who were struggling for land reforms with increasing militancy.

factories—especially in the industrial triangle of Turin, Milan and Geneva. Various unions had erupted struggle for worker's right. For Gramsci, the councils were very different from trade-unions. Trade unions worked within the framework of bourgeois society; whereas the Factory Councils were conceived to be instrumental for the revolutionary transformation of Italy into a future socialist state. Bordiga attacked these ideas as 'syndicalist' and accused Gramsci of underestimating the power of the State.

L'Or. ine Nuovo group, despite its syndicalist tendencies, now clearly perceived the tremendous role of masses in the making of socialist state. It realized that mere seizure of power without mass support connot be successful. Councils were required to make masses aware of the goals of revolution. In April 1920, employers in a bid to cripple factory council movement, declared lock-out. The workers occupied factories in protest and appealed to other factories and other cities to follow the lead. Appeals were also made to PSI and trade unions. The strike spread to Piedmont, continued in metal industry in Turin for one month and paralysed Turin for ten days. Yet it failed as no organization came to its hely. The *L' Ordine* group was thoroughly disillusioned with the PSI; and so was Bordiga, albeit for different reasons.[1] Bordiga called a meeting of left factions of PSI. He himself favoured electoral abstentionism'.[2] Gramsci wanted non abstentionist platform based on *Comintern guidelines.*[3] Bordiga hostility for conciliar

1. Bordiga disapproved of maximalist view of PSI and favoured their expulsion. In their place, he wanted strict adherence to political plan of party.
2. Bordiga wanted the party to abstain from elections because he felt, bourgeoisie with their power and wealth use elections to strengthen their privileges.
3. At the second Congress of Comintern held in Moscow in July 1920, the executive committee bublished Twenty-one conditions to which parties desirous of joining Comintern must conform. Among other things, these conditions stressed on maintaining discipline in party, even at the cost of a split, over issues of principle and 'unconditional support' of every member party to any Soviet republic in its struggle against counter-revolutionary forces. It further stressed that decisions of Comintern Congress and executive committee were to be binding on all member parties.

movements and his indictment of *Nuovo group* for their exclusive emphasis on economic sphere ignoring the main objective of overthrow of state by a party, drew into open differences within the *Nuovo group*. Tasca urged a return to traditional organizations. Terracini and Togliatti leaned towards maximalists. Bordiga's theory of 'objective forces'[1] clashed with Gramsci's philosophy of praxis. Gradually Gramsci too came to realize the need for a party, but Bordiga could never understand the role of the masses and the need to make them conscious.

Gramsci wrote in 1920 ; "The existence of a cohesive and strongly disciplined Communist Party, which through its factory, trade union and co-operotive nuclei, co-ordinates and centralises within its own executive committee all of proletariat's revolutionary activity, is the fundamental and indispensable condition for attempting any Soviet experiment."[2] In the second Congress of the International Lenin described this article as "fully in keeping with the fundamental principles of the Third International.[3] After the Congress, Bordiga gave up abstentionism but Serrati refused to expel reformists, thus strengthening Bordiga's resolve for creating PCI and excluding the 'centrists' from it. Bordiga differed with the International over the question of winning over majority of working class and stressed on a pure, doctrinaire, rigid course. His view was that let the masses follow the party. The question of winning the masses, according to him, was the concern of 'centrists' of the PSI. Bordiga opposed

---

1. Bordiga believed that international developments in the realm of economics created revolutionary situation on international scale. He asked all communists to wait for objective international conditions, that wonld inevitably carry the masses to revolution. This view excluded daily struggles of masses. The spontaneous movements were to be ignored by the party . . . 'the single, exclusive organization of the proletariat.' This view also generated passivity among the ranks of the party and alienated it from masses.
2. Gramsci, "For a Renewal of Socialist Party," quoted in Introduction to *Selections from Prison Notebooks*, p. XI.
3. *Ibid.*

mass movements not controlled and guided by the party, like the Turin movement. He enjoyed a dominant position among left socialists and communists of PSI. He criticised United Front policy of Comintern ;[1] his differences with Gramsci thus remained intact. While Itlian delegates were returning from Second Comintern Congress at Moscow in September 1920, occupation of factories in Milan started. The time of confrontation with workers on the threat of lock-out at a factory, was again chosen by employers but proletarian response was impressive. The occupation spread and with it became clear the impact of the idea of *L'Ordine Nuovo* on the working class. Gramsci threw himself wholeheartedly in the movement and constantly tried to encourage workers to maintain production. The reformists favoured owners. The PSI called for insurrection and looked to Turin for leadership. Togliatti fearing for workers, refused to act first. The Reformists who till then controlled unions now offered leadership of trade-unions to PSI, which being indecisive was refused. The PSI sought ways to diffuse the crisis. The unions under reformists refused to take 'political' decisions confining themselves to economic sphere alone. The occupation petered out. The government waited patiently without taking any armed measures that might have precipitated the crisis and when the PSI did a volte face and stopped all activity, the government offered amnesty.

The 'missed out' revolution, gave impetus to fascist forces to carry raids on behalf of the landowners of the North ; it also deepened the differences within the PSI. The factions of left socialists, Bordigans and Council-communists, decided to have a split to the left, breaking from reformists and maximalists. The immediate issue to be taken up was adherence to the twenty-one conditions of the Communist International. At the

---

1. United Front of Comintern advised Cummunists to win over the majority of working class. In pursuance of this goal, all labour organizations, including reformists, were to join to attain the chief tasks of overthrow of bourgeois order, establishment of dictatorship of the proletariat.

Leghorn Congress of PSI held on 29 January 1921, the maximalists under Serrati pleaded exceptional conditions of Italy and, made compliance with International difficult ; but it failed to ; have any effect on the left groups and they marched out of the conference under the leadership of Bordiga. As their manifesto circulated in November 1920 had claimed, the new party was based on Bordigan ideas and had totally rejected the positions of *L'Ordine Nuovo.* The main uniting point of divergent left groups was thus break with reformists. and maximalists, With the formation of the PCI, Bordiga continued to dominate the PCI for the next two years. The inaugural Central Committee of the new party consisted of fifteen members including Gramsci (but Togliatti was not included). The all powerful five members Central Executive of the party consisted of Bordigans[1] who thus had almost total control over the decisions of the party.

In 1921 May elections, PCI won only 15 seats ; PSI won 122 seats, and fascists captured 35 seats. The revolutionary surge was subsiding and Comintern favoured United Front Policy to enjoin masses. The PCI favoured United Front from below in an effort to disclaim the PSI and the reformists. The Rome Congress of the PCI in 1922 reiterated its distrust of the PSI. Gramsci was sent to Moscow to represent the PCI in the Comintern.

In the meanwhile Fascism was gaining ground. The increasing violence during the end of 1920 and early 1921 against peasants' and workers organizations continued ; and, whenever Communists tried to return force by force, the liberal state intervened on behalf of the fascists. The intransigence of Bordiga advocated waiting for the objective revolutionary conditions to ripen, and the party refused to seek alliance against fascists. Gramsci could forsee the danger and declared fascism as enemy number one.[2] He realised that Fascism was

---

1. Members of Central Executive were—Bordiga, Fortichiari, Terracini, Grieco and Repossi.
2. As far back as 1921, Gramsci had perceived that fascism is not a pure class phenomenon; it is "an unchaining of elemental forces which cannot be restrained under the bourgeois system. . ." See, Gramsci, *Selections from Political Writing*, Vol. II, p. 38.

not merely an illegal arm of the State ; it was a movement of the petty bourgeoisie. He singlehandedly sought allies against fascism and worked for the United Front from below. In October 1921 a strike in the metal industry witnessed the failure of the workers and a passive acceptance of the fascist alternative. By 1922 fascists had taken control of the whole town ; State remained paralyzed, and, in October 1922 'March on Rome' successfully established Mussolini in the government. The membership of the PCI was dwindling. *Il Communista* was banned. *L'Ordine* too was occupied by police. Gramsci realised that "Fascism was an attempt to resolve the problems of production and exchange with machine guns and revolvers".[1] Gramsci always felt that Fascism was a pettybourgeois phenomenon. The rootless, destructive, ignorant strata of society filled with pride at its participation in War, went to fascists in search of an apparatus of glory. It had no class base, yet it had curbed proletarian revolution on the one hand, and triggered the collapse of the state on the other. In order to counter it, Gramsci held that the PCI must be a part of masses and not only an 'organ' as Bordiga professed. The Comintern, PCI and other Leftist groups completely failed to comprehend the threat posed by fascism until it was too late to check it.

The PCI continued to regard the PSI as the main enemy. The stress of PCI under Bordiga was not on the concept of class struggle but on the dictatorship of the proletariat, exercised by the proletariat "alone, in a single organization, excluding other classes, and with energetic coercive force".[2] As the party decided to go alone and give no direction to workers on immediate issues, the spontaneous anti-fascist efforts of workers petered out and the resistance of workers to fascism, even though heroic, remained unorganised and defensive in Character.

---

1. Gramsci, "Italia e Spagna" *Socialismo e Fascismo L'OrdineNuovo* (1921-22), Finaudi, Torino, 1967, p. 101.
2. Bordiga, *Il Soviet*, 15 February 1920, quoted in Davidson a *The Theory and Practice of Italian Communism*, p. 105.

As Gramsci alone had realised the far reaching impact of fascism, he favoured party's support to the popular movement known as *Arditi del Pepolo*. Defying party's policy of forming a 'united front from below', he contacted other anti-fascist organizations but was isolated within the PCI. The PCI leadership asked workers to develop their own defence bodies and continued to regard PSI as the main enemy. Togliatti, the new editor of *Il Communista* since August 1921, also decried *Popolari*. But the PCI decided to enlist the masses of working class in their defence against fascists. In pursuance of 'united front from below', the PCI had established a communist Union Committee in 1921 and by September had made considerable progress in capturing the leadership of a large number of unions. But communist dominated unions faced threats from both fascists and employers. The fascists also formed their trade-union federation in November 1921 and as fascist led unions got favours from employers, gradually the communist attempts to counter fascism in factories were unsuccessful. In these circumstances, the second congress of PCI was held in Rome in March 1922.

At the Rome Congress, Bordiga and his supporters declared that the proletariat could only come to power violently and under the leadership of the Party. The Party must maintain purity despite its small numbers. It should work with proletariat to organise and win over workers. The party should formulate tactics and should not worry about day-to-day events. It decried bourgeois government and democracy and favoured united front from below instead of alliance with other parties. These showed party's belief in unchangeable theory to the negligence of daily struggles of masses. The joint front of trade-union *Alleanza del Lavoro* was denounced as a bureaucratic form of unity. Even though all factions of the party approved of these, the Comintern disapproved of intransigency of the party line. As the Fascist Party had already been formed in November 1921 and its centralised activities were on the increase, this intransigency of PCI proved very costly for the anti-fascist movement. A minority group within the PCI led by Tasca fought for acceptance of Comintern line. The Comintern, at this juncture, was advocating formation of alliances and 'united front' with all potential allies. The PCI had rejected the policy at the Third World Congress in June-July 1921. At another meeting of Executive of Comintern in January 1922, PCI again refused to accept Comintern policy of united front, even when PSI was asked to expel reformists as a precondition for joining the Comintern. The Rome Congress reiterated this stand. The Comintern tried to search for alternative leadership but Gramsci refused to desert Bordiga. Gramsci then went to Moscow in May 1922 as delegate to Comintern.

In October 1922, Mussolini came to power after 'March on Rome'. The repression against left intensified ; and PCI maintained that Fascism was another fact of existing bourgeois state. As the Comintern at its fourth World Conference in November 1922, tried to secure the support of the right wing of PCI, Gramsci decided to participate in the commission that was to decide terms for unity of PSI and PCI. Bordiga, however, refused. The hard terms for fusion put by Gramsci resulted in failure of implementation of agreement of unity. In Italy, the tirade against communists was intensified. In January 1923, Bordiga was arrested.

The Comintern asked the PCI to accept atleast on individual basis those members of PSI who accepted Comintern policies, but even this was not acceptable to PCI. Bordiga in a manifesto sent from jail, repeated his arguments. The majority of PCI executive now realized, under threat of expulsion from Comintern, that the adherence to Comintern was the cause of the birth of the PCI. The Gramscian approach was one of understanding Italian situation and to lead political campaign for action. The majority of PCI was against Comintern. In late 1923, Bordiga was released and refused to accept Comintern's views and issued a new Manifesto.

Gramsci in January 1924 distanced himself from Bordigan line. The sectarian approach of Bordiga, Gramsci felt, had generated a passivity in workers. He also favoured formation of a 'Centre' position. In November, Gramsci went to Vienna and from there, he tried to win support for his views. As the views of PCI were not widely discussed in party forums, because of government's repressive regime, ranks regarded Gramsci as a substitute of Bordiga and supported him.

In May 1924, Gramsci returned to Italy and decided to attend the Como Congress. The differences between Bordiga and Gramsci came into open here. While maintaining that Gramsci and the majority were 'continuers' of groups that had formed PCI, Gramsci advocated that in the changed situation, the need is to win back the population which had followed the industrial proletariat. Bordiga blamed PCI's changed attitude towards PSI for the loss of party's strength and stressed that the party was 'not in a hurry,'[1] affirming the correctness of abstentionist policy. He also refused to acknowledge that organization of other classes, if they agreed to accept the PCI line, was necessary. He remained intransigent and sectarian. Gramsci accused Bordiga of following the line of Trotsky. He appealed to make "the Party of the widest masses of Italians, which realizes the hegemony of the proletariat within the vast schema of the alliance between the working class and the mass of peasants".[2] Gramsci, however, failed to secure the support of Federation ; Bordiga, on the other hand, received large support from them. When Bordiga left to attend the Fifth Comintern Congress, Gramsci started dialogue and discussion with various Federations and sent Togliatti to Fifth Comintern Congress as the representative of Majority[3] in July.

In the meanwhile, the PCI following Gramsci's leadership had given up abstentionism and had participated in the April, 1924 elections. Gramsci's attempt to form electoral

---

1. Quoted in Gramsci, *Selections from Political Writings*, Vol. II, p. 251.
2. Gramsci, *La costruzione del partito communista 1923-1926* Finaudi, Turin, 1972. p. 182.
3. Majority of Central Committee of PCI was led by Gramsci and Minority of Central Committee was led by Bordiga. This was formed sometimes in 1923 when differences between factions over Comintern issue sharpened.

bloc with other anti-fascist forces was turned down by the party. PCI's twenty-four deputies got elected including Gramsci. After the elections, fascist repressions led to the murder of PSU deputy Matteotti, and all opposition parties seceded from parliament to meet separately on Aventine Hill in Rome, Gramsci's discussion with Federations informed the rank of party about the differences between Gramsci and Bordiga. Gramsci was still urging a policy of alliance with peasants and Comintern too was advocating slogan of "workers' and peasants' government ; this changed political situation hightened the polarization within the PCI.

An analysis of Fascism revealed that its rise led to prudence among masses who preferred passivity to resistance. This tendency, Gramsci believed, was destined to disappear but the party had to adopt moderation in order to combat it. He favoured PCI's participation in anti-parliament of groups opposed to Mussolini formed after the death of Matteotti.[1] He found it a means to intensify mass movement against Fascism. The PCI under Gramsci started regaining its lost strength. The membership of party rose from 8696 in 1923 to about 17,000 in December 1924. The PCI penetrated South, the islands, and consolidated in the Centre of Italy. Simultaneously it involved peasantry and middle classes. The trade-unions were also soughtto be reinducted. At many places workers formed unions in defiance of fascist bans. The rank and file of PCI also appreciated the role of Gramsci in reviving the strength of the party. Bordiga was defeated but in the middle of 1925 he again surfaced on account of his interaction with the Comintern.

At the Fifth Comintern Congress held in June 1924, the Russian leaders stressed that Social-Democracy is the left wing of fascism. The need is for 'united front' from below. Bordiga was satisfied and was made a member of the Comintern Executive. Failure of Comintern to perceive the true nature of fascism led to a neglect of Gramsci's since. Con-

---

1. G. Matteotti, a socialist deputy was Kidnapped and murdered by Fascist thugs in 1924.

firmed in the correctness of his stance, Bordiga returned to Italy to pursue his policies without involving the Majority of the PCI. The fourth Enlarged Central Committee of International condemned Gramsci's attempt to build mass support against fascism. As against strengthening the organization, the Comintern stressed need for political struggle, based not on alliance and compromise but on revolutionary ideas. Now the rank and file was with Gramsci and middle cadres with Bordiga. The Russian and Italian fascist leaders contact[1] were criticised by Gramsci. With a renewed offensive by fascisli against the only organised, dedicated opposition party, the PCI, the need arose to abondon its sectarian stance. With the end of parliamentary practices in 1925, Gramsci left Bordiga out of deliberation within the party. In order to combat Bordiga's views decisively the Majority decided to condemn his Trotskyism.

The Trotskyism was condemned by the Majority more for Bordiga's association and less for its own implications. The views of Trotsky that German revolution failed to materialize because theory was neglected there, found favour with sectarian Bordiga. The fallacy of ignoring masses, their organization inherent in Trotsky's line were exposed by Majority of PCI. Despite Bordiga's intransigence, Gramsci did not favour his expulsion as it might adversely affect the morale of workers, resulting in loss of the party. Gramsci went to Moscow to present his views and ultimately won its support. Bordiga was isolated both in the party and at the Comintern. PCI the under Gramsci accepted the need of Bolshevization of workers for first hand knowledge of Marxism. Gramsci drew his own conclusions from the debates and stressed on educational role of the party. The political climate of country presented various hazards in this task. By 1924 end, fascists forced many communists to resign from organized committed internal commissions of various factories. The policy to negotiate only with fascist unions also was

---

1. Soviet Italian trade agreement 1924. For details see Davidson. *The Theory and Practice of Indian Communism*, p. 158.

aimed at undermining the base of communists. The Bolshevization, for Gramsci and Togliatti, meant contact with masses in political activities, combat sectarian tendencies by educating the masses. In April 1925, PCI started a correspondence school; its motto was; "nothing else but the theoretical consciousness of our immediate and supreme ends, and of the way we can translate them into action".[1] Translation of major works in communism were provided and traditions of *L'Ordine Nuovo* were resuscitated. The press of party was also expanded. *L'Unita* reached a circulation of 40,000 by end of 1924 and weekly journal *La Stato Operaio* 10,000.[2] The education was such as to make it practically relevant with group discussions and teachers being chosen from amongst these groups. The views of Majority of PCI were reflected in party press but Bordigan views were also presented in 1925. The renewed activities alarmed fascists and regular censorship and silencing of press by violence saw the end in this activity by August 1925. Only instruments of PCI now were the illegal papers. Gramsci wanted this to continue by mass contacts, couriers to lower level of party and by secret meetings. He stressed the importance of peasants, petty-bourgeoisie under the hegemony of proletariat to change the scenario. He analysed the change of fascism from petty-bourgeoisie to big capital in order to centralise the economy. This had alienated the petty-bourgeoisie. If the Northern proletariat was weak, Southern pessantry would follow petty-bourgeoisie. So the need was to prevent this by proletariat-peasant alliance. In this connection, he felt, as the South was under influence of Catbolic priests, the left of Catholicism might also be contacted. This schema had an important role for intellectuals. The Bordigan mechanist and fatalist views of party was countered by Togliatti by stressing the organizational will of masses to intervene in the process of change

---

1. Gramsci, *La Costruzione del Partito communista*, 1923-26, pp. 49-50.
2. All these figures are taken from Davidson, *The Theory and Practice of Italian Communism.*

actively. This was the main theme of Lyons Congress of PCI held in January 1926 in France.

The Far Left under Bordiga presented a separate thesis and Gramsci presented the main draft. The main thrust of Bordiga was that party is an organ of working class. He termed the tendency to regard party as 'part' of working class, as statistical identification of party and class. Bordiga also disapproved of organization by cells, as in his view, it generated a corporate spirit in party. Affirming party as vanguard, Bordiga also denounced the view that party must in all situations be in contact with masses. The need for "immediate success" obscured the need to win stable position. The attempt to take into account, change in objective situation was also, for Bordiga, dangerous and leading to 'eclecticism'. He affirmed faith in an immutable line. Bordiga denounced 'Bolshevization' as mechanical imposition of methods suited to Russian Party. United Front tactics also came into criticism.

Gramsci replied to these contentions. He asserted that in Italy bourgeois in itself was weak and could dominate only with the help of peasantry. Therefore, the main task of party was to win over peasants and lead them. Fascism, too, could be countered by mass political action of this type. The organization of workers into cells was to stop the political division of working class. The problem of PCI and Russian Party were similar—that of unifying the working class. The party in this task sought to reorganise party on the basis of factory cells. The tactics of party—united front, anti-parliament, participation in *Arditi del Popolo*—were aimed to join the mass movements against reactionary regime. The difference between democratic and reactionary regime generated these tactics. Highlighting this, Gramsci said : "The truth is that in today, in a reactionary situation, we are struggling to organize a party, while in ademocratic situation we would be struggling to organize an insurrection".[1] The party, therefore, is a part of working class, linked with all sections of class and

---

1. Gramsci, *Selections from Political Writings*, p. 323.

giving direction to mass movements. He lamented that the "party has not been seen as the result of a dialectical process in which the spontaneous movement of the revolutionary masses and the organising and directing will of the centre converge".[1]

The next few months saw desperate struggle of party against fascism. The debate in International over the issue of Trotsky was viewed in Italy in terms of Bordiga's alliance with Trotsky. Gramsci was hesitant initially, but later on accepted the treatment meted out to Trotsky in the interest of the party unity. The Trotsky issue also generated difference between Togliatti, the PCI's representative at Comintern, and Gramsci. The former accepted the Russian party's stand because of needs of Russian party and Russian stress on unions as communist organization. Gramsci judged the issue in Italian perspective and from this point stressed 'Bolshevization' and the need to adopt 'democratic centralism'. The PCI continued to support Gramsci. His national-popular basis to make revolution was found politically viable and historically sound. The Italian analysis, relations of forces, and the importance of organizing peasantry, were the main themes of *Notes on Southern Question* started in October 1926 : it, however, could not be completed as a result of the crackdown by fascists.

Gramsci was arrested on November 8, 1926.

After his arrest, Gramsci painstakingly developed his political philosophy in the *Prison Notes*. These Notes were the culmination and synthesis of his political experience and practice till 1926, and of profound deliberations indulged dialectically in the Fascist prison. His extensive study of Croce, polemical writings and critique of the Fascist ideology, etc., helped him to evolve his own worldview and develop his philosophy of praxis. He articulated his views on politics as an autonomous science and on the role of the intellectualls. In discussions with his fellow prisoners, he stressed the role of party as the organic intellectual of the working class, and the

---

1. Gramsci quoted in Introduction to *Selections from Prison Notebooks*, p. lxii.

need of a militant organization capable of combating the strategy and tactics of the Fascist state. He also insisted on the political need of creating a Constituent Assembly to win allies against the ruling class, and thus pave the way for the eventual victory of socialism. He maintained that the victory of the working class and the defeat of fascism could be found in the historical process...that is, through a Marxist analysis of the real forces operative in the society. And, it is this thesis that sharpened his theory of historic bloc and of hegemony.

Frail constitution, constant transfers from one to another prison, adverse conditions—all these combined to severely damage Gramsci's already weak organism. On International protests, he was released from the prison and shifted to a clinic where he died on April 27, 1937 leaving behind a large numbers of disjointed, crypic writings.

IV

It is our effort to gleam from the active, fertile life of politically active Gramsci and from his writings as a prisoner the running threads of his political philosophy, now that we are aware of the background in which he functioned and developed. It is manifest that the worldview of Gramsci was developed on a clear understanding of the philosophy of praxis. He imbibed the essence of historical materialism by undertaking a critique of past philosophies, notably of Croce, and by combating positivism inside the party. This understanding of philosophy also made him highlight the elements of politics and its dialectical relationship with economics and history. The study of politics brought into relief the predominant role of 'the intellectual'—the 'intellectual' being the 'Modern Prince' or the 'party'. The relationship of the masses and the party thus revealed to him not only the elements of the party, but also fields of activity of the party and the necessity for it to penetrate the superstructure in order to destroy the hegemony of the ruling class and establish a 'United Front' of workers and peasant under its (Party's) leadership to establish a new State.

As has been said,[1] philosophy to Gramsci is not a systematic set of doctrines. It is rather the very 'life' of 'thought' itself; it is an experience that humanity undergoes. In other words, 'philosophy' is the 'philosophy of praxis', and it includes problems relating to worldview, intellectuals, politics, state, hegemony and political party; viz. the entire gamut of activities designed to change the existing order and to establish a new classless State.

It is the burden of the following pages to take up these problems one by one, and analyse them in order to unfold the cardinal points of Gramsci's political philosophy.

1. See above Section I.

2

Ideational Influences on Gramsci

Philosophy, as has been said, is not a systematic set of doctrines; it is an experience that humanity undergoes. As such, it entails a critique of past philosophies. Gramsci political philosophy was developed in a specific milieu and we need to understand those ideas and thinkers who helped in the formation of this background, and specifically those who shaped Gramsci's thinking and later on spurred him to clearly formulate his philosophical, political position.[1]

Gramsci was aware of socio-economic condition of Southern Italy and of its poverty due to exploitation. This awareness not only led him to study the Italian historical development but also those thinkers who had involved themselves with the task of changing the system. Machiavelli was the first such thinker. When Gramsci reached Turin, the views of Croce were very much in the air and they had a profound impact on his development. Via a study of Croce, Gramsci started a study of Kant and Hegel. The political climate of Turin with its revolutionary zeal also turned him towards the PSI and he studied Labriola, a prominent Italian

1. Here only the main ideas of thinkers who influenced Gramsci are taken; specific themes will be taken in subsequent relevant chapters.

Marxist thinker and George Sorel who had greatly influenced the socialist movement of Italy. Again, the Soviet Revolution opened new vistas for Gramsci and he tried to imbibe the ideas of Marx, Engels and of Lenin to an extent. His participation as the PCI representative in the Third International led him to have a discourse with such personalities as Bukharin, Trotsky and Luxemburg. Further, the political practices of Gramsci, his stress on praxis and hegemony and thereby his differences with mechanistic Marxists gave birth to a faction that charged him with being a Bergsonian. In prison, Gramsci analysed the phenomenon of Taylorism that was at that time effecting production relation; its Italian counterpart, Fordism, also interested him. Lastly, the issue of leadership forced him to study even the views of elitist thinkers and Pareto, Mosca and Michels.

All these ideational threads were interwoven—directly or indirectly, positively or negatively—in the fabric of Gramsci's political philosophy.

Niccolo Machiavelli (1459-1527) the Italian thinker of the sixteenth century particularly inspired Gramsci's writings. Gramsci's major themes—i.e. politics as science and its autonomy; a weil-knit leading party etc—have Machiavellian overtones. There is even a comparison of Marx and Machiavelli in Gramsci. The essence of Machiavellian thought, for Gramsci, is relevant for all ages in theory and in practice both; it is relevant for educating "those who are not in the know of political practice i.e. the revolutionary class of the time."[1] Emphasising the importance of relating Mark to Machiavelli, Gramsci says : "Marx and Machiavelli. This subject can involve a double task : a study of the real relations between the two as theorists of militant practice, of action; and a book that would extract from Marxist theories a coherent exposition bearing on political actuality on the model of the Prince. Its subject would be : the political party in its relation with classes and the State. Not the party as sociological category, but the party

1. Gramsci, *Selections from Prison Notebooks*, p. 135.

that seeks to found a State."[1] As such Gramsci saw the need to study Machiavelli in a historicist manner. "A reconstruction of times and need which Machiavelli saw in them"[2] is a precondition of study according to him. Two of Machiavelli's major works—*The Prince* and *Art of War* were minutely analysed by Gramsci.

At the end of the Middle Ages, Italy was divided into small states torn by religious problems and political dissentions. The comparatively stable states were busy in manipulating the balance of power in Europe. Under such a situation, Machiavelli realized the need for unity for 'Italy to become what France was'. Although he addresssed *The Prince* to the Midici; in reality its appeal was to the masses to unite and let their will prevail. His aim was to create a modern Italian State, capable of defending itself. The Jacobinist approach fascinated Machiavelli.[3] *Art of War*, ostensibly a book on military, deals with the tactice by which war can achieve the political aims. Machiavelli advocates an alliance with other forces to establish a national militia that could project a 'myth' to capture the imagination of the masses. The 'Prince' too is 'mythical', embodying half human, half animal qualities; these qualities in modern parlence could be referred as 'hegemony' and 'coercion', respectively. The inclusion of peasants in the notional militia reveals Machiavelli's awareness of the need to involve peasants in the state to provide it stability and mass base.

---

1. Gramsci quoted in Glucksmann, *Gramsci and the State*, p. 22.
2. Davidson, "Gramsci and Reading Machiavelli". *Science and Society*, Vol. 37, 1, (1973), p. 67.
3. Jacobinism has been used to denote any revolutionary movement which is determined to impose its aims at whatever cost. According to Gramsci, "the term 'Jacobin' came to be used for a politician who was energetic, resolute and fanatical, because fanatically convinced of the thaumaturgical virtues of his ideas, whatever they might be". It's constructive elements were "having made the demands of the popular masses one's own". See, Gramsci, *Selections from Prison Notebooks*, p. 66.

Machiavelli's aim was to find out ways for the liberation and unity of Italy. And for this, to whom could be the guardianship safely confided?—The Prince, the aristocracy, or the people? If the people are not corrupt, Machiavelli prefers their collective judgement to that of the Prince or the nobility. But he is a relativist and has no unqualified confidence in the people. Given his general view of man for him all—the one, the few and the many—are suspect. Therefore to achieve freedom and unity for the country, Machiavelli advocated ideological hegemony (winning the love of the people) as well as coercion (brute force). This unique analysis at a time when religion interfered greatly in the affairs of the state, reveals Machiavelli's understanding of purely political nature of the issues facing his Times. This political ingenuity makes Machiavelli relevant today; and also a constant object of study by such Italians as Croce and Gramsci, besides others.[1]

Gramsci's reading of Machiavelli finds many parallels of the latter in modern concepts. For him, (Gramsci) the revolutionary party connot be other than the 'modern' Prince. The reformist currents of today are to be criticised in the same vein as Machiavelli criticised corporatism. For Gramsci, Machiavelli carried "a critique of the present" and presented "an original conception of the world. This conception of the world too could be called 'philosophy of prasis' or 'neohumaism', in as much as it does not recognise transcendent or imminent (in the metaphysical sense) elements, but bases itself entirely on the concrete action of man, who impelled by historical necessity works and transforms reality."[2]

Kantian metaphysics, particularly the concept of "thing in itself", interested Gramsci much. As far as Kant's epistemology is concerned, he believed that perception and conception are the two elements that form our knowledge. Although our knowledge begins with experience but mature and genuine knowledge needs to be properly processed through

---

1. Prominent members of this 'Machiavelli' school were Gaetano Mosca and Pareto.
2. Gramsci, *Selections from Prison Notebooks*, p. 249.

reason. Without sensibility or experience we would not perceive an object, and without conception we cannot understand the object percieved. Ultimate reality for Kant, abides in the realm of the transcendent; it lies beyond all experience. Consequently the 'ultimate reality' for the metaphysical substance is unknowable. The only world man experiences is the sense-world, the phenomental world produced by substance or matter, it is with this world that man can establish any enpirical contact. The phenomenal world is the world of appearance; it is a show world. The ultimate reality remains unknowable, therefore man cannot establish sense contact with it. In fact, it is this ultimate reality, this metaphysical substance, this thing-in-itself, that praduces the phenomenon. Man perceives the phenomenon, but is unable to know the substance. The ultimate reality, the thing-in-itself, is composed of "noumenon, the object of 'non-sensuous intuition', phenomena' are immanent and 'noumena' are transcendent. The world is thus divided into (a) 'phenomena' or the sensible world and (b) 'noumena', or the intelligible world. The sensible world is that in which we live and move and have our existance; the intelligible world is the real world which is contacted solely by understanding. Accordingly, the real world is a reconstruction in the human mind, fashioned by the laws of understanding. In other words, the reality of things is different from the phenomenon through which we have knowledge of them. The whole of reality is not contained in the phenomenal world.[1]

Gramsci queries : "What are phenomena? Are they something objective, existing in and for themselves, or are they qualities which man has isolated in consequence of his

---

1. These views of Kant later on gave birth to Neo-Kantianism. After the decline in the influence of Hegel in Germany, and the subsequent spread of positivist and materialist philosophical culture, a revolt against positivism took the form of a return to Kant as a source for new methodology and philosophical foundation for the cultural and historical sciences. This was neo-Kantianism. Broadly speaking neo-Kantianism adhered to a division between the sciences of nature and those forms of knowledge [which take human culture and historical phenomena as their object.

practical interest (the construction of his economic life) and his scientific interests (the necessity to discover an oder in the world and to describe and classify things, a necessity which is itself connected to mediated and future practical interest). Accepting the affirmation that our knowledge of things is nothing other than ourselves, our needs and interests,...it is difficult not to think in terms of something real beyond this knowledge...not in the metaphysical sense of a 'noumenon,' an 'unknown God' ar an 'unknowable', but in the concrete sense of a 'relative' ignorance of reality, of something still unknown, which will however be known one day when the 'physical' and intellectual instruments of mankind are more perfect,..."[1]

Kant's ethics is a democratic one inasmuch as it insists on the motto that what is right for one is right for all and what is immoral for one is immoral for all. This is due to the fact that moral principles are categorical;they are unconditional and hold true under any all circumstances. This is the meaning of what Kant has termed as the 'categorical imperative'; since moral and immoral actions must stem from an 'autonomous will', every person by virtue of his being human is autonomous; that is every human being has a free will, and no power on earth can force one to will other than he chooses for himself. And since human beings are endowed with an autonomous will, they possess dignity and are of infinite intrinsic worth. Thus the essence of Kantian ethical theory is reverence for the moral laws and respect for the categorical imperative. Gramsci offered a critique of this. He observed: "What is meant by 'similar condition'? The immediate conditions in which one is operating, or the complex and organic general conditions,..."[2] we find that Kant's philosophy "is linked to the philosophy of intellectuals as a cosmopolitan stratum".[3]

Hegel—who does not seem to question Kant's account in its basic principles—also finds Kant's notion of the categorical

---

1. Gramsci, *Selections from Prison Notebooks*, p. 368.
2. *Ibid.*, p. 373.
3. *Ibid.*, p. 374.

imperative defective. He, in fact, shares Kant's view in regard to the binding nature of the 'ought' inasmuch as it is a direct intuitive perception. However, he finds Kant inadequate in his Failure to discover the concrete details or the substance of binding duty. The abstract ideal of duty is formed and does not tell man what his duty is. In other words, Kant gives an account of subjective conscience, but fails to give it a concrete (objective) base. It is at this point that Hegel puts forth his conception of social righteousness or *Sittlichkeit.*

The key to Hegel's philosophy of man and politics lies in his 'logic' and in his 'phenomenology' of spirit'. He always thinks of the central factor in the shaping of individual and collective lifi as the development of reason. In the logic, Hegel maintains that every proposition negates previous conceptions of the world and every given truth contains its opposite or nagation wthin the dialectic of 'though'. There is self movement of the notion and in this dynamism every incomplete idea is replaced by a more complete one and the process continues. Thus, the very notion of 'being' implies 'non-being'; and from this emerges the union of the two, or 'becoming'. 'Becoming', in other words, is the wider idea in which both 'being' and 'non-being' are marged. The actual reality, therefore, according to Hegel, is neither 'being' or its opposite 'non-being'; but it is a process of 'becoming' and vanishing. It is this process which sums up human consiousness in all its ramifications, Consciousness is the whole complex of the ethical word or of social righteousness (*Sittlichkeit*). And *Sittlichkeit* in its turn is the body of established institutions, mores and tradition into which the individual is born and through which the Universal spirit enters the human Consciousness. It is at this level of social ethics that Hegel analyses institutions. The dialectic which is inherent in thought finds its reflection in the individual and social behaviour of men.

In other words, in the objective—ethical world conflict occupies an important place in shaping both the social-right eousness and the individual self. The two bases of this dialectic in the objective world are family and the civil society. Family stands for natural society based on the ties of love. But, paradoxical as it may seem, family also nurtures 'individuality' in man and as soon as the child attains adulthood he leaves family and enters the world of Civil Society characterized by conflict and competitions. The basic assumption here is that of a civil society in which private individuals and corporations are pursuing their own interests in their own way. In short, both the family and civil society have limited ends. To fulfil themselves they need the authority of the universal state, which is the Highest spiritual manifestation of the Universal Spirit. It is in the state that the natural government of the family and the imposed external government of the civil society are synthesised into a higher self-government. It is because of this reasoning that the state is indeed 'the march of God on earth' (Hegel's expression), if God is taken to be the evolving Reason.

It is obvious that Hegel's doctrine of historical dialectic, the significance of history, the relativity of the right and the good, and the notion of the group or the class mind played an important role in the development of Marxism. Togliatti has admitteed that both Gramsci and he "reached Marxism by the same route as Marx himself, i.e. starting from classical German philosophy, from Hegel."[1] A question arises here : what is the Gramscian understanding of Hegel ? Putting the issue in a historical perspective, it is Gramsci's view that the organic intellectuals of bourgeoisie require the Hegelian concept of the Absolute State in their justification. He says : "What is political for productive class becomes rationality for the intellectual class."[2] Hegel represents the aspirations of bourgeois class, the then historically progressive class. It is not authoritarian. He "belongs to a period in which the spreading development of bourgeoisie could-be asserted : all mankind will be dourgeois."[3] Pursuing this expansion of the state, Hegel dwells upon the mechanism of state-control and

---

1. Togliatti, 'La nostra ideologi', *Opere 1917-1926*, Vol. I, quoted in Christine Buci-Glucksmann, *Gramsci and the State*, p. 382.
2. Gramsci, Notebook I, 150 quoted in *Ibid* , p. 382.
3. Gramsci, *Selections from Prison Notebooks*, pp. 258-59.

institutions of civil society. "Hegel's doctrine of parties and associations as the 'private' woof of the State. This derived historically from the political experiences of the French Revolution, and wasto serve to give a more concrete character to constitutionalism—The State does have and request consent, but it also 'educates' this consent, by means of political and syndical associations ; these, however, are private organisms, left to the private initiative of the ruling class".[1] The civil society is the pre-political society. The concept of civil society suggests that state is autonomous from the previous stage of cultural and ideological dominance, i.e. of religion. Civil society has two facets—of need and of labour. This concept highlights the economic sphere in contrast to previous thinkers who stressed the legal aspect in the development of state. It implies that civil society is the stage of private initiative as Gramsci has developed in his theories.[2] He contends that Hegel presents the doctrine of an 'integral state' by separating state from religion and civil society. This state is a unifying factor and all classes regard it as superior. The logic and relationable of this integral state are not fathomed by all and sundry ; only a handful of intellectuals understand it. These intellectuals act as mediators between the state and the common people by establishing their dominance in civil society. Thus, the intellectuals of Hegel have a positive role to play. This position is required in order to carry out a critique of Croce who did not adhere to this schema of Hegel.

As has been said, it was via Croce that Gramsci studied Hegel. And, it is interesting to note that Hegel's influence worked in sharply different directions. For example, Croce's (1866-1952) theory veered towards liberal Hegelianism, whereas Giovanni Gentile became associated with Mussolini's Fascism. Both were Italians and Gramsci's contemporaries.

In fact, Neo Idealism is mainly the work of Italian thinkers, (chief among them being Croce and Giovanni Gentile). The school presents a view of the world which is

---

1. *Ibid* , p. 259.
2. For Civil Society and State see Chap. VI.

deeply influenced by specific Italian characteristics. The keynote of the neo-Idealists is that thought is the living reality. The only living thing is Idea or Mind, and history is the history of the Mind. There is no given Absolute Universe towards which this world must strive. Mind in itself is self-creating and it also analyses, studies, interprets the things that it creates. Since mind creates 'reality', it is History ; and History in its turn is present reality. The selfcreative mind becomes philosophy when it interprets. Philosophy, then, is History and History is Philosophy. Philosophy is the interpretation of an activity which mind creates, so history of philosophy is history of mind. This is also the philosophy of mind. The universe is constantly developing and continuously becoming, a process that has no end or completion. As it is a continuous process, no moment is ever complete and at every stage a doubt spurs mind to create a new moment. This is the process of developing of history and is a circular movement since at no time can completion be reached. There is no place for transcendence in this view of the world. The centre of this world is 'Man', not historically determined man but a metaphysical entity. The state for neo-Idealists is an ethical entity.

For Croce, experience is the only thing whose existence is a certainty for us. It is a whole and it is mental. The distinction between experience and object of experience is created by mind. One can say that the external world is not apart or given, rather it is created by mind through the concrete whole of experience. Thus mind an Absolute, whole is reality, which creates itself and its surroundings. There are various movements of reality through which one preceives various forms of experience. The first form of reality is knowing ; it is contained in two stages—one is 'intuition' and is expressed by ethics ; and the other is the conceptual thinking and is studied by logic. The second form of reality is practical activity which is logically dependent on the logical thinking. Again, the practical activity is contained in two stages of economics and ethics. Thus, reality is constituted of these two forms and their four stages. All stages are interlinked and no stage can exist in itself. This is the 'dialectics of distincts' of Croce on which are based his theories of state, history and development.

The reality is a mental activity not of the individual mind but of some supra-individual mind. In Croce's schema culture and ethico-political element has a dominant place and the element allows for the role of particular and immediate in historical change. "When people have faith in a certain ideal, there is historical splendor"[1] otherwise there is a decadence. There is no predetermined course of history as Hegel had postulated. This puts the responsibility of the world over the shoulders of man, the protagonist of History to createan ethico-political state. It is this moral goal that was given to the youth of Itlay; and an appeal was made to them for executing the vast responsibility. Denouncing any role of materialism, Croce's views on ethics precluded role of external forces. It is therfore rightly said: "The recognition that man's personal conscience or individuality is necessary to safeguard the moral world is an important Crocen contribution."[2] For him (Croce) History is at every moment and in every phase of its development, liberty, "Man is a microcosm, not in the natural sense, but in the historical sense, a compendium of universal history".[3] This truth that history lives within us has led philosophers "astray into their theory of a history tobe constructed *a priori* from pure and abstract logic and free of all documentation though they later contradicted themselves when, making an outward show of a synthesis, they sought a collaboration between the supposed *a priori* on the one side and the supposed *a posteriori* on the other."[4]

At another place, Croce says that "devotion to the state is collaboration with it putting the best part of ourselves into its political life—our affection...our ideas. Such a particip-

---

1. Gennaro in Introduction to Croce, *Essays on Marx and Russia*, Fredrick Ungar Pub. Co. New York, 1966, p. 11.
2. *Ibid.*, p. xii.
3. Croce, *History as the Story of Liberty*, George Allen & Unwin Ltd., London, 1949, p. 20.
4. *Ibid.*

ation is what is called liberty."[1] Croce goes on to assert: "History reveals this love of a state in action..."[2] As men attain a moral ideal within a state, they love it. The consent of men to state is one where consent implies moral approval. The revolutions try to restore consent for a new form of state. Thus, the history of civilization is unfolded in the history of state and consists of perpetual conflicts and conciliations. The movement is towards equality and peace. These moments of change are not the end of life but through this man may try to raise conflicts to higher levels. Naturally, the intellectuals occupy a dominant position in this schema of Croce. As a matter of fact, Croce aroposed an aristocracy, albeit on open one, in place of blood recruitment to educate the masses upto a certain level of religious consciousness of concepts. As men are not adept in all fields, intellectuals work for intellectual and moral reform of the masses through religion. Croce conceived the upliftment of masses through religion because they (the masses) are incapable of comprehending the rationality of Mind. This stress on values of culture, and the role of men in establishing these values, led Croce to undertake a critique of Marxism. In the complex web of problems faced by Italian cultural and political life in the decade 1900-1910, Croce became the theoretician of the liberal state, and chief antagonist of positivism and Marxian socialism. He exposed the mechanistic materialism and positivist of the Second International as tenets of Marxism. In fact, Croce's study of Marxism may be divided into two phases—a revisionist phase (1890-1911), when he tried to expose deficiencies of Marxism; and 1911 onwards phase, when he tried to evolve a philosophy of his own to replace Marxism. He attacked Marxian theories for being more of a political ideology rather than philosophical or economical treatises. Accusing Marx of "substituting for Hegel's God which was called the 'Idea', his own, which he called 'Matter',

---

1. Croce, *My Philosophy*, George Allen and Unwin Ltd., London, 19:9, p. 57.
2. *Ibid*, p. 58.

(both) come to the same thing, something which works behind the scenes of history."[1] Croce denied mechanism and provided for role of culture in the process of change.

Gramsci regarded Crocean philosophy as progressive one, though in a 'speculative' form being tied to the apronstrings of Hegelian methodology and disregarding positivism. Croce's stress that history is based on fact and "Knowledge was the end product of relationship between Consciousness, Idea and Fact and not Ideas and Fact alone",[2] made his philosophy significant for Gramsci who accepted Crocean notion of history as a creative process ; he also favoured use of Hegelian methodology. In Gramsci's eyes, Croce represented the most advanced phase of modern thought inasmuch as at the centre of Croce's thought lay the concept that history is an ethico-political manifestation, and the realization on a political level, of the strongly felt 'ideology of groups' and leaders. But it is exactly here that Gramsci's criticism of Croce begins. Gramsci approved of the task of philosophy to implement a "moral and intellectual reform", but criticised Croce for ignoring the worldview of masses, thereby ignoring class struggle and strengthening the hands of aristocracy in perpetuating the exploitative system. Via a critique of Croce, Gramsci sought to fulfil the Marxian task of countering the highest ideology of the time in ordor to establish the hegemony of the philosophy of praxis.[3]

---

1. *Ibid.*, p. 64.
2. Alastair Davidson, *Antonio Gramsci—The Man, His Ideas*, Austrailian Left Review Publications, Sydney, 1968, p. 29 (Introduction by John Playford)
3. It is interesting to note the vital role Croce played in the formulation of Gramsci's though. Croce, essentially an idealist thinker, reached this position via a study of Marxism. He learned his Marxism chiefly from Cabriola. However, he later claimed that he was responsible for the eclipse of Marxism in Italy. This Marxist turned liberal occupied a prominent place in European thought for about three decades and wrote extensively on ethics, aesthetics and history. He was regarded as the "lay Pope" of Italy. Gramsci

(*Contd.*)

Gentile (1875-1944) accepted Croce's thesis that experience is a unified whole but rejected his four moments theory because mind cannot be at once a whole and single source of four moments which are as real as the whole. For him, mind is the only reality in this Universe. The object of experience is within experience itself; self-consciousness is a synthesis of two phases—in the one mind appears as subject, and in the other as object. The philosopher is then the maker of reality. Philosophy is the study of the process of knowing itself of mind; thought is a creation of mind and in thinking about thought one creates thought. Philosophy is the development of thought and is identical with it. "Nothing is, but thinking makes it so in the act of its own self-formation". Experience is thus immenent in individual experience and is a whole "Experience is the one thing of whose reality we are assured; therefore, the rest of reality must be in the likeness of experience."[1]

Gentile's writings represent a reactionary neo-Hegelianism with his concept of 'ethical state'. The ethical state becomes a real divinity and conceived to be greater than individuals. In practice, such a concept manifested the actual (fascist) state which became the embodiment of the divine on earth. An ardent champion of fascism, Gentile used Hegelianism to justify the concrete politics. Gentile's writings lead to 'corporate' tendencies by establishing an interaction between economics and politics—a point notably missing in Croce. It is also noteworthy that the dominance of legal aspect that was stressed by Croce is also not present in Gentile (who is anti-legal). Gramsci says: "For Gentile history is entirely State history, while, for Croce it is

---

was very much influenced by Croce and carried a Critique of Croce. He realised the wide influence of Croce and therefore concentrated a large amount of study in carrying out a comprehensive rebuttal of Croce. Even then Gramsci is regarded by some as a 'Crocean', a Hegelian marxist. For detail evaluation of this point, see the last chapter.

1. Quotes of Gentile are taken from C.E.M. Joad, *Introduction to Modern Philosophy*, Clarendon Press. London, 1934, pp. 60-61.

'ethical-political'....Gentile sees the economic corporate phase as an ethical phase within the historical act : hegemony and dictatorship are indistinguishable, force and consent are simply equivalent ; one cannot distinguish political society from civil society ; only the State, and of course the State-as-government exists".[1]

Needless to say that Croce and Gentile, both the neo-Hegelians, influenced the Italian political theorists of their times in one way or the other—that is to say, either negatively or positively. Gramsci, as seen above, was no exception to it.[2]

The thesis and formulations of Marx and Engels were eclipsed by anarchist ideas in Italy as Bakunin's appeal lay chiefly among peasants and Italy had largely an agricultural economy in the last decades of the nineteenth century. The rise in labour class and its organizations started an effort to understand Marx's thesis in the national perspective of Italy and was taken up by the Italian Socialist Party (PSI). But the PSI failed to account for the role of imperialism and world market that had in fact given rise to petty-properiety as main from of agricultural production. Italian industry was also a product of monopoly capital's investment, a fall out of imperialism. It therefore, gave birth to 'labour aristocracy' ignoring the peasant masses, and PSI was its leading force. It became the burden of Antonio Labriola to search for socialist moorings of PSI and make them the basic tenets of Marxism. Although influenced by Hegel in his formative years, he was yet strongly attached to Italian traditions, and, as such he imparted peculiar Italian features to his version of Marxism. Another significant fact is that he was primarily a professor and not a party activist.

Labriola (1843-1904) is regarded as the father of Italian socialism. As the sources of Italian socialists were limited on account of limited translation of Marxist texts, Italian

---

1. Gramsci, *Selections From Prison Notebooks*, p. 271.
2. Another neo-Hegelian Mondolfo had turned to Marxism and will be taken up along with thinkers of the Marxian school.

socialists received their socialism from the texts of Achille Loria[1] which were positivistic. Marxism was regarded by Italians either as evolutionary theory or fatalism. Antonio Labriola brought up in neo-Hegelian ideas, and set out to fight against this vulgarization of Marxism around eighteen ninetees. He staunchly opposed the efforts of newly emergent socialist groups to include 'sympathisers of socialism' and consequently withdrew from practical affairs after the formation of the PSI. "The contribution of Communist Manifesto", according to Labriola, was the "new conception of history". It is not a schema for change, but contains "the minute art of understanding case by case what could and should be done."[2]

Marxism presents a materialistic conception of history ; but it never meant a reduction of all phenomena to economics. Man's being determines their consciousness and consciousness is a part of history. The materialist conception studies the known history of men, and this in turn, is made possible by the dialectical relation of men and their activities. It starts with seemingly isloated facts whose economic base is not easily found. To understand these facts, men had to start from the highest development of thought conceived as the outcome of certain practices. Thus, historical materialism explains its origins. The history is characterised by class struggles and other subjects are influenced by this. Science, for example, seems to follow a progress of reason but it is based on social need. Marxism is a philosophy of praxis ; and upholding this, Labriola denounced positivism and fatalism. It is "Form life to thought and not from thought

---

1. Achile Loria (1857-1943) was an academic economist and propounded the theory of 'historical economism' whereby "economic development is reduced to the course of technical change in the instrument of work". See Gramsci, *Selections From Prison Notebooks*, p. 163.
2. Labriola, "In Memory of the Communist Manifesto", *Essays on the Materialistic Conception of History*, pp. 40-41.

to life : this is the realist process."[1] The positivists by stressing only empirical science and ignoring the philosophical aspect, diluted the Marxian philosophy. Without practicipating in workers' movement, intellectuals presented a simplistic version of *Weltanschauung* that held the working class as the subject of history. This can only be remedied, according to labriola, by the publication of the works of Marx, their dissemination among masses and diffusion of Marxian ideas among the working class. Unfortunately Labriola was isolated among Italian socialists. Despite Engels' support of Labriola's anti-positivist stance (which was manifest in Engels' criticism of Loria in the preface of the third volume of *Capital* written at the request of Labriola), Labriola's works remained neglected during 1900-8 period, when theory was virtually dead in the PSI.

Labriola started correspondence with Sorel in a bid to make knowledge of Marx's works wide among masses. We find echoes of Labriola in Gramsci's tirade against mechanism and determinism. Labriola asserted : "It might easily happen that where the socialist movement is still in its beginning, appeal may be made for lack of personal direct experience—as often happens in Italy—to the authority of a text from the Manifesto as if it were a precept, but these passages are in reality of no importance."[2] This view can be compared to Gramsci's notion that "Philosophy does not supply formulae to be applied to problems,"[3] Even the early Gramsci had a clear perception of it in "The Revolution Against *Capital*".[4] Similarly, Labriola's rejection of the view that capitalism and bourgeoisie are inevitable part of the development and indeed provide the terrain for new struggles ; form the backbone of Gramsci's thought. Gramsci has also taken from Labriola the essence of historical materialism." To Labriola :

---

1. Labriola, *Socialism and Philosophy*, Charles H. Kerr & Co. Chicago, 1934, p. 71.
2. Labriola, *Essays on the Materialistic Concept of History*, p. 11.
3. Gramsci, quoted in Glucksmann, *Gramsci and The State*, p. 372.
4. See Chapter I.

"Historical materialism is in a certain sense all there is to marxism...A philosophical method for the general understanding of life and universe as a critique of political economy reducible to certain historical phase, an interpretation of politics above all of these political movements which are necessary and servicable for the march of working class towards socialism."[1] It seems ironical that Labriola's work was eclipsed by the criticism of Marxism, by his own pupil. For Labriola, socialism was not only a break with the past but it also signified a total revolution based on a critical attitude ; it is autonomous, independent and original. "It is rather scientific experiment," and for someone who has reached it, it is science that has arrived at its perfection. Labriola's views on Marx is worth quoting : "His politics was, as it were, the practice of his historical materialism, and his philosophy was inherent in his critique of economic relation, this being his way of dealing with history."[2] This amply illustrates that Marx was the "philosopher of science."[3] Gramsci explains : "Labriola distinguishes himself...by his affirmation ...that the philosophy of praxis is independent which contains in itself the element of a further development, so as to become, from an interpretation of history, a general philosophy."[4]

George Sorel (1847-1922), french theorist, approved of Labriola's writings. He wrote to Labriola that due to the absence of intellectuals from the worker's movement, proletariat sometimes succumbed to vulgar interpretation of *Weltanschauung* that made class the subject of history. He agreed with Labriola that *Capital* is not the "Bible of socialism."[5] However, both parted company on the means and nature of the transformation of existing society into

---

1. Labriola *Socialism and Philosophy*, p. 23.
2. *Ibid.*, p. 91.
3. *Ibid.*
4. Gramsci, *Selections From Prison Notebooks*, p. 390.
5. G. Sorel, *Reflections on Violence*, Colliers, New York, 1961, p. 186.

socialist society. Sorel moved towards extreme voluntarism ignoring the concrete reality and adopted anarcho-syndicalist postures. He agreed with Labriola on the need for change, for revolution, but violence pervaded his whole philosophy. He along with Croce, declared that there is a crisis in Marxism. At one time he had supported the revisionist ideas of Bernstein[1] but later on withdrew himself from that stand. His hatred of intellectuals led him to reject 'theory' as such, the product of the intellectuals. He denounced the "fortress of the intellectuals—namely the State and Political Parties."[2] For this reason, any revolution led by the intellectual is bound to create a privileged group. The intellectuals, he thought, decry workers' strike and violence in order to aid and abet bourgeoisie with professed desire for peace. Sorel's hatred for decadent bourgeois intellectual was very much a type of self hatred.

Sorel glorified spontaneous violence and believed in the myth of general strike. The 'myth' eptomised all the sentiments which reflect the aims of socialism against capitalist society and recaptured the glory of socialism. The persistent use of strikes would lead to strong organization of workers and weaken the exploitative state. It would bring out heroism and voluntarism of the workers and rekindle the sublime ideals of socialism. The revolution by producers creates specific institutions of proletariat or syndicates. The critics try to see parallels between Factory Council Movement of Gramsci and Sorel's concept of syndicates as institutions specific to working class as such. The concept of Sorel starts with spontaneity and stops at the level of trade union consciousness. Moreover,

---

1. Bernstein (1850-1932) asserted that growth of cartels, monopoly capital, trusts also saw separation of ownership and control leading to socialisation of production. So the number of capitalists is increasing. Increase of social wealth leads to strengthening of capitalism. He foresaw in this way a harmonious development of capitalism leading towards socialism in an unbroken process.

2. G. Sorel, "The Decomposition of Marxism", translated in I. Horowitz, *Radicalism and Revolt Against Reason*, also quoted in Glucksmann, *Gramsci and The State*, p. 50.

Sorel's general strike is a passive activity and does not envisage a conscious striving for hegemony, a key concept of Gramsci. Gramsci is, no doubt, influenced by Sorel's stress on importance of workers in revolution, he was supported in his Factory council Movement[1] by Sorel, *albeit* for different reasons. Sorel's movement was purely economic and he always condemned politics. This is not so in the case of Gramsci for whom politics occupies an important position. The young Gramsci was much influenced by the revolutionary postures of Sorel and workers' role in the process, but, he never accepted his view totally. The mature Gramsci realized the limitations of Sorelian doctrine and carrieda critique of its short-comings.

The Sorelian influence continued to prevail even in Italian socialist circles and new ideas emerged only when the PSI was severely affected by differences between the 'left' reformists and the 'extreme' left. The new ideas were formulated by Rodolfo Mondolfo (1877-1977). Mondolfo, had been a neo-Hegelian. He started his works on Marxism with a comparison of Feuerbach and Marx. His studies were published in literary journals of the time, and his discussions were accessible to the academic circles only.[2] He had no contact whatsoever with the masses. Mondolfo tried to show that humanism and praxis of Marx originated to a great extent from Feurbach's[3] ideas. Marx's originality was the

---

1. See for details of Factory Council Movement in Gramsci, Chap. V. Sorel supported Factory Council Movement of Italy in the fond hope that these councils will develop into Syndicates and lead to a General Strike.

2. Mondolfo contributed chiefly to academic journals and rarely to popular journals like *Critica Sociale*. All his writings are collected in Mondolfo, *Umanismo di Marx studi Filosofici 1908-1966*, Einaudi, Turin, 1968.

3. Feurbach's (1804-1872) aim in his critical philosophy was to reduce theology and speculative philosophy to anthropology. To do this, the religious mentality and its philosophical variant—Hegelian metaphysics—had to be exposed as false consciousness. Feuerbach took as his starting point the sensuous, concrete man, and saw God

realization of the need not only to interpret the world, but also to change it. In this context Mondolfo felt that Labriola's historical materialism was appropriate; his shortcoming was that he could never specify how knowledge could become a social force and what practice was required for this? Mondolfo tried to fill this gap with his attempt to prove that "men make their destinies" and are dominated by conditions of life. The change could be brought about not only through political action, but also by testifying every proposition in practice. It is significant to note here that this view of Mondolfo has no resemblance with the pragmatists: because for them, the momentary contingency, the here and now is so important that they end up by justifying the immediate action to the detriment of the long-term goal. Marxism, on the other hand, effects a synthesis of thought and action. Mondolfo in this way, emphasised voluntarism against intellectualism.[1] He stressed impulsiveness against fatalism yet had differences with Sorel who ignored the movement of history. He condemned crude Marxism[2] and pleaded for a new theory for the PSI.[3] He differed with Labriola on the question of class struggle. A class can be called that only with the attainment of 'consciousness' and a theory of 'critical-practical'

(the object of theology) and the Absolute Spirit (the object of speculation) as objectifications and projections of purely human qualities into a distant beyond. To him, consciousness of God is self-consciousness; as such God is the expressed self of man. Marx moved ahead of Feuerbach and asserted that man is no abstract being 'squatting outside the world'; man is the part of the world, the state, the society. And, therefore, the real task no longer is one of criticism, but that of providing a practical critique means to change the perverse social and political conditions. In other words, it means "human sensuous activity, practice". This is the core of the philosophy of praxis.

1. The impulsive moment, Mondolfo asserted, was neglected in Hegelian rationalism.
2. For Mondolfo, Marxism is a 'voluntarism' of praxis, and will is autonomous whereas in crude Marxism all theory is neglected.
3. He Insisted that the PSI instead of being reformist, needed a theory and accentuation of class struggle.

is essential for it.

Labriola and Mondolfo were, in brief, two such prominent socialists who dealt with the need for a theory of change in the socialist movement in Europe. Labriola had realized the effect of imperialism and suggested practice. Towards this goal he confirmed to the indoctrination of marxist's educational tasks. Mondolfo, however, suggested the nature of practice of forming class parties to intensify the class struggle without taking into consideration the phenomenon of imperialism. Both these Italian Marxists, thus, complement each other. For Mondolfo, Marxism was 'critical-practical'. He says: "Man operates, according to the impulse of his needs and actuating his will, but the result of his action then becomes in turn a condition, limiting and at the same time stimulating, his future activity. In this *reversal of praxis* is the true meaning of the dialectic of the real, the true value of the economic is historical science."[1]

Apart from these Italian Marxists who had deep influence on Gramsci (by virtue of their influence over the PSI, as well as by virtue of their attempts to give their versions of Marxism to the Italian left), the European and Soviet left leaders also had their role in making Gramsci to clarify his formulations. It is in this respect that an overview of the ideas of V.I. Lenin, Rosa Luxemburg, Leon Trotsky and N.I. Bukharin falls into the line.

Vladimir Illych lenin (1870-1924) needs no introduction. He was the main architect of October Revolution in Russia and is regarded as the developer of Marx. Even though Gramsci had not read many works of Lenin, he was certainly aware of the events of Russian Revolution and the role of Lenin in effecting the Revolution. Lenin, too, was aware of the activities of *L'Ordine Nuovo* group led by Gramsci and had endorsed its policies.[2] Lenin's various theoretical

1. Mondolfo, 'Rivista di filosofia', p. 109, quoted in A Davidson. *Theory and Practice of Italian Communism*, p. 67.
2. At Second Conference of International held in Petrograd, 19 July 1920.

concerns—such as the critique of economism, revisionism and metaphysical materialism, coupled with his concepts of a world-view, party, hegemony and of the state—are all present in Gramsci's philosophy in various forms. It is indeed remarkable that Gramsci had reached Leninist formulations despite his typically Italian background of marxist studies and his limited access to the works of Lenin.

Lenin presented a detailed, coherent arrangement of Marxist political theory of class struggle, and suggested organizations and tactical skill in support of these. He actively led the struggle against the economistic and reformist tendencies of the Second International leading to its demise and the formation of the Third International. Lenin highlighted the failure of the party leadership in articulating the demands of the working class. Taking up an analysis of the class conflicts and relations between various classes in Russia, he realised that proletariat on its own and on the basis of limited economic struggle cannot attain the consciousness required to carry out the revolution. On its own, proletariat could attain only the bourgeois level; whereas the need was to expand the *weltanschauung* of the working class among masses. He felt that the relationship between economic and political moment and the relations of forces were based on the degree of homogeneity and organisation of each class in relation to the state. The phase were only economic-corporate interests are recognised is the primary (the lowest) stage : it is at the level of struggle for economic rights that the second (higher) of the trade union consciousness emerges, this develops into the third stage of political consciousness giving birth to the struggle for hegemony. Lenin emphasised that the party has to keep these levels in mind in order to prepare themselves for the overthrow of the exploiters. Towards this, he suggested formation of mass organisations in order to keep the masses organised for day-to-dav struggle under the guidance and leadership of a close-knit party, the vanguard for revolution.

The vanguard party is the consciousness of the proletariat; it leads and guides them towards socialist revolution. To carry out the revolution successfully, Lenin saw the need to seek the support of peasantry which is a natural ally of the working class. Lenin's views on revolution and its tactics were mainly based on an analysis of the national factors, preparedness of the ruling classes and proletariat's ability to carry it out under the party. Although the analysis of the national factors were predominant in Lenin's scheme; yet he also did not overlook to scan the phenomenon of imperialism that had gripped Western countries and helped them to sustain the capitalist system.

Imperialism had led to the development of monopoly-finance-capitalism, leading to economic stagnation. It also gave birth to bribed aristocracies of labour in advance industrial countries. These aristocracies benefitted from the continuation of capitalism, thrived on the exploitation of the workers of the other countries (colonies), and hampered the process of revolution. The beneficial influence of imperialism from the point of view of proletariat was the spread of exploitation in the colonies and birth of revolutionary conditions in the world; and these conditions intensified the demand and necessity of international revolution in order to strengthen the socialist revolutions.

Lenin emphasises on the fact that the prime aim of the revolutionary process is the overthrow of the State. For him: "the State is a special organisation of force : it is an organisation of violence for the suppression of some class."[1] Subsequent to the overthrow of the exploitative state, the proletariat has to establish a dictatorship of the proletariat in order to combat the threat to the nascent state and also to destroy the ideological control of the erstwhile ruling classes. The stage of dictatorship is also the phase of establishing hegemony of the working class and its allies. Thus, hegemony for Lenin, is a class strategy to complete the revolutionary process and it is achieved during this phase of dictatorship.

Gramsci asserted that there can be no comparison between Marx and Lenin in order to create a hierarchy. Both represent two essential phases. As Marxism is both science

---

1. Lenin, *Selected Works*, Vol. 2, Progress Pub., Moscow, 1960, p. 320.

and action, Lenin has effected the passage from 'science to action'. Lenin "advanced philosophy as philosophy in so far as he advanced political doctrine and practice."[1] Gramsci's concept of hegemony starts from where Lenin has left; and he develops it to analyse western, developed societies. In the subsequent chapters[2] Lenin's impact on Gramsci is discussed. One wonders how Gramsci developed and emulated great heritage of Lenin without having had the opportunity of an access to his works.

Rosa Luxemburg, (1870-1919) a contemporary of Lenin, also had far-reaching effect on the debate over relationship between the masses and the party. Rejecting the prevalent reformist views, she stressed that social reforms are only a means towards the goal of revolution and any stress on the first without preparation for the revolution ultimately denies the objective necessity of socialism. She carried a vociferous attack of Bernstein's theories, but she supported Kautsky's[3] parliamentary struggle combining revolutionary theory and reformist practice. Differing from Lenin, Rosa stressed the importance of trade-union struggle and claimed that through trade union struggle, proletariat acquires class consciousness. She denounced vanguard role of the party and accused Lenin of imposing 'terrorist' leadership over the party. She stressed on 'spontaneity' of masses as against 'centralism' of the party. She, however, never rejected totally the need for a 'central' leadership but wanted 'a self-centralism' of the proletariat. She mistook Lenin's party as a sectarian, that was separated from the masses. She stressed on the role of the party as an 'agitator' and not as an 'organiser'. In fact, Rosa's limited view of the party was to a large extent the result of the short-comings and the short sightedness of the German Social Democratic Party.

---

1. Gramsci, *Selections From Prison Notebooks*, p. 365.
2. See Chap. VI.
3. Kautsky (1854-1938) German historian and economist, was opposed to revolutionary Marxism and was criticised by both Engels and Lenin for distorting Marxism.

Her concept of revolution is also formed on the basis of her emphasis on the element of spontaneity. To her, 'spontaneity' is embodied in mass strikes. As a matter of fect, this view was an attempt to include political reformism of trade unions and political action in the making of revolution. The notion of mass-strike also stressed the point that economic and political elements are inseparable from each other. However, this view overlooks the fact that mass-strike does not lead to revolution or create revolutionary conditions; rather it is the revolutionary conditions that spur on mass-strikes and symbolise a revolutionary period.

The concept of mass strike also shaped Luxemburg's views on imperialism. She claimed that as capitalism expands and more pre-capitalist societies are exploited, situations lead towards a collapse of capitalist system and gradually and inevitably make way for the application of the socialist principles. Her conclusions, however, were not widely accepted and the 'automatic breakdown theory' was not supported by facts. Lenin disapproved of these theses.

Gramsci criticised Rosa as she "disregarded the 'voluntary' and organisational elements which were far more extensive and important in those events than—thanks to a certain 'economistic' and spontaneist prejudice—she tended to believe." Dwelling on different tactics—of frontal attacks (or manoeuvre) and war of position—Gramsci stressed that one or the other tactics is adopted on the basis of an analysis of "immediate economic element (crisis etc.)" and basic long-term crisis of relation of production. He accused Rosa of adopting somewhat direct and simple association that exists between economics and politics and the tactics of frontal attack. Yet he realised the theoretical importance of strategy of war of manoeuvre enunciated by Rosa, and said Rosa's *The General Strike The Party and The Unions* is one of the most significant documents theorizing the war of manoeuvre in relation to political science."[1] By utilizing the immediate economic crisis,

---

1, Gramsci, *Selections From Prison Notebooks*, p. 233.

proletariat is encouraged to attack the enemy, throwing enemy forces in disaray. This provides "ideological concentration on the common objective to be achieved."[1] Rosa's stress on philosophy's development "following the necessities of practical activity"[2] is reflective of the need of historical factors to raise questions consonant with the social understanding of a social class. But, despite all this, he felt, Rosa failed to take account of crucial factor of hegemony of the ruling classes and the resulting necessity of adopting an alternative strategy of war of position before embarking on a frontal attack on the State.

Leon Trotsky's (1877-1940) theory of permanent revolution and Bordiga's association with him led Gramsci to dwell on him in detail. Trotsky believed that Russian capitalism was not self-sufficient in investing its own surplus, and required state-investment borrowed from the Western countries, leading to frequent crisis and displacements. However, the proletariat class was created by this borrowed capital, and the Russian social system could not cope up with this twin phenomena. It is in the absence of a middle class that the autocratic centralised machinery of the state had to resort to absolutism. This peculiar factor made proletariat forces stronger in an economically backward country and revolution became easier than in countries with advanced capitalism. The small working force was sufficient to bring about a revolution and mobilize the peasantry. But Trotsky believed that after the revolution, the working class would have to continue "an uninterrupted revolution" to effect the "liquidation of absolutism and feudalism."[3] It is here that the Russian proletariat needs help from the European proletariat. The European proletariat, he urged, should carry frontal attacks on state to accelerate the process of world revolution. This theory, however, failed to take account of the specific

---

1. *Ibid.*
2. Gramsci, *Selections From Prison Notebooks*, p. 392.
3. Trotsky, *The Permanent Revolution and Results and Prospects*, Pathfinder, N.Y. 1969, p. 81.

national factors of countries other than Russia. It also failed to take account of the hegemony of ruling classes and the strength of the capitalist superstructures. Gramsci accused Trotsky of ignoring the dialectic between state, class and society that takes place on the national terrain.

N.I. Bukharin's (1888-1938) views were regarded as mechanistic by the Russian Social Democratic Party in 1929. Gramsci, too, after initially partially accepting Bukharin's views during 1924-25, made a full study of Bukharin in prison and sharply attacked his premiss as being 'mechanical'. Bukharin had claimed that historical materialism is a sociology or even a class ideology of the proletariat. The common sense of masses is a unified conception of the world. Common sense is the philosophy of masses and it is to be opposed to the traditional philosophy of intellectuals. He asserted that philosophy of praxis is 'sociology' whereas 'true' philosophy is philosophical materialism. Sociology is a proletarian science based on laws of natural sciences. This schema ignored the role of historical materialism and reduced marxist philosophy to a class 'ideology'. The model of natural sciences, Gramsci felt, led to a simple cause and effect relationship ignoring the complex nature of dialectical relations and the phenomena of base and superstructure. This schema also ignores the theory of praxis, or the unity of theory and practice. Gramsci believed that Bukharin by dividing Marxism into two—sociology and philosophical materialism—destroys the revolutionary essence of dialectics "which is relegated from its position as a doctrine of knowledge and the very marrow of historiography and the science of politics to the level of a subspecies of formal logic and elementary scholastics'"[1]

Apart from dialectics, Gramsci feels, metaphysics too is treated in a superficial manner by Bukharin. The attempt to reduce everything to a simple cause and effect pattern has led Bukharin to characterize Marxism as a 'sociology' of philosophy of praxis. Metaphysics is simply a specific

1. Gramsci, *Selections From Prison Notebooks*, p. 435.

philosophical formulation for Bukharin. These views lead only to an evolutionary development because it follows the laws of regularity and causality.

For Bukharin, science is also defined on the pattern of natural sciences, having a standard method and ignoring the specific need and methods of each branch. Morever, in this analysis there is no place for accounting for error of individuals and all views and opinions come under the head of 'commonsense' and the coherence of worldview is absent. The criticism of subjective conception of reality, is also undertaken from the point of view of commonsense and an attempt by Bukharin to establish the objective reality of external world on the tenets of natural sciences is, according to Gramsci, unsound. Objective does exist apart from man "but when one affirms that a reality would exist even if man did not, one is either speaking metaphorically or one is falling into a form of mysticism."[1] Bukharin adhered to the belief that stress on 'material' objects to the exclusion of historical elements reinforces orthodox and thereby immutable ideas. The overt stress on methods of natural sciences led Bukharin to uphold that prediction is possible in social sciences with the laws of natural sciences. This leads to economism and fails to account for subjective elements or the role of 'human will' in historical change. Bukharin's whole attempt is satirically summed up by Gramsci : "Reading the *Manual* one has the impression of some one who cannot sleep for the moonlight and who struggles to massacre the fireflies in the belief that by doing so he will make the brightness lessen or disappear."[2]

Apart from these Hegelian and socialist currents, Gramsci was also much influenced by sociological theories of Vilfredo Pareto (1848-1923), Gaetano Mosca (1858-1941) and Michels (1876-1936). Their ideas are regarded as precursors of Fascism. Pareto, disgusted with parliamentary practices, craved for stability even at the cost of moral freedom. He

---

1. Gramsci, *Selections From Prison Notebooks*, p. 446.
2. *Ibid.*, p. 433.

advocated a rule of aristocracy. This aristocracy is not hereditory or blood based. Based on a system of social equilibrium, the elite is identified on the basis of ability of "take and hold power". He divided society into two strata—"a superior stratum, of which governors form part and an inferior stratum, in which the governed fall."[1] Pareto advocated theory of Free Trade. He separated economy from political developments and regarded state as regulating the free development of Free Trade. His theory of 'circulation of elite' showed the change in ruling elite personnel with change in production. The process of circulation of elite, he claimed, witnessed the rise of neo-elite to the elite category. He said : "This phenomenon of new elites which through an incessant movement of circulation, rise up from the lower strata of society, mount up to the higher strata, flourish there, and then fall into decadence, are annihilated or disappear this is one of the motive forces of history."[2] His stress on use of force to ensure survival of ruling elite made him a farerunner of fascism.

Mosca (1858-1941) criticized democracy and advocated individual liberty. He realised that in every society ruling class is always small. If it is recruited from people of common religions, moral beliefs and from economically stable groups it is less likely to be corrupt. He wanted complete power for this elite ruling group. He criticised "the irresponsible and annonymous tyranny of the elements which win elections in the name of the people."[3] He preferred the government of the 'wise' elements of society, in other words, government of the elite.

Michels (1876-1936) claimed that in all organizations power tends to concentrate in a few leaders whatever may be the form or system or constitution. This suggested that "who

---

1. V. Pareto, *The Mind and Society*; quoted in Buci-Glucksmann, *Gramsci and The State*, p. 52.
2. S.F. Finer (Ed.), *Vilfredo Pareto: Sociological Writings,* quoted in Jame Joll, *Europe Since 1870*, Penguin Books, Hamondsworth, Sussex, 1976, p. 130.
3. Mosca quoted in Joll, *Ibid.*, p. 128.

says organization, says oligarchy and it exposed the control of elite groups of men over institutions of state. The writings of Michels were directed against democracy and the facade of equal opportunities. Thus, for Michels, the 'iron law of oligarchy' exposed the control of elite groups of men over institutions of state.

All the three belonged to the school 'new liberalism' of the early twentieth century that saw the eclipse of democratic elements of liberalism. The school was ready to accept a strong 'state' in order to safeguard its economic interests. The utilitarian belief in providing for happiness of all and everyone in a rational society deteriorated in the need to impose the rule of a 'few to ensure unhindered development of the free trade, ete. The attempts of the elite theorists with their enunciation of 'positivist sociolgy of elites' converged in an attempt to formulate a sociology of intellectuals. It provided for a narrow role of politics by restricting political activity to an elite, Gramsci severely criticised these attempts to deny the proletariat their rightful place in the process of governance and combated these ideas in his famous theory of intellectuals.[1]

A major influence on Gramsci is that of Bergson. He was accused by Bordiga[2] of being a Bergsonian because of his stress on Council Movement and on role of 'human will' in the social transformation. Although Bergson's work is concerned primarily with psychology and philosophy it also spills over in politics. He studied mechanisms by which the human beings acquire knowledge of the external world. He denied the reality of external/objective and stressed on its 'intuitional' character; i.e. reality, he said, is perceived from within. This perception of reality is a process, existing in time and space. As such for Bergson, reality is instinctively grasped.

Bergson's concept of *elan vital* may be analysed here. His masterpiece *Creative Evolution*, provides the basis of

---

1. See Chap. IV.
2. Bordiga, "Is this the time to form Soviet", *Il Soviet*, 1 January, 1926, quoted in Glucksmann, *Gramsci and The State*, p. 166.

Vitalism. *Elan vital* is 'vital impetus' in contrast to mechanistic theorise of life that present a "gradual building up of the machine under the influence of external circumstances". Bergson suggests that there is "an original impetus" of life, the life being a "tendency to act on inert matter." This suggests an extreme voluntarism and stress on chance. "The direction of this action (i.e. action on inert matter) is not predetermined; hence the unforeceeable variety of forms which life in evolving sows along its path."[1]

At a meeting in November 1917, a PSI leader accused Gramsci of being a 'Bergsonian' and 'voluntarist'. The Factory Council movement was also accused of voluntarism and Bergsonian on account of its effort to direct the spontaneous uprising of the masses. Gramsci, contradicting this accusation, stressed that it is leadership that guided this spontanreity. He emphasised : "It was educated, directed, purged of extraneous contamination; the aim was to bring it into line with modern theory."[2] Even in Prison writings Gramsci had used Bergsonian terminology 'vital impulse' to explain concrete will or man but he provides a new connotation to the term.

Another important topic of Gramscian analysis is the phenomenon of Taylorism, prevalent in America. Techniques of scientific management expounded by F.W. Taylor[3] came under this purview. It advocated mechanisation, mass production and techniques to standardise the work. Gramsci's critique is dealt with later on;[4] here it is sufficient to point out that it started a whole series of measures of technical, scientific expansion and greatly affected production relation. Another significant American phenomenon was Fordism,[5] it provided

1. Bergson quoted in Gramsci, *Selections From Prison Notebooks*, p. 127.
2. Gramsci, *Selections From Prison Notebooks*, p. 198.
3. F.W. Taylor (1856-1915) author of *Principles of Scientific Management*.
4. See Chap. VI.
5. Propounded by Henry Ford, who founded Free Trade School in 1916 for educating the workers in the ethics of life.

for a regulated life for workers. It was also criticised by Gramsci. Fordism justified interference in all aspects of workers life in order to increase production. This entailed a mechanised life for workers to the extent that their private lives and their role in production processes were completely regulated. The workers were, thus, turned into a mere wheel in the vast machine system. The irony is that this complete mechanization of workers lives was affected behind the facade of humane and aetruistic aims. The ultimate aim was to increase production and destroy the trade unions and other organizations of the workers and to make workers conform to a social and moral order that helps producers to tighten their grip over subordinate classes who then voluntarily adopt this very exploitative system.

A birds-eye-view-journey through various ideas and currents of though above was undertaken with the intent of searching the ideational roots of Gramsci's political philosophy. This exercise would also be helpful in analysing Gramsci's world view, or a critical conception of the world, which took shape by a long polemic with many of the above mentioned thinkers and their ideas.

3

Gramsci's Worldview

An analysis of the main themes of political philosophy of Gramsci presupposes a sketch of the schema for the study. Gramsci himself syas : "It is necessary, first of all, to reconstruct the process of intellectual development of the thinker in question in order to identify those elements which were to become stable and permanent..., distinct from and superior to the 'material'...which served as a stimulus to him."[1] In the previous chapters an attempt has been made to establish the material and the intellectual development of Gramsci's philosophy. Now, the 'permanent' elements are to be "determined by intrinsic factors"[2] in the development process.

And, the 'intrinsic factor' of his political philosophy is his worldview or *weltanschauung*.

According to Scruton, a *weltanschauung* is "A general conception of the world, in which beliefs, values and metaphysical presuppositions are all woven together so as to instil the world with significance, and facilitate the transition

---

1. Gramsci, *Selections From Prison Notebooks*, pp, 382-83.
2. *Ibid.*

from thought to action."[1] Another source explains worldview as "perspective of life, conception of things."[2]

Gramsci felt an urgent need for the "production of new *Weltanschauungen* to fertilise and nourish the culture of an historical epoch, and philosophically directed production according to the original *Weltanschauungen*. Marx is the creator of a *Weltanschauung*."[3] It is significant to note that even the Young Gramsci was clear about his political orientation despite his somewhat idealist formulation as is evident from these words : "Socialism is an integral vision of life; It has a philosophy, a faith and a morality."[4]

Gramsci accepts that he faced a problem in the study of Marx, inasmuch as his (Marx's) work did not contain any systematic and comprehensive presentation of his worldview; and as such he (Gramsci) felt the necessity to "search for the '*leitmotiv*'."[5] It is paradoxical, however, that the same problem, which he found in Marx, is inherent in the study of Gramsci as well. The problem arises mainly because it is difficult to classify Gramscian writings as purely 'political' or 'philosophical'. He searched for manifestations of philosophy in all spheres of life—language, religion, culture, education, etc.; and politics pervaded all his philosophy. Against this backdrop the elements of his worldview require to be sifted not only from his philosophical deliberations, but from his entire writings.

Since Gramsci's worldview is not expounded in specific themes, it has to be approached via an analysis of his writings on Croce and Bukharin, and a review of Marxism of the Second and the Third International. He carried out a critique of different forms of revisionism and aberrations of Marxism

---

1. Roger Scrution, *A Dictionary of Political Thought*, Pan Books in association with the MacMillan Press, London, 1982, p. 493.
2. Runes (Ed.), *Dictionary of Philosophy*, Vision Press, London,1982, p. 335.
3. Gramsci, *Selections From Prison Notebooks*, p. 381.
4. Oramsci; quoted in Christine Buci-Glucksmann, *Gramsci and The State*, p. 4.
5. Gramsci, *Selections From Prison Notebooks*, p. 383.

in his quest to define the main thrust and unique contributions of Marxism.

Gramsci proposes a new way of conceiving philosophy 'from below' rather than from the top as was the practice in the past. He starts with the postulate that each man acts according to a particular set of views. A conception of the world contains theoretical as well as practical conscious activity. *Weltanschauung* is an "original and integral conception of the world".[1] As has been hinted in the first chapter, Gramsci had clearly perceived that the 'real' philosophy of each man is contained in his actions, thereby illustrating that there may be a contrast between professed goals and action. The contrast between theory and practice is evident even if a whole social group is taken, especially when the group is in the process of evolving its own view of the world reflected in its practice; because the 'practical' aspect of the worldview is always subordinated to the dominant view of the world taken theoretically. As such, there are a number of worldviews when societies are not culturally and structurally unified.

According to Gramsci, until the advent of Marxist philosophy, there was a tendency to keep philosophy apart from practice. Marx was the first to demand a unity of theory and practice; he advocated taking a look at history from the viewpoint of different classes. Gramsci concurs : "A worldview is philosophical it is represents the intellectual and moral life of an entire social group."[2] Marxism is the worldview of the proletariat. In every epoch there are a number of worldviews and one always makes a choice among them. When the choice is critical and when philosophy becomes the theory of a class, it fulfils the historical function. But this is a long drawn struggle. "The process of development is tied to a dialectic between the intellectuals and the masses."[3] The organic intellectuals[4] of every class try to evolve a

1. Gramsci, quoted in Glucksmann. *Gramsci and The State*, p. 2 7.
2. *Ibid.*, 357.
3. Gramsci, *Selections From Prison Notebooks*, p. 334.
4. For details of organic intellectuals, see chapter IV.

worldview consistent with their place in the production processes. The old conceptions are gradually substituted by the efforts of thinkers who 'prove the rationality of their ideas by participating in political processes through various organisations such as political party. But philosophy is a "response to certain specific problems posed by reality, which are quite specific and 'original' in their immediate relevance.[1]

Philosophy, therefore, cannot be separated from politics. In other words, philosophy is not to be studied simply as an epistemology : it is organically linked with politics. Gramsci's worldview can be evaluated as a unity of theory and practice—praxis. His 'theory' is, in fact, an 'epistemology of politics' as the terrain necessary to comprehend the cultural revolution in a developed capitalist country. The union of politics and philosophy analyses philosophy in its superstructural arena and politics as that which produces knowledge.[2]

Gramsci is emphatic in his assertion that philosophy is common to all men. While initiating a discussion on the study of philosophy, he saps : "It must first be shown that all men are 'philosopher', by defining the limits and characteristics of the 'spontaneous philosophy' which is proper to everybody. This philosophy is contained in : 1. language itself, which is a totality of determined notions and concepts and not just of words grammatically devoid of content; 2. 'common sense' and 'good sense'; 3. popular religion."[3]

Language is the most immediate tool to perceive the world and interact with others. A limited knowledge of a standard language of a place and confinement to the knowledge of a dialect necessarily limits one's worldview as there is no exposure to wider problems of society. This implies, "that 'language' is essentially a collective term which does not presuppose any single thing existing in time and space. Language also means culture and philosophy..."[4]

---

1. Gramsci, *Selections From Prison Notebooks*, p. 324.
2. In the subsequent chapters, we would try to verify the concepts outlined in this chapter in order to evaluate his theoretical formulations against concrete historical situations.
3. Gramsci, *Selections From Prison Notebooks*, p. 323.
4. *Ibid* , p. 349.

Thus, language is tool of cultural assimilation by the hegemonic ruling class. A social group has a language that corresponds to the cultural level it has attained. Morover, even in every individual there are residues of past cultures as well as his particular strata of languages, Language is essentially a means of communication. Cutting away from a dialect straightaway, without overcoming cultural stages cannot be very effective in propagating a new worldview, as the language is essentially determined by the social being. Unless the social distinctions and cultural disparties are removed, a new language cannot be imbibed by the masses whose conception of language contains these elements. The gap between the language conception of masses and intellectuals is also revealed in the literature. The popular literature is an expression of subaltern groups and is therefore undeveloped. It is not correct, aceording to Gramsci, to say that the so-called 'literary' writings are 'ideological' manifestations of ruling classes and hence are to be rejected by the masses. Rather, the need is to analyse the 'literary' writings in order to comprehend the unified conception of ruling classes as well as to identify the permanent features of this literature that are borrowed by and transmitted into popular language. Moreover, every philosophy expresses itself through the agency of language and provides certain connotations to existing terms, it also coins new idioms and metaphors. Needless to say that 'philosophy' finds its shape and content through the language. Language, thus, is an intrinsic part of every philosophy.

'Common sense', according to Gramsci, denotes the ideas, aspirations, ways of living and thinking of subaltern social groups. A history of common sense is a history of these groups. Its use as a collective noun implies that it is not a single unified concept. There are a number of common sense in every society. In common sense, the conception of the world is "uncritically absorbed by the various social and cultural environments in which the moral individuality of the average man is developed."[1] The fragmented, incoherent view

1. *Ibid.*, p. 419.

guides the actions of such social groups whose philosophy it is. The history of common sense, as it is not documented, can only be understood by understanding the history of philosophy, because common sense is the "folkore' of philosophy."[1] There are residues of past philosophies and religions in common sense. There has been a tendency in idealist as well as some other schools to separate philosophy of intellectuals from the philosophy of masses or common sense. Spontaneous philosophy is "simply a generic term for grouping together the set of sentiments, ways of living and thinking that are specific to the subaltern strata, and it paves the way for a new and specifically Gramscian object : a history of these subaltern strata."[2]

As at any given point of time, there are a number of worldviews existing among subaltern strata; it can be said that philosophy of an epoch does not reflect the consciousness of an epoch and history of philosophy does not contain the history of subaltern strata. Yet, it is necessary to understand history as the history of class struggles. Thus, common sense assimilates the conceptions of intellectuals in anin coherent and fragmented way. However, the philosophical revolutions of every epoch are sooner or later filtered into the common sense. Gramsci, thus, says : "These systems influence the popular masses as an external political force, and element of cohesive force excercised by the ruling classes and therefore an element of subordination to an external hegemony. This limits the original thought of the popular masses in a negative direction, without having the positive effect of a vital ferment of interior transformation of what the masses think in an embryonic and chaotic form about the world and life."[3]

Gramsci finds religion as an element of fragemented common sense. It is "a unity of faith between a conception of the world and the corresponding norms of conduct."[4] He,

---

1. *Ibid.*
2. Glucksmann, *Gramsci and The State*, p. 225.
3. Gramsci, *Selections From Prison Notebooks*, p. 420.
4. *Ibid.*, p. 326.

then, queries : "But why call this unity of faith 'religion' and not 'ideology', or even frankly 'politics'?"[1] It is not that ideology refers to a "system of ideas"[2] and politics "a conscious action in pursuit of a common social goal"?[3] Croce had characterised religion as fit only for the masses and Gramsci's point of view is : "For Croce, religion is a view of the world that is accompanied by a morality conforming to it, in a mythological form."[4] Religion tries to maintain a doctrinal unity between all strata—higher or lower. The Church, for example, claims to be equal for all and having a uniform level for all strata : but actually it (church) always had an elite who managed its affairs. Religion, then "is the most grandiose attempt to reconcile in a mythological form the real contradictions of historical life."[5] This type of religion, Croce affirms, proposes to leave behind the masses in their ignorance, but maintains a facade of equality before the Divine Being. However, religion did at one time organise people in one unity of faith, and through the organizational capacity of the Church did succeed in preventing the ideological aberration between the masses and the intellectuals.

The views of Gramsci on spontaneous philosophy reveal that for him there is "no epistemological break between the philosophy of the masses and that of the philosophers. The distinction between the two is less a qualitive than a quantitative one."[6] The healthy nucleus of common sense is to be made coherent in order to arrive at the *Weltanschauung* of Marxism.

Gramsci starts the search for critical philosophy through as critique of spontaneous philosophy. "Every social stratum has its own common sense and its own good sense which are basically the most widespread conceptions of life and of man.

1. *Ibid.*
2. *Ibid.*, p. 375.
3. *Ibid.*, p. 3:6.
4. Gramsci, quoted in Glucksmann, *Gramsci and The State*, p. 354.
5. Gramsci, *Selections From Prison Notebooks*, p. 405.
6. Glucksmann, *Gramsci and The State*, p. 226.

very philosophical current leaves behind a sedimentation of ommon sense; this is the document of its historical effectiveness. Common sense is not something rigid and immobile but is constantly transforming itself."[1]

Philosophy is an intellectual order and therefore among the masses, it can be "experienced as a faith".[2] But Gramsci poses the question of faith in whom? and himself replies : "In particular in the social group to which he belongs in so far as in a diffuse way it thinks as he does."[3] But any new conception is very unstable while facing the established *weltanschauugen* that perpetuate the ideas of ruling classes. The Marxist philosophy, in order to consolidate as a worldview, carries a critique of past philosophies as well as a critique of the common sense. "The philosophers have only interpreted the world, the point now is to change it", is the credo of the new philosophy.

It means that "philosophy must become political, practical, if it is to continue to be philosophy".[4] This philosophy seeks to transform the world so much so that the "foundation of a directive class (i.e. of a State) is equivalent to the creation of a *Weltansehauung*."[5] The unique specificity of Marxism carries a critique of common sense in order to bring about a revolution in the very methods of knowledge and to provide methods to transform the way of life. Thus Marxism or philosophy of praxis is 'intellectual and moral reform' and dialectics connects the two terrein of its function.

Gramsci used "philosophy of praxis" in a critical sense. He derived this sense from Labriola's usage. It was not a unity of thought and action in 'Spirit' or 'pure action' as

---

1. Gramsci, *Gli Intellettuali e L 'Organizazione della Cultura*, quoted in Cammett, *Antonio Gramsci and The Origins of Italian Communism*, Stanford, Univ. Press, 1967, p. 57.
2. Gramsci, *Selections From Prison Notebooks*, p. 339.
3. *Ibid.*
4. Gramsci, quoted in Glucksmann, *Gramsci and The State*, p, 344.
5. Gramsci, *Selections Erom Prison Notebooks*, p. 381.

Gentile[1] averred; rather it was the "concrete historical activity of men engaged in transforming the material productive forces"[2] that are organized in a definite form. Marxism of Labriola' was "born on the battle field of communism. As a revolutionary doctrine, it is above all else the intellectual consciousness of the present proletarian movement."[3] This outlines two approaches of study—first a break with past philosophies, and second, a revolution based on dialectical understanding.

As the philosophy of praxis is grounded in concrete historical reality, it puts an end to all idealist philosophy. For both Gramsci and Labriola, philosophy of praxis is autonomous, independent and original. "A new science proves its efficacy and vitality when it demonstrates that it is capable of confronting the great champions of the tendencies opposed to it"[4] but certain currents of Marxism fail to grasp this essential critical task. This task is vital to continue the struggle for hegemony, to make its viewpoint acceptable to the masses.

Here a critique of Bukharin is in order to isolate the points of Marxism from its aberration and to identify the precise theory of Gramsci. In fact, Bukharin's chief error lies in not understanding the dialectics. He divides Marxism into two categories...first, a sociology based on the method of the natural sciences, and second a philosophy which he also calls the dialectical materialism. Bukharin regards "dialectic as a branch of formal logic" but this is not so. Gramsci explains : Separated from the theory of history and politics philosophy can not be other than metaphysics", Gramsci's analysis further reveals that Bukharin's treatement of dialectics is more concerned with laws of causality and regularity, making it "one

---

1. For Gentile praxis is unit of subject and object in 'Spirit' as pure action (see chapter I). Gramsci called his own praxis 'impure act' to contrast it against Gentile's thesis.
2. Glucksmann, *Gramsci and The State*, p. 360.
3. Labriola quoted in *Ibid.*, p. 361.
4. Gramsci, *Selections From Prison Notebooks*, p. 433.

manifestation of the 'search for God"[1] rather than a historical methodology. This fails to take account of the role of politics or the class struggle. Yet another current[2] tries to reduce philosophy to mere 'class ideology' and eliminates dialectic between philosophy and practice.

The stress on materialim as the philosophy of Marxism, at the same time, postualting separation between dialectical and historical materialism, fails to perceive the element of dialectic in this relationship. Both tendencies stressing either a materialism or ideology, fail to perceive the role of culture and intellectuals in the task of building socialism. As the role of intellectuals is taken up in later chapters, suffice to say here, that what is needed is "to make culture, and practical function coincide.'[3] This is a task assigned to intellectuals, in order to achieve the expansion of Marxism.

'Dialectics' and 'Praxis' are, in fact, two sides of the same coin. Dialectics is "the doctrine of knowledge and the very marrow of historiography and the science of politics".[4] The Marxist philosophy develops dialectically. It is impossible to identify 'dialectics' as a science or a method because such terms limit its capacity to transcend past philosophies and to effect a cultural reform. Philosophy of praxis or Marxism brings out the contradictions in society, and unlike past philosophies that tried to resolve contradiction "becomes the very theory of these contradictions."[5] Gramsci succinctly says : "*If the environment is the educator, it too must in turn be educated.*"[6]

---

1. *Ibid.*, pp. 436-37.
2. E.G. in Stalin for whom dialectical and historical materialism, are one : Thus it denies specificity of dialectics in dialectical materialism.
3. Gramsci, quoted in Glucksmann, *Gramsci and The State*, p. 210.
4. Gramsci, *Selections From Prison Notebooks*, p 435.
5. *Ibid.*, p. 405.
6. *Ibid.*, p. 435 (Emphasis added).

The dialectics of reciprocity developed by Gramsci emphasises that the philosophical systems are the most articulate expression of an epoch, and in the long run, they even furnish that epoch with the needed conceptual apparatus for its continued activity. Thus a dialectic between objective conditions on a given terrain and subjective conditions of its relation to state apparatus, preclude any determinism or prediction of processes of change. Causality and dialectics are different, "In reality one can 'scientifically' fore see only the struggle, but not the concrete moments of struggle, which cannot but be the results of opposing forces in continuous movement, which are never reducible to fixed quantities since within them quantity is continually becoming quality."[1] As philosophy of praxis is the very theory of contradictions in history and society, it carries a critique of all philosophies that are contained in the superstructure. It itself becomes a superstrcture. "Hegemony realized mean the real critique of a philosophy, its real dialectics."[2] The error of Bukharin was not to understand this intervention of philosophy.

For Bukharin, the philosophy of philosophers and of non-philosophers are separate ; and the later is an ideology. Ideology regards philosophy as system of truth and thereby excludes it from the conjuncture in which it intervenes and leads to a division between the philosopher and the non-philosopher. This fails to take account of the advanced historical situation that a class may represent and the ideologically backward worldview of this class. Gramsci feels that this division can only be overcome by the active intervention of praxis in order to establish hegemony. Bukharin fails to compehend the critical dialectical relationship between philosophy and ideology. As the practical consciousness of a group may be vastly different from his explicit theoretical consciousness, the contradiction can be identified by the intervention of philosophy that tries to make practice more

---

1. *Ibid.*, p. 438.
2. *Ibid.*, p. 381.

coherent. Gramsci insists that the philosophy rectifies theoretical truth when it becomes a "stimulus to know better the concrete reality of a situation that is different from that in which it was discovered" and "in its capacity to incorporate itself in that same reality as if it were originally an expression of it."[1] Thus a critique of Bukharin exposes the fallacity of his dictum : "The 'mode of production' determines also the 'mode of conception' : "theoretical activity is a 'step' in the reproduction of social life."[2]

The reiteration of Marx in 1859 'Preface' to *A Contribution to the Critique* of *Political Economy* sums up Gramsci's stand that "ideological form in which men become conscious of this conflict and fight it out" does not make superstructure directly dependent on material forces of production alone. And the acceptance of this, calls for a new approach to Marxism in order to overcome its aberrations and to meet the challenge of other philosophical systems.

In other words, Gramsci stresses that, in order to combat revisionist tendencies, a critical analysis is to be taken of "Idealist revision : Sorel, Croce, Bergson, neo-Kantianism, orthodox revision, i.e. that of the 'official Marxisms': concerned to find a Marxist philosophy at all costs, they finally did find one, but in a kind of modren version of vulgar meterialism or neo-Kantianism".[3] The tendency of Idealist revision championed the cause of such intellectuals who were primarily concerned with evolving and developing the ideologies of the dominant classes. They tried to absorb the progressive features of Marxism in order to infuse themselves with historicity, and at the same time strengthening their specific interests. Gramsci's anti-Croce stand is an attempt to prove this point and this necessitates a summary of Croce's critique of Marxism.

Croce had proclaimed the death of Marxism because of

---

1. *Ibid.*, p. 201.
2. Bukharin at London Congress of History and Science, 1931, quoted in Glucksmann, *Gramsci and The State*, p. 256.
3. Gramsci, quoted in Glucksmann, *Gramsci and The State*, p. 332.

its stress on political practice. He thus analysed Marxist transformation into reality. In his own words: "This transformation would consist in substituting practice for philosophy, the revolutionary for the philosopher. A transformation moreover, which is highly understandable, since there can be no doubt but that thought denies itself in action, and action in thought".[1] Carrying this plea further, Croce asserted that Marx overthrew philosophy in general and his practical activity replaced Marxism. Thus, for him, there can be no Marxist philosophy.

Gramsci's assertion was that what Marx attacked was not philosophy as such but what was so far regarded as philosophy. Marxism postulates a unity of theory and practice as against all past philosophies that stressed only one element of philosophy. It is true that Gramsci and Croce both realised that there was the need for "Overthrow of traditional posing of philosophical problems, dissolution of philosophy understood in the traditional way."[2] But then both parted company. For Gramsci, the task of philosophy was to solve the problems arising out of historical process. However Croce's problematic led him to divide philosophy into two—philosophy of philosophers, and of non-philosophers, were the latter is the inheritor of the former. The philosophers have a scientific philosophy and the philosophy of masses becomes religion in the ultimate analysis. Gramsci felt that this schema makes intellectuals the sole contenders of knowledge. Croce, thus, not only celebrated death of Marxism, but also took the "rational core of Marxism and translated it into speculative idealism."[3] By dividing philosophy, Croce presents a homogeneous theory of history that discounts the role of politics in transformation.

The Crocean formulations regard man as the creator of history. The 'man', for Croce, is not a 'historically

---

1. B. Croce, *Conversazioni Critiche*, Laterza, Bari, 1918, p. 298.
2. Gramsci, *Il Materialismo Storico e la Filosofia di Benedetto Croce*, Einaudi, Turin, 1966, p. 180.
3. *Ibid.*

determined man'. It is a 'spirit' or a 'universal man', a metaphysical entity. The history of man is a history of idea. As man is the creator there is no transcendental element in progress. History is the absolute 'becoming' and dialectically develops to attain liberty. History for Croce is reduced to a "formal history, a history of concepts or to a history of intellectuals".[1] The dialectic of distincts is a conceptual dialectic and had four moments of spirit ethics, logic, art and economics, Politics is a 'mere' passion for Croce. The true sciences are moments of philosophy. In this dialectics, there is complete negation of conflicts and synthesis is the fusion of thesis and antithesis, whereas in Hegelian schema, synthesis is a transcendence of initial forms by new forms. As the only reality for Croce is Mind, synthesis is established *a priori* and there is no conflict in the progress of history. These concepts of metahistorical man, fusion of conflicts and *a priori* development of liberty—all try to eliminate the revolutionary alternative and serve the ideological function of ruling groups. Croce's true sciences are possible, Gramsci declares, only in structurally unified, homogeneous societies of future or classless society. In conflict-ridden societies, politics is a science.

The critique of aberrations of marxism (for example of Bukharin) as well as of idealist revision (for example of Croce) stress the need for a restatement of Marxist theory that is based on an organic relationship between theory and politics, philosophy and science. A study of such dimensions takes the role of culture and education is effecting the transition from theory to practice or the attainment of praxis. The sources of Gramsci's Marxism were both Italian (i.e. Croce and Gentile and Labriola) and international (i.e. Lenin, Bukharin et al.).

The sum and substance of the whole argument is that in Gramsci's view the philosophy of praxis is not to be studied simply as an epistemology, as it is organically linked with politics. The theoretical problems do not exist as

---

1. *Ibid.*, p. 304.

pre-established and can always be overlaid by ideological and cultural formations alien to it. Thus before embarking upon the specific formulations of Gramsci, it is necessary to reaffirm Marx's views and their 'actualization' in Lenin's practice. The fact that Lenin "continued and actualized Marx" reveals Marxism's capacity to ensure "transition from Utopia to science, from science to action."[1] Marxism would disappear with the disappearance of class struggle. Gramsci declares that it is the "only philosophy that actively intervence in the conjuncture".[2] It can best be understood by taking into account the practice of Lenin. In fact it was the first Italian Marxist thinker Labriola who not only suggested the term 'philosophy of praxis' for Marxism but also stressed the necessity to construct the views of Marx sceintifically.

No wonder, that Gramsci's study of Marxism is pervaded by historicism. Historicism is both philosophical and political as it is a philosophy of transformation into praxis. Gramsci rejects any concept of history that is transcendental or metaphysical and asserts:"We deny the need for any *apriorism*, whether it be transcendental in the sense of religious faith, or historical as with the privileges of the bourgeoisie".[3] This idea is further developed to encompass in its meaning a politics. The philosophy of praxis is "*absolute historicism or absolute humanism*".[4] The unity of theory and practice makes it possible for praxis theory to be a "crowning point" of past philosophies. It is the 'heir' to the classical idealist philosophy not only because of the embodiment of theory into practice but also because of its continuation.

Thus, according to Gramsci, Marxist philosophy is a new philosophy. There is a need to overcome the gap between philosophy and action of the members whom it intends to engage—i.e. those 'who are not' in the know of

1. Gramsci, *La Construzione del Partito Comunista*, p. 273.
2. Gramsci, *Selections From Prison Notebooks*, p. 405.
3. Gramsci, *Scritti Giovonili*. Einaudi, Turin, 1958, p. 117.
4. Gramsci, *Selections From Prison Notebooks*, p. 417 (Emphasis added).

political practices' is to be overcome by taking into account the intervention in the field of culture. However, this is not a direct relationship of dependence of theory on practice. Gramsci admits : "In the new developments of historical materialism, the deepening of the concept of the unity of theory and practice is as yet only in its initial phase ; there are still residue of mechanism. Theory is still spoken of as a 'complement' to practice, almost like some kind of accessory".[1] The unity of theory and practice is dialectical and Gramsci asserts that it "is not a mechanical fact, but a historical becoming".[2] This formulation of historicism is very close to Lenin's formulations that "unity of theoretical idea (of knowledge) and of practice...and this unity precisely in the theory of knowledge."[3]

Gramsci felt that the prevalent tendencies of Second International that stressed materialism to the deteriment of 'historical' in the term 'historical materialism' and because of this it discounted the role of ideas in the process of change. Moreover, this view neglects the superstructures that are vital for revolution. Hegemony of a class postulates a critique of mechanism. Historical materialism is different from these. "It is well known, moreover, that the originator of philosophy of praxis (Marx) never called his own conception materialist and that when writing about French materialism he criticises it....Thus he never uses the formula 'materialist dialectic', but calls it 'rational' as opposed to 'mystical' which gives the term 'rational' a quite precise meaning."[4] When conventional terminology is used, it is necessary to return to the cultural sources in order to identify the exact value of concepts. As Labriola says that "the expression 'materialist conception of history' if seized by verbatim may be restricted to formal

---

1. Gramsci, Notebook 8,228, *Quaderni del Carcere* (Ed. Gerratna). Einaudi Turin, 1975.
2. *Ibid*.
3. Lenin, Philosophical Notebooks, *Collected Works*, Vol. 38, Progress Publishers, Moscow, 1979, p. 219.
4. Gramsci, *Selections From Prison Notebooks*, pp. 456-57.

definition and erroneous belief that this is an easy thing to reduce into terms and into simple and palpable expression, the agitated and immense complexus of nature and history and that it is easy to picture the multiform and complicated interlacing of causes and effects."[1] It is vital to understand "how historical materialism can incorporate a crucial role for consciousness without losing in the process, the essentials economic core that constitutes it uniqueness."[2] While "Marx is essentially a historicist,"[3] 'historical' both qualifies materialism and dominates it in historical materialim Carrying a critique of historical economism, Gramsci says "many people find it very convenient to think that they can have the whole of history and all political and philosophical wisdom in their pockets concentrated into a few short formulae. The forget that the thesis which asserts that men become conscious of fundamental conflicts on the level of ideology is not psychological or moralistic in character but structural and epistemological".[4] Lenin's contribution of hegemony to historical materialism explains the role of superstructure. Gramsci, therefore says : "Illich" had "advanced Marxism not simply in political theory and in economics, but also in philosophy (i.e. by advancing political doctrine, he would also have advanced philosophy).[5]

We now come to the relationship between history, philosophy and politics as envisaged by Gramsci, in the philosophy of praxis. He insists that the history of philosophy cannot be studied apart from the class struggle. The Cvocean view is derived from Hegel that philosophy is history. The only living concrete reality is thought and in order to comprehend the whole of world it is necessary to understand

1. Labriola, *Essays on Materialistic Conception of History*, Charles H. Kerr & Co., Chicago, 1908, p. 92.
2. Femia, *Gramsci's Political Thought*, Clarendon Press, Oxford, 1981, p. 66.
3. Gramsci, Notebook. 4, 11, *Quaderni del Carcere*.
4. Gramsci, *Selections From Prison Notebooks*, p. 164.
5. Gramsci quoted in Glucksmann, *Gramsci and The State*. p. 351.

history of thought or of philosophers' philosophies. For Gramsci this is a sectarian view. For him, the conceptions of leading groups, the worldview of broad popular masses and the interconnections between these, mark the philosophy of praxis. The philosophy, then is "*a caltural struggle seeking to transform the popular mentality and diffuse the philosophical innovations that prove historically effective.*"[1]

Thus philosophy becomes a moment in the theory of superstructures. It is "the translation into the terms of a realistic historicism of the subjective conception of reality."[2] History of philosophy is thus a history of conflict among classes having different worldviews. Hence philosophy is politics and politics, as already discussed, is a science.

The philosophy of praxis is also concerned with the question of knowledge and its objectivity. Praxis is "the concrete historical activity of men" for "transforming a definit organised"[3] matter. The attempts by mechanists to replace 'idea' of Hegel with 'matter' and then arrive at Marxism is a wrong problematic. The relationship between subject and object, men and nature does not postulate a dualism between phenomena. For Gramsci, 'human history' should be viewed as the history of nature. The philosophy of praxis cannot be broken into parts of economics, politics and philosophy. As philosophy has no object in the sense that science and metaphysics have and unity of Marxism is organic, there can be no dualism in Marxism.

Men become conscious of structural conflicts at an ideological level is an epistemological affirmation. The unity of theory and practice is also of importance for the theory of knowledge. Moreover, the striving for hegemony[4] is also epistemological in so far as it gives rise to a new ideological field ; it is a reform of consciousness and of methods of knowledge. This analysis of Marx's 'Preface' to *Critique of*

---

1. *Ibid.*, p. 356 (Emphasis added).
2. Gramsci, 'Notebook' 10, 10, *Quaderni del Carcere.*
3. Glucksmann, *Gramsci and The State*, p. 236.
4. For the concept of hegemony, see chapter VI.

Political Economy led Gramsci to evolve a concept of ideology that is novel and needs careful scrutiny.

His concept was evolved out of a critique of Croce's concept of ideology as an illusion and Bukharin's concept of ideology as a 'system of ideas'. Croce reproached Marx for treating ideology as apperance. According to Gramsci, croce has misunderstood Marx by reading ideology as a direct influence of structure and yet distinct from it. Its limited efficiency to change the world even when it thinks itself capable of this task, also strengthened this belief. It is also, in a negative sense, an "arbitrary elucubration"[1] of individual. This view is very close to Marx in *German Ideology* of which was unaware.

As against these negative concepts there is a positive connotation of the word (ideology) to be analysed historically in terms of the philosophy of praxis is a superstructure. "For Marx, the ideologies,... have an objective and active reality" without being the mover of history and Gramsci explains that "it is the social reality in its productive infrastructure whih creates ideologies".[2] It is true that they have limited historicity and tend to disappear. The term 'ideology' initially mean a 'science of ideas' and later on, implied a 'system of ideas'. Bukharin too subscribed to this view whereby ideas were considered to be the result of sensations. He, however, confused historical materialism with metaphysics of matter, thus equating it with ideology. For Gramsci it "is a conception of the world that is implicity manifest in art, law economic activity, in all manifestations of individual and collective life".[3] This is relationship of ideology and the superstructure. As a matter of fact, there is a dialectical relationship between ideologies and material forces.

---

1. To quote Gramsci exactly "the name ideology is given both to the necessary superstructure of a particular structure and to the arbitrary elucubrations of particular individuals". See Gramsci, *Selections From Prison Notebooks*, p. 376.
2. Gramsci, Notebook 4, 15 *Quaderni del Carcere.*
3. Gramsci, *Selections From Prison Notebooks*, p. 328.

To quote Gramsci, an analysis of various socio-economic forces reveal that, "the concept of *historical bloc* in which precisely material forces are the content and ideologies are the form, though this distinction between form and content has purely didactic value since the material forces would be inconceivable historically without form and the ideologies would be individual fancies without the material forces."[1] In this way, masses intervene to shape their own history. Since the superstructure is not directly influenced by structure, it (the superstructure) only reflects the tendencies of development and not hard, fixed laws. The tendencies may or may not materialize. The ideology of the dominated classes cements the basis of these classes. The organic ideologies are born on the terrain of historical necessity and are essential to organise the masses. It is rooted in the immediate and conjunctural problems of the class whose ideology it is; in contrast to it the philosophy has both immediate and future interests of an entire social group. In ideology, masses implicitly or explicitly, elaborate their relation to the world. Organic ideology is a conception of the world and its corresponding rules of conduct.

And it is exactly this fact that in Gramsci's view "establishes human subjectivity as a core element of Marxism."[2] Marx argues for a reciprocity between subject (man-in society) and object (the material world). Gentile had tried to unite subject and object in spirit as, 'pure act'. But denying it, Gramsci countered that it is an "impure act'. It is a critical activity of mem in transfroming a definite organized matter (the material productive forces). It cannot be reduced to a single unit in spirit or matter. The praxis theory does not give precedence to either subject or object, it is rather the elaboration of relation between the two, between men and nature, it is historical activity of transformation of men and nature.

It is in this context, that Gramsci asserts that "matter as such therefore is not our subject but how it is socially and

1. *Ibid.*, p. 377.
2. Femia, *Gramsci's Political Thought*, p. 4.

historically organized for production."[1] There can be no daulism between man and nature. Marxism does not simply replace the sp!rit with 'matter.' The relation is dialectical and organic.

In handling the question "what is man"? Gramsci opines that this question is relative in the sense that through this query "we want to know what are we and what can we become," and the extent to which man can make himself. The answer of these would be—man is the "*process of his actions*".[2] He further claims: There does not exist, historically, a way of seeing, and acting which is equal for all men"[3] i.e. biological equality or law of nature are not applicable in philosophy. Catholieism and past philosophies stumble when they conceive 'man' as limited to spirit. The practice of catholicism reveals that contrary to its professions, only men with some property or economic facilities were given political rights, or the right to transfrom the society. This implied recognition of man in material assets. Man is a social being, and a society of things presupposes human society. "What is man" is a question pertaining to" "man in general" or to 'human nature.' If man is related to his social, economic being then there cannot be 'man-in-general' and human nature is therefore an 'ensemble of relation'. Human nature is, thus, quite specific and historic and can belocated "in the entire history of the human species."[4] There can never be uniformity in human nature that can be related to history, as it is manifested in the idea of becoming. The socio-economie equalities in history exist to that extent of which men are conscious. The striving of man, towards these socio-economic equalities is measured in length of 'progress' or 'becoming'. Progress is an ideology whereas becoming is a dialectical and a historical movement. The extent of state of becoming, i.e. extent to which man dominates his environment is the yardstick of comparison of

---

1. Gramsci, *Selections From Prison Natebooks*, p. 465.
2. *Ibid.*, p. 351 (Emphasis added).
3. *Ibid.*, p. 352.
4. *Ibid.*, 356.

human nature. The mastery of external world or material forces is the means to achieve human nature. The common sense regards all men as equal on biological grounds and has residue of catholicism (sons of God). In fact, humun nature is the unity of theory and practice.

The relation of man to nature is also important. Kantian noumenon, distinguishes between 'thing--in-itself' and phenomenon through which we have knewledge of them. Subjectivists, on the other hand, believe in the concept of reality as we know it. But since all philosophy is historical and not definitive, it is difficult to believe that reality changes objectively with changes in ourselves. The hiatus between objective world and man is created by religion which believe that God created the world first and the man afterwards. This leads common sense to deride subjectivisit conception. But in reality it is the founder of modern philosophy in its most advanced form in so far as it gave birth to and was superceded by historical materialism. For Gramsci: " 'Objective' means exactly and only this; we consider objective that reality that is ascertained by all men, that is independent of every point of view, be it merely particular or that of a group. Actually even this is a particular world view. However, this view as a whole and for the direction it indicates, can be accepted by the philosophy of praxis, whereas one should object the view of common belief, even though it reaches the same material conslusions."[1] The above relation of objective or rather 'humanly objective' to 'human consciousness' is very close to the following views of Marx: "When you ask about the creation of man and nature, you are abstracting in so doing from man and nature. You postulate them as non-existent yet you want me to prove them to you as existing. Now, I say to you-Give up your abstraction and you will also give up your question? Man alone, bestows sense on objectivity".[2] For

1. Gramsci, "Science and Scientific ideologies" *Tilos*, No. 41, pp. 153-54.

2. Marx. *Economic and Philosophical manuscripts*, Progress Publishers, Moscow, 1977, p. 107.

Grameci also the issue is the same; Can there "exist an extra-historical and extra-human objectivity? But who is the judge of this objectivity"?[1] Science is tied to the needs of man. It is praxis, the activity of man that constitutes our view of objectivity. Since nature is always mediated through praxis, praxis or labour is an epistemological category. One man's experiences become objective only when they attain the coherent integration with the experience of others, forming a social body of knowledge and exercising hegemony on that society. This hegemony, in turn, helps in the formulation of world view of individuals and this absorption into an already existing body of knowledge is the process of knowledge. There is a rence between objective and givenness. "Not every thing given is objective. Matter as such is not our subject but as it is socially organized for production."[2]

Philosophy intervenes in the problems and modifies them; Marxist methodology and worldview are not separate. The worldview contains the method of reformation and of hegemony. As has already been shown, relationship between men and nature is not one of subject and object in idealist sense. Gramsci therefore insists that the natural sciences are not the model for philosophy. Within the ambit of historical materialism, thinking cannot be detached from being nor man from nature (of which he forms part); and historical activity cannot be detached from matter nor the subject from the object.

The methods of natural science deprive Marxism of its inherent element (active praxis), and are evolutionary. The Marxian 'historical necessity' only entails that material conditions for transformations are ripe but it has no emphasis on determinism as Bukharin thought. Science struggles for knowledge of the objectivity of the real but the important thing is not the knowledge of the objectivity of the real as such, *but the approach to it*; in other words, it is man-reality relationship. It is the active element that intervenes in

---

1. Gramsci, *Selections From Prison Notebooks*, p. 445.
2. *Ibid.*, p. 465.

philosophy to develop the relation. Viewed in this perspective, superstructure is a part of the struggle to transform the structure; and science is also a superstructure as much as it serves the needs of man and is conditioned by the infasturcture. It is subject to class-struggle and is sometimes dormant under the effect of dominant ideology (religion). Thus though it is never objective and has ideological nature, yet it can never be identified with class subjectivism. One can accept the science of other classes without their ideoligies.

This analysis reveals that "Unity is given by the dialectical development of the contradictions between man and matter (nature-material forces of production). . . . In philosophy (the unity centre is) praxis, that is, the relationship between human will (superstrure) and economic structure".[1] The conscious activity or voluntarism as whll as spontaneous activity should be viewed in this perspective. Gramsci believes in two types of voluntarism—one pretends to being "an organic form of historical— political activity" and strives to recruit "ensemble or 'Superman". The other type is the "initial moment of an organic period which must be prepared and developed".[2] Both these activities fail to comprehend the dialectical relationship between subjective and objective factors. The active intervention of humans is possible by understanding the measure of freedom. As Gramsci explains "possibility is not reality: but it is in itself a reality."[3] The extent to which a human will can intervene depends on making this possibility into a reality. In a highly revealing passage, Gramsci replies to all those who stress either spontaneity or voluntarism in the mistaken bilief of mastering over objective processes. He asserts "That the objective possibilities exist for people . . . has its importance, or so one would have thought. But the existence of objective conditions of possibilities or of freedom is not yet enough: it is necessary to know' them, and know to use them. And to want to use them. Man in this sense, is concrete will, that is

1. Gramsci, *Selections From Prison Notebooks*, p. 409.
2. *Ibid.*, p. 204.
3. *Ibid.*, p. 438.

the effective application of the abstract will or vital impulse to the concrete means which realise such a will."[1]

This understanding can only be based on a knowledge of historical materialism and it has to be always in a dynamic process.

It follows that the philosophy of praxis based on historical materialism is itself historic i.e, it is a temporary philosophy. It is not eternal in the sense that it eternally goes on to resolve the contradiction; it does not only resolve the contradiction but is a part of that very contradiction. And, this element in Gramsci's philosophy involves an analysis of 'truth' which also cannot be absolute.

The above assumption makes it evident that Marxist philosophy is not a system "Philosophy-Politics—Economics—If these three activities are the necessary constituent elements of the same conception of the world...there must necessarily be, in their theoretical principles, a convertibility from one to others and a reciprocal translation into the specific language proper to each constituent element".[2] It thus follows that philosophical and historical materialism are not divisible into two. The kernel of historical materialism is the transformation of praxis. As it is not a system and cannot become a perfect dogma or faith, it is concerned with the question of truth. In fact an understanding of the problem of truth is a precondition for the study of worldview.

II

There has been various connotations attributed to the concept of truth. For a lay man, truth is like a precept, something fixed and universal. However the scientific study requires a systematic analysis of the term. The common usages of the term permeate the concept of norms also. The incessant search for a definition of truth led many to find it in certain immutable laws of nature. The development of nature, on the

1. *Ibid.*, p. 360.
2. *Ibid.*, p. 403.

basis of certain laws, led these thinkers to believe that these natural laws are applicable even to human society. This current also permeated Marxist thought. On the other hand, crass materialists sought 'truth' in the practical activities of man, condemning each and every attempt to scientifically synthesise theory and practice. The idealist school, envisaged truth as universal and as such inherent in 'Idea' or 'Spirit'. They conceived the truth as spirit, a transcendental concept. The 'spirit' which they though travelled through various stages of change to attain ultimately the Absolute Idea, and this Absolute Idea was the only 'truth'. For neo-Hegelians like Croce, although there was no transcendental truth, yet, 'absolute' truths were there. Ethics, Aesthetic, logic, etc. strove towards the 'absolute' idea of truth.

From amongst this medley of concepts, philosophy of praxis evolved its own concept of truth. And to reiterate, philosophy of praxis is historical materialism. Marxist philosophy is situated in the class struggle. Gramsci views other philosophies as inorganic because these are contradictory creations. Only the philosophy of praxis is the organic philosophy because it inheres in dialectics—the theory of contradictions. Unlike other philosophies, it is the philosophy of the masses and tries to bring consciousness among them. It identifies the class struggle, the inherent contradictions of the systems and endeavours to solve them. The philosophies of the ruling groups try to diffuse the situation and solve the contradictions peacefully in order to preserve the status-quo. This is not the case with praxis which is itself a theory of contradictions. It, therefore, does not wish to resolve crises peacefully. It bases itself on a critique of ideologies, on the whole of superstructure so much so that it itself becomes a superstructure. By elevating the common sense of masses to the level of philosophy, it becomes organic. All this is done according to the laws of historical materialism or the methedology of marxian thought. Philosophy, thus, suggests a course of action as well as a uniform, coherent worldview. The historical materialism is transient and would be eliminated with the disappearance of contradictions.

The 'historical materialism' is the philosophy of praxis and is itself 'historic'. It has not yet been superseded. As has been explained philosophy does not imply a conception of social totality with the function of true consciousness of its epoch. Philosophy cannot be categorised as such on account of its own history, i.e. there is no such thing as philosophy of a 'period'. The philosophy of praxis would be superseded by the supersession of class-struggle itself. As it is grounded in the class-struggle and is an organic component of the struggle, it is capable of intervening in the political practice. "The philosophy of praxis does not tend to resolve contradiction in history and society peacefully, but is the very theory of these contradictions".[1] As it is the philosophy of historically progressive class i.e. proletariat, it attacks the ruling classes. It teaches the subaltern classes, who want to learn the art of government and have an interest in knowing every truth, even the most disagreeable.[2] Thus the praxis theory carries a critique of all past philosophies in order to arrive at a coherent worldview. The philosophy of praxis takes into account the objective conditions as well as the intervention of the subjective 'will' in the historical conjuncture. There is a difference between truth and fact. Every truth is subjective. There is a need to understand what constitutes knowledge and subjective and objective in order to distinguish 'truth' and define it.

Gramsci had carried out a dissertation on Kantian concept of 'noumenon' and 'phenomenon'. According to Kant,[3] 'noumenon' is the 'thing-in-itself' and it is through 'phenomenon' that we understand this. This suggests that reality is not contained in what we perceive, there is something transcendent, beyond ourselves that constitutes reality. However, by their stress on reality as what one can see and

---

1. Gramsci quoted Glucksmann *Gramsci and The State*, p. 224.
2. *Ibid.*
3. For details of Kantian philosophy, see Chapter II.

perceive, the vulgar marxism (materialist)[1] and positivism[2] had created a reaction against the Kantian view. This gave rise Neo—Kantianism.[3]

Different from both these schools, Gramsci's historicism enabled him to blend the unity of thought and action in the theory of knowledge. According to Gramsci, knowledge is not confined to observable phenomena alone; there is a "relative" ignorance of reality, of something still unknown, which will however, be known one day when the 'physical' and intellectual instruments of mankind are more perfect, when that is, the technical and social conditions of mankind have changed in a progressive direction.

The Kantian concept of Ethics also came under heavy reproach. Kant's dictum that "Act only on that maxim whereby you can at the same time will that it should become a universal law",[4] presupposes a norm in 'similar' conditions, that in reality do not exist. Gramsci insists that activity of each man is located in specific historical conditions, in a given milieu. So there cannot be uniform rules of action. 'The Kantian maxim "presupposes a single culture, a single religion "world-wide' conformism."[5] As each man tends to justify one's action which he does not necessarily apply to others, it has to be analysed in the historical perspective. The Kantian notion describes an agent, who is "the bearer of the 'similar conditions' and indeed their creator."[6] This agent tries to

---

1. Vulgar materialism, according to Gramsci, denies that unity is given by dialectical development of contradiction between workers and productive forces. Vulgar Marxists regard machines as producers of value independent of men who run them.
2. Positivists Gramsci analyses, regard natural sciences, as the only true scieuces and try to study all development with the methods of natural sciences, they are in search of 'essential causes to 'predict' the future.
3. For neo-Kantianism—see chapter II.
4. Kant, quoted in Gramsci *Selections From Prison Notebooks*, f.n. p. 373.
5. Gramsci, *Selections From Prison Notebooks*, p. 374.
6. *Ibid.*

create a 'model' which others must emulate; or, it can be treated as a model of behaviour established by the ruling hegemonic group of society. Such a model can at the most be an ideology and never a 'truth' as such.

Gramsci has also analysed the term itself and its relation to truth. Ideology originally meant 'a science of ideas' but gradually it came to mean a 'system' of ideas. The theoretical 'ideology' of philosophy suggests that philosophy is system of truth. But this is a fallacious impression created by hegemonic class to achieve an 'interclass' aura and to make people conform to the values consistent with the perpetuation of exploitative system. Yet, even Marxism has become an ideology. As Gramsci has aptly remarked, there are technical reasons behind this inversion. "If the philosophy of praxis affirms theoretically that every 'truth' believed to be eternal and absolute has had practical origins and has represented a 'provisional' value (historicity of every conception of the world and of life), it is still very difficult to make people grasp 'practically' that such an interpretation is valid also for the philosophy of praxis itself, without in so doing shaking the convictions that are necessary for action."[1] The need to generate faith among masses makes philosophy of praxis on ideology, a "dogmatic system of eternal and absolute truths.[2] The thought of Bukharin, Gramsci says, confuses "matter" which is eternal and absolute with materialism and interprets the latter as the basis of laws of development, fixed and immutable.

In fact, objective and subjective conditions characterise truth. Every truth has only provisional value. Therefore, one must not conceive of a "scientific discussion as a process at law in which there is an accused and a public prosecutor whose professionol duty it is to demonstrate that the accused is guilty and has to be put out of circulation."[3] In fact, the search for truth is the concern of every philosophy in order to

---

1. *Ibid.*, p. 406.
2. *Ibid.*, p. 407.
3. *Ibid.*, p. 343.

attain an organic coherence. "It seems necessary to leave the task of researching after new truths and better, more coherent, clearer formulations of the truths themselves to the free initiative of individual, specialists, even though they may continually question the very principles that seem most essential."[1] This search of truth is most useful if it adopts a scientific method Gramsci declares : "In scientific discussion, since it is assumed that the purpose of discussion is the pursuit of truth and the progress of science, the person who shows himself most 'advanced' is the one who takes up the point of view that his adversary may well be expressing a need which should be incorporated, if only as a subordinate aspect, in his own construction."[2] This is precisely what philosophy of praxis does; it assimilates the historic element of past philosophies, and carries a critique of the past in order to evolve a philosophy of the masses. The philosophy of praxis being the worldview of historically progressive class, its truth no doubt are relevant for its present, but in themselves, these truths cannot be static and everlasting. There have been regressive tendencies in Marxism itself to treat theory as if it has a value of itself. "The problem arises of whether a theoritical truth, whose discovery corresponded to a specific practice, can be generalized and considered as universal for a historical epoch. The proof of its universality consists precisely in its becoming a stimulus to know better the concrete reality of a situation that is different from that in which it was discovered, when it stimulated and helped the better understanding of concrete reality, in its capacity to incorporate itself in that same reality as if it were originally an expression of it."[3]

The above definition entails an epistemological as well as a political value for change. The truth is thus a knowledge of reality and tools to transform this reality. The search for truth, then, cannot be the preserve only of intellectuals or

---

1. *Ibid.*, p. 341.
2. *Ibid.*, p. 344.
3. *Ibid.*, p. 201.

political activists or of any other exclusive group. It is the duty of all and in fact, all men act in the belief of being in the right. What characterizes truth is historical perspective and critical approach towards problems, i.e. a scientific method. The quest for truth must be left to scientist individuals who may or may not attain it. The constant questioning of the basis of all premiss, the rejection of 'all time' norms is the terrain of individuals. There should not be an exclusion from this search on account of differing worldviews. In fact, what appears utopian thought now, may materialise into reality in a future era but the scientist must be rooted in historic condition. Even scientific truths are "not definitive and final, then science too is a historical category."[1]

There has been different opinions regarding Gramsci's concept of truth. The problem of 'faith' of masses in a course of action is raised. How can the masses participate in a worldview, that is itself a part of contradiction and tries for its own liquidation, that is to resolve the contradictions with the disappearance of which it would become redundant. Gramsci has tried to solve this problem. He concurred that "philosophy can only be experienced among masses as a faith,"[2] but insisted that the task of philosophy is to elevate the consciousness of the masses to the level where they can perceive the philosophy and actively participate in the world-view. Moreover, the disappearance of exploitative state alone would not suffice. The moral and intellectual reform of the masses is a precondition for uniform worldview and that can be attained only with the prevalence of classless society and elimination of all forms of exploitation. Gramsci therefore maintained that there are many pitfalls in adopting a universal and static definition of truths. As we have seen above, everyone "acts according to one's culture. The so called norms of society that proclaim a code of conduct postulate a single

---

1. Gramsci translated by Finocchiari, 'Science and Scientific ideologies', *Telos* 41, p. 155.
2. Gramsci, *Selections From Prison Notebooks*, p. 339.

culture, single religion and single worldview."[1] So long as there are classes in society, exploitation remains and hence there cannot be a single culture and worldview. The norms of behaviour and code of conducts are proclaimed by hegemonic classes in order to perpetuate their exploitative system and to quell any rising of discontent on the basis of socially accepted norms.

In rsume, it can be observed that Gramsci's worldview contains three core elements—philosophy of praxis, historical materialism and problem of truth—and these are organically and inherently connected with each other. In fact, there is one and only one continuum and the three elements are its integral and constituent points. The worldview is manifested in 'praxis' dialectically through language, common sense, culture, etc.; in other words, it is manifested in historical materialism. 'Historical Materialism' operates dialectically both in philosophical and material moment; it is the interaction of 'subject' and 'object' in praxis. Again, the dialectical moment of philosophical and historical materialism and of praxis contains 'Truth' which in its turn is dynamic, and not static.

The kernel of this worldview is to prepare masses to think coherently and to undertake a revolutionary politics. The ESSENCE of Marxism becomes the basis for POLITICS in Gramsci's philosophy. In fact, the task of the philosophy of praxis is to infuse in the masses the significance of acting consciously. Let Gramsci speak himself : "If a mass of people are led to conceive the present reality in a coherent and unified way, this is a far more important "philosophical fact' than the discovery by a 'genius' of a new truth that remains the property of small group of intellectuals."[2] In other words, "*the real philosophy of each person is contained in the politics.*"[3]

---

1. *Ibid.*, p. 374.
2. Gramsci, quoted in Glucksmann, *Gramsci and The State*, p. 380.
3. *Ibid.*, p. 366 (Emphasis added).

Philosophy, then, is contained in Politics; and Politics is Praxis. Praxis in its turn is Unity—a Unity of theory and practice, thought and action, subjective and objective arrived at dialectically. It is the Intellectuals who are the agents of this Unity; they are the link through which theory and practice, Subject and Object, thought and action are united in a dialectical manner.

4

Concept of Intellectuals

The Gramscian concept of 'truth' reveals an important function of philosoph; it is to attain organic coherence in order to criticise past philosophies in the process of evolving the worldview of the proletariat. The moral and intellectual reform of the masses is to be taken up by the intellectuals as a precondition for a future victory of the working class. Thus, the concept of intellectuals—their origins, evolution and functions—is integrally linked with the question of the world-view and becomes the core of Gramsci's political philosophy.[1] But, before embarking on Gramscian concept of intellectuals, it is necessary to understand the popular meaning of the term

---

1. It is interesting to note that as early as 1927, Gramsci wrote from the Milan prison to his sister-in-law Tania that he intended to undertake a "research on the history of Italian intellectuals, their groupings in relation to culture currents, their various modes of thinking, and so on." This study "from a 'disinterested' point of view" was aimed at examining "the popular creative sprit, in its diverse phases of development" This schema for study was adopted in *Prison Notebooks* and runs almost through his letters from prison. See Gramsci, *Letters From Prison*, (Introduction by L. Lawner), Quartet Books, London, 1973, pp. 79-80.

as well as the meaning imparted to the term by various liberal and sociological theorists.

The general meaning attributed to intellectuals is of one "having the power of understanding"[1] or having 'rational' power. Its literal meaning is "of, appealing to, requiring the exercise of intellect," and "given to mental pursuit."[2] An intellectual is a person who has the specific task of mental faculties, one assigned the role of meditating and expounding new ideas. Priests, teachers and philosophers come under the purview of this term. More often than not, the general masses regard all those people as intellectuals who are ostensibly the makers and custodians of social norms and morality. The inclusion of scientists and researchers in the category of intellectuals lends credence to the common sense belief that intellectuals are detached formulations of social norms and moral order. Thus, in common parlance intellectuals are characterised by their function of mental exercise in society, they are detached from social groups and are makers and custodian of social and moral norms. The religious and cultural functionaries are predominant among the intellectuals. There have been various thinkers and commentators who have sought to reinforce this view giving it an academic sanction.

Before the advent of advanced capitalism, the term, 'intellectual' was mainly confined to artists, social scientists and religious-cultural representatives; but gradually with the advent of industrialised societies, technocrats, managers, scientists, etc., too were included in the intellectual category. This wide spectrum of activities makes it very difficult to demarcate the class boundaries of intellectuals and thereby reinforce among the masses the image of intellectuals as 'special', remote group, and as parate social stratum.

The liberals, also reinforce these attributes of intellectuals but they do not do so solely on the basis of their social position. They do it because they trust their capability

---

1. E.M. Kirkpatri (Ed,), *Chambers Twentieth Gentury Dictionary*, Allied Publishers Pvt. Ltd., Bombay, 1983, p. 654.
2. Caulson, Carr, Hutchinson, *Oxford Illustrated Dictionary*.

to mould people's thinking. American sociologists give a particular stress on the occupational role of the intellectuals. They exclude managerial class and civil services from this category because of the occupational role entrusted to them (intellectuals) for forming public opinion. For Lipset, "all those who create, distribute, and apply culture, that is, the symbolic world of man, including art, science and religion"[1] constitute intellectuals. For Parsons, "intellectual is an individual forming part of a definite system of culture."[2] And therefore differing sharply from those performing managerial functions. For Schumpeter, intellectuals "are in fact people who wield the power of the spoken and written word", they have "the absence of direct responsibility for practical affairs."[3] For Robert Brym, they are independent "of their social attachment" and are involved chiefly in "the production of ideas"; this also includes "students in post-secondary institutions who are apprentices to these occupational roles."[4] The American view, thus, reinforces the separate social substratum of intellectual.

The European commentators emphasise on the moral values and ideological principles of intellectuals. Coser says: "Intellectuals exhibit in their activities a pronounced concern with the core values of society. They consider themselves special custodians of abstract ideas like reason and justice and justice and truth, jealous guardians of moral standard that are too often ignored in the market place and the houses of power."[5] This superior role assigned to intellectuals gives them a moral authority and strengthens the common usage of the term. For Aron, the intellectuals are necessarily "aloof

---

1. S.M. Lipset, *Political Man*, Doubleday and Col. Inc. New York, 1960. p. 311.
2. T. Parsons, "The Intellectual : A Social Role Category". *On Intellectuals*, Doubleday, New York, 1969, pp. 3-4.
3. J.A. Schumpeter, *Capitalism, Socialism and Democracy*, Harper and Brothers, New York, 1950, p. 147.
4. R.J. Bryms, *Intellectuals and Politics*, George Allen and Unwin Co. London, 1950, p. 147.
5. L.A. Coser, *Men of Ideas*, Free Press, New York, 1965, p. viii.

from any sort of menial practical activity, not involved even in administrative, managerial, political activities."[1] Under the growing impact of Marxian analysis of society in terms of class conflict, Edward Shils, Boranetsky, D. Bell, Galbiarti, et al., have included the bureaucrats and specialists in the sub-stratum intellectuals. P. Boranetsky for example, envisages the "creation of a category of creative organisational work, which is destined to supersede the class of proletarian and capitalists in the post-industrial society."[2] Shils believes, "Intellectuals are the aggregate of persons in any society who employ in their communication and expression and with relatively higher frequency than most other members of their society, symbols of general scope and abstract reference, concerning man, nature and cosmos. The high frequency of their use of such symbols may be a function of their own subjective propensity or of the obligations of an occupational role."[3]

All these modern definitions reinforce the popular meaning of the term providing it a special role, a separate sbustratum. Some include in this category wider sections of the new society and some other adhere to their traditional functions. It is interesting to note in this connection that some of the sociological thinkers of nineteenth century, in order to strengthen liberal ideas of free trade, tried to portray political power as separate from socio-economic power, as balancer of the political society. These thinkers propounded theories of elite[4] who were superior to and separate from the general populace.

Gramsci finds in the idea of this school—an attempt to establish intellectuals as a separate class. Let him speak for himself: "Mosca's so-called 'political class' in nothing other

1. Aron, quoted in Nadel, *Contemporary Capitalism and Middle Classes*, Progress Publishers, Moscow, 1983. p. 252.
2. P. Boranetsky quoted *Ibid.*, p. 255.
3. Edward Shils, *On Intellectual Theoretical Studies*, Doubleday, New York, 1969, p. 4.
4. See chapter II above.

than the intellectual category of the dominant social group. Mosca's concept of 'political class' can be connected with Pareto's concept of the *elite*, which is another attempt to interpret the historical phenomenon of the intellectual and their function in the life of state and society."[1] It is in the context of identifying intellectuals with the elite that a brief presentation of ideas of these elite theorists thinkers could not be out of the place. More so because the function of the philosophy of praxis is to "combat modern ideologies in their most refined form."[2] It was necessary for Gramsci to take account of the ideas of Mosca, Pareto, Michels and Croce, in order to combat them.

Mosca, Pareto and Michels belonged to the school that places intellectual at a higher pedastal. They proposed the theory of 'positivist sociology of elites'. The theory originated when the upsurge of masses led to the discomfiture of rulers; and to deprive the masses of any power, the elite rulers evolved a 'principle' to maintain their stakes in the government. The parliamentary institutions thus posed a threat to their hegemony and a conservative liberalism sought to curb it.

Pareto's circulation of elite theory tried to conserve power within the ruling group by a rotation of rulers. The system of social equilibrium represented a theory where politics is merely guided by action and laws; it thus separated economy and social structure from the legal political institution. This analysis was based on functional and positivist lines, representing a simple cause and effect relationship between politics and the ruling class. Thus, the circulation of elites was considered to be determined by the ability of the elite to hold on to power. The society too was simplistically divided into two classes; and all political, social organizations were based on this categorization. The governed were thought to be an inferior stratum and rulers a superior stratum. The aristocratic views of Pareto, thus, represented

---

1. Gramsci, *Selections From Prison Notebooks*, f.n. p. 6.
2. *Ibid.*, p. 392.

an attempt to curb parliamentary democracy and the rise of the masses. The intellectuals, being a superior stratum, hold the key to the perpetuation form of a government.

Gramsci contends that for Mosca also the stimulant was the same, i.e. need to crush popular consciousness. However his tone seemed slightly different as it was more liberal and disguised. Mosca opined that the government of the select elite was required to be constituted of capable men and these capable men belong to a political class that produces rulers. He claimed; "whatever its historical base and its form, all government is the achievement of an organized minority: of a *political class* and the transition from one epoch to another involving internal changes in its own formation, recruitment and operation.[1] Mosca tempers his exclusive elite government theory by a stress on the juridical aspect of the government in order to determine whether it is good or bad. Thus, though he does not 'provide an unqualified support to the intellectuals, yet he gives them an exclusive privilege to rule.

Michels and Croce also share the idea that the intellectuals form a separate class; they are a leading elite. Later on, Sorel also followed this theory.

Tracing the historical development of 'elite' idea, it is found that as the early twentieth century saw an upward trend in workers consciousness, the idea of intellectual elite was countered to subdue and even to annhilate the worker's aspirations, Michels propounded a theory of elite and attributed social unrest to an over supply of intellectual who, when not absorbed in society form a proletariat of intellectuals in search of economic form a proletariat of intellectuals in search of economic security, thus ignoring the contradictions in production relations as cause of unrest. These ideas were rebutted by Sorel who adopted another extreme approach by stressing on a revolution of producers by producers alone. He analysed the existing state as "a body of intellectuals invested with privileges and possessing so-called political means for defending itself against the attacks of other groups

1. Quoted in Glucksmann, *Gramsci and The State*, pp. 52-53.

of intellectuals and to acquire the profits of phublic offices. Parties are organized for the acquisition of these public posts which are imitative of the state."[1] The condemnation of political parties and intellectuals led him to decry any organised attempt at revolution and Marxist theory. The intellectuals who, "have the explotation of politics as their only vocation,"[2] must be excluded from the proletarian plan of action. Marx Weber, on the other hand, developed the idea of parliament as an agency to recruit the ruling elite, thus hiding the truth of 'rule by few' and giving it a democratic veneer.

Now a glance over Lenin and Bordiga's concept of intellectuals. Both played an important part in the development of Gramsci's ideas. Lenin believed that intellegentsia "is not an independent economic class and therefore is not an independent plitical forces."[3] However, they "occupy a special position among the other classes, attaching themselves partly to the bourgeois i.e. by their connections, their outlooks, etc., and partly to the wage-workers as capitalism increasingly deprives the intellectual of the independent position."[4] Each class develops its own intellectuals who represent its interests. The need is to win over intellectuals of other classes in order to strengthen the revolutionary proletariat. This required an assessment of the nature of intellectuals of various classes. The intellectuals of bourgeoisie according to Lenin, consisting manily of petty-bourgeois elements, are by their origin and by economic position, reactionary and ought to be effectively exposed. But that section of intellegentsia who have working class background and who have managed to get education ought to be won over by the proletariat because they are by nature revolutionary. In such a situation, Lenin feels that if

---

1. Sorel, "The Decomposition of Marxism", *Radicalism and the Revolt Against Reason*, p. 244.
2. Sorel, quoted in Glucksmann, *Gramsci and The State*, p. 50.
3. Lenin, *Collected Works*, Vol. 2, Progress Publishers, Moscow, 1982. p. 380.
4. *Ibid.*, vol 4, p. 202.

bourgeois intellectuals join the workers' movement, they have to be put under the control of the working class. Lenin is aware of the various hardships on the way. He says : "The intelligentsia is always more individualistic than the proletariat, owing to its very conditions of life and work, which do not directly involve a largescale combination of efforts...The intellectual elements, therefore, find it harder to adapt themselves to the discipline of Party life,...(elevating) their instinctive anarchism to principle of struggle."[1] This fact leads him to declare : "We shall never rely on the intellectuals, we shall only rely on the vanguard of the proletariat that leads all workers and poor peasants",[2] for "it is wrong to confuse the 'intellectual forces' of the people with the 'forces' of bourgeois intellectuals".[3] In short, Lenin contends intellectuals have an important role in building socialism after the revolution. The proletariat, therefore, must extract from the bourgeois intellectual all that is beneficial for their development. Those intellectuals who understand, appreciate and enthusiastically join the worker's movement, would be welcome to join them, where as the recalcitrant ones would be annihilated after the revolution.

The views of Bordiga were entirely different from that of Lenin. For Bordiga, intellectuals are an exclusive group or the vanguard of the movement. They control the party of the proletariat (being the intellectuals of proletarit) and formulate its policies. At the appropriate time, the party call upon the mass to join the struggle. The views of parts must strictly be based on an orthods textual Marxism. He pleaded that "there should not only be "discipline in fact but in thought"[4] also, and favoured abstentionism so that party has time to prepare for revolution distregarding needs for change in specific Italian circumstances.

---

1. *Ibid.*, vol. 7, p. 453.
2. *Ibid.*, vol. 28, pp. 213-14.
3. *Ibid.*, vol. 44, pp. 284.
4. Bordiga, "Discorso del Relatore della frazione astenzionista" quoted in Davidson, *Theory And Practice of Italian Communism*, p. 92.

In fact, Bordiga is not concerned with raising the cultural consciousness of the masses. His bid to counter cultural aristocracy of leaders led him to deny any place to intellectual activities among the masses. This stress on politics alone, to the exclusion of other elements, is not beneficial for the worker's movement, because they are not equipped with the facility to win over the intellectuals of other classes. It is evident even from Gramsci's early orientations and writings, that he thought it vital to raise the cultural level of the masses; and this precisely is the burden of intellectual activities. Gramsci strongly denounced the elitism of Bordigan concept, and even before his incarceration, as a political activist be tried to evolve his concept on a Marxist analysis of the social basis of intellectuals.

Gramsci came to grips with the issue after an analysis of economic and socio-political conditions of south Italy. In his "Notes on Mezzogiorno" (Southern Question), written in 1926, Gramsci discussed the problem of the South, its poverty and backwardness as compared to the North and tried to highlight the reasons behind this state of affairs. The discussion continued in incarcaration where, initially during 1929-30, the these of Southern Question were reinforced. South had always been like a colony of the North, culturally backward, underdeveloped and exploited. The feudal vestiges and domination of big landlords there led to the perpetuation of a reactionary culture' North on the other hand, witnessed an advancement of culture with the emergence of industrial intellectuals. The different development of the North and the South also implied varied relationship of their intellectuals with the State. The intellectuals of the South played a mediatory role between landlords and peasant masses through controlling the apparatus of the state the bureaucracy and the clergy, etc. The Southern masses were under the ideological domination of great intellecuals like Croce and of the mediating bureaucracy. Its backward culture was a prerequisite for the development of the North, and hence these groups perpetuating domination were vital to preserve the interest of the ruling class. North, on the other hand, had different class relations and the mediating role was performed by trade unions and political parties. The intellectuals of the North did not exercise direct control over apparatus of hegemony as was the case in the South.

This particular study of Italy led Gramsci to identify various categories of intellectuals. The South, according to him, was governed by the 'traditional' intellectuals, whereas in the North 'organic intellectuals' of the working class dominate. The former constituted the flexible but extremely resistant armour of the agrarian bloc; and the latter was 'the factory technician' type, who served as link between the working-class mass and the capitalist class. Taking up the problem of stratification exclusively in the South, Gramsci saw that there were three social layers—"the great amorphous, disintegrated of mass of peasantry; the intellectuals of the petty and medium rural bourgeoisie; and the big landowners and great intellectuals."[1] The rural bourgeois origin of the Southern intellectuals led them to adopt virulent anti-peasant postures and consequently pushed them to join the bureaucracy in order to maintain the exploitative system. This analysis showed that (a) in the South traditional intellectuals dominates and (b) these intellectuals led by Croce tried to diffuse the discontent of peasants, prevented them from becoming revolutionary. How these intellectuals managed to diffuse the social disintegration is analysed by Gramsci. The economy, as has been shown, had helped creat 'an agrarian bloc' of landlord and intellectuals and served as 'overseer' of Northern Capitalism". Along with this agrarian bloc, the great intellectuals of South who "had all the necessary gifts to satisfy the intellectual needs of the most sincere representatives of the cultured youth in the South" tried to "steer (this youth) along a middle way of classical serenity in thought and action." These intellectuals, led by Croce had "fulfilled an extremely important 'national' function. He has detached the radical intellectuals of the South from the peasant masses, forcing them to trke part in national and European culture; and through this culture, he has secured their absorption by

1. Gramsci, *Selections Erom Political Writings*, vol. II p. 454.

the national bourgeoisie and hence by the agrarian bloc."[1] The need of the time, therefore, as Gramsci viewed, was to evolve intellectuals of peasants and workers. But this was not an easy task because: "Intellectuals develop slowly...They represent the entire cultural tradition of a people, seeking to resume and synthesize all of its history. This can be said especially of the old type of intellectual : the intellectual born on the peasant terrain."[2] And this is the reason why it was difficult to secure their loyality for an alternative system of thought. The proletariat needed to win over intellectuals of other classes; but this task could be fulfilled only by securing an organic break in the mass of intellectuals. In other words this could happen only when the intellectuals join the revolutionary proletariat by realizing it as a historically determined class. And for acquiring this realization, peasant masses and workers needed to be organized in order to break the existing historic bloc of intellectuals and also to win over intellectuals of the other classes.

Picking up the thread from the "Southern Question", Gramsci continued his research on the concept of intellectuals while in the fascist prison. The rise of Fascism as a bourgeois reaction to the crisis of times presented to him a new set of questions. What precisely led to the rise of Fascism, he thought, could be traced back to the relations prevailing in Italian society from the time of its unification. And this study entailed not only an analysis of relations between different classes but also a study of intellectuals.

Gramsci reasoned that the traditional terminology put intellectuals on a separate and somewhat higher pedastal on account of their specific task of intellectual and mental faculties. He, however, disagreed with this view. His contention was that since all men having an intellect use it to formulate their conception of the world, all are intellectuals. Since all men are intellectuals, there can only be categories of intellectuals in a society made up of intellectuals. He thus,

---

1. *Ibid.*, p. 460
2. *Ibid.*, p. 462.

denied any special niche to intellectuals in the society on the basis of their functions alone. The term intellectual has had a limited meaning only because so far people had misused it by confining it to a particular kind of activity of men and broadly classifying their activities as intellectuals or non-intellectual. Gramsi's assertion, however, was that all activities were part of the system and as such must be studied within the ensemble of activities. It is in this sense that all men can be referred to as intellectuals. In Gramsci's words: "The term ientellectual must be taken to mean not only those social strata who are traditionally termed intellectuals, but in general the whole social mass that performs functions of organization in the broad sense: whether in the realm of production, culture or public administration."[1]

In fact, Gramsci's concept of intellectuals is a logical culmination of his worldview. As all men have an intellect, a worldview and act accordingly, all men are intellectuals. He, thus, provided a peculiar connotation to the word intellectual, entirely different from the traditional terminology. He opined that the intellectuals do not exist on the level of ideas alone; they are firmly rooted in the mode of production and production-relations in every society. What distinguishes them is their role as organisers of their class and society, and this also characterizes their division into categories along functional lines. There is no unitary criterion to identify intellectuals and it is an error to look "for this criterion of distinction in the intrinsic nature of activities, rather than in the ensemble of system of relations in which these activities have their place within the general complex of social relations".[2] One can, therefore, say, that worker is not identified by his physical labour alone, but by the condition in which he is forced to do a particular work in the process of production; i.e. his activities in the ensemble of relation determine his place.

---

1. Gramsci, quoted in Glucksmann, *Gramsci and The State*, p. 28.
2. Gramsci, *Selections From Prison Notebooks*, p. 8.

In *The Prison Notebooks,* Gramsci identifies two methods of the formulation of intellectuals. First "Every social group, coming into existence on the original terrain of an essential function in the world of economic production, creates together with itself, organically one or more strata of intellectuals which give it homogeneity...not only in economic but also in the social and political fields."[1] But, these intellectuals find "categories of intellectuals already in existene and which seemed indeed to represent an historical continuity uninterrupted even by the most complicated and radical changes in political and social forms."[2] This is the second method. The first can be labelled as the organic and the second as the traditional inttellectuals. Organic intellectuals are those members of society who articulate the aspirations and interests of the class of their origin whereas traditional intellectuals have an inter-class aura about them. To be specific, Gramsci speaks of two categories of intellectuals—traditional and organic. Traditional intellectuals have historical and organic intellectuals have sociological trait.

With the changes in the modes of production, the class character of the socitey also undergoes a change and new groups emerge. These new social groups require representatives to formulate and articulate their interests in the emerging economic erder. It is this necessity that, generates the 'organic' intellectuals, who, thus become the deputees of the class of their origin. The organic intellectual is closely bound with the class of its origin and acts as its representative in various aspects, yet he represents "for the most part 'specializations' of partial aspects of the primitive activity of the new social type which the new class has brought into prominence."[3] Thus, it becomes clear that such groups as the feudal lords and bourgeoisie were initially organic intellectuals of the respective classes of their origin. The peasantry however, was unable, on

1. *Ibid.*, p. 5.
2. *Ibid.*, p. 7.
3. *Ibid.*, p. 6.

account of its role in the world of production, to evolve its organic intellectuals. It is clear that "the intellectuals of historically (and concretely) progressive class, in the given conditions, exercise such a power of attraction that, in the last analysis, they end up by subjugating the intellectuals of other social groups; they thereby create a system of solidarity between all the intellectuals with bonds of a psychological nature."[1] The peasantry alone cannot win over intellectuals of other groups as it seldom attains class consciousness on its own. Its (peasantry's) intellectuals are absorded by the system as by its place in production relations, it (peasantry) strives to possess land, thereby strengthening the prevailing systems. In other words, it (peasantry) has to be led by the worker's intellectuals.

The extent to which organic intellectuals participate in direct political process varies in different systems. The capitalist stage of development gave birth to bourgeoisie and proletariat classes and the exploited proletariat (the historically progressive class) has to win over the intellectuals of the other classes. The intellectuals of the proletariat are directly bound up with production unlike the other classes. The intellectuals of the bourgeoisie play a direct role in the formation of class by having a clear perception of their situation in social relation for attaining hegemony. The intellectuals of proletariat, however, do not have the capacity to organize their class on their own. It, therefore, falls on the shoulders of 'collective' intellectual or the political party to organise and lead them. The intellectuals of proletariat act as mediator between leadership of the party and the masses. They have an essential role in the political process of organising politically the class in a dialectical relationship with the party. They are "qualified political intellectuals, leaders and organizers of all the activities and function inherent in the organic development of an integral society, both civil and political."[2]

Gramsci envisages the traditional intellectuals, as the

---

1. *Ibid.*, p. 60.
2. *Ibid* , p. 16.

group that do not easily give up their right as the deputies of dominant class and try to project a semblance of continuity between the past and the present society. As Marx rightly says' "Men never relinquish what they have won but this does not mean that they never relinquish the social form in which they have acquired certain productive forces. On the contrary, in order that they may not be deprived of the result attained and forfeit the fruits of civilization, they are obliged, from the moment when their mode of carrying on commerce no longer corresponds to the productive forces acquired, to change all their traditional social forms."[1] The changes in economic structure, then do not directly effect the superstructure. The traditional intellectuals lose their relation with the class of their birth and acquire an inter-class aura. "One of the characteristics of the intellectuals as a crystallized social group (one, that is, which sees itself as continuing uninterruptedly through history and thus independent of the struggle of groups rather than as the expression of a dialectical process through which every dominant social group elaborates its own category of intellectuals) is precisely that of connecting itself, in the ideological sphere, with preceding intellectual category by means of a common conceptual nomenclature."[2]

The most common example of traditional intellectuals is ecclesiastics whose control over various institutions of society was all pervasive at one time. Their role in Italian history is particularly very influential. They were born with landed aristocracy However, with the demise of this ruling group, (landed aristocracy) the ecclesiastics gave up certain of their privileges but continued their monopoly in the religious field. As a matter of fact, according to Gramsci; teachers, philosophers, artists etc.—all those who consider themselve as autonomous of mode of production and without organically being related to any class are in reality members of the 'traditional' intellectual.

---

1. Marx, in a letter to Annenkov, compiled in Marx, Engles, *Selected Works*, pp. 660-61.
2. Gramsci, *Selections From Prison Notebooks*, p. 452.

In addition to the above types, intellectuals can also be catergorised on the basis of location; and there are two categories of intellectuals in this regard—rural and urban. The emphasis on the "Notes On Southern Question" is on the relationship between these categories, and also between these and the geographical categories. Putting together all these categories, one may broadly find the presence of rural and urban bourgeoisie, peasants, and workers. The base of Fascism also can be understood by keeping in mind these categories of intellectuals. The rural and urban intellectuals differ on account of differences in production processes; and the resultant cultural difference is to be studied in order to understand their class origins. The cultural development is a slow process and witnesses vast socio-economic disparties as is evident from the North-South position. The role in the process of production determines to a large extent, the relationship between a class and the state. Intellectuals of the urban society have grown up with industry and they function as a link between producers and workers. The rural intellectuals are generally traditional who bring the feudal lords and peasants into the system.

It is in this context that Gramsci explains the phenomenon of Fascism as emerging out of an alliance between the rural petty-bourgeoisie (or bureaucrats) and the urban capitalists. It is here that the problems about the very nature of Italian state demand explanation. Gramsci's assertion is that at the time of Risorgimento (Italian unification) the dominant group had failed either to produce sufficient number of intellectuals or to win over intellectuals of other classes. The unification, thus, remained weak as no single worldview could be evolved. As a matter of fact, this fragile Italian political system led to an unstable political facade. And, the inherent weakness of the system tempted the Fascists to capture power and to exercise dominance through force. In fact, the excessive reliance of Fascism on force betrays an absence of its organic intellectuals. The urban intellectuals, by actively participating in the production processes, are aware of political processes and have a duty to organise the class of their origin. They, therefore, are in command of the activities of their class and strive to achieve direct control over the state. The rural intellectuals, having largely the function of mediation between landlords and peasants and between government and the other classes do not have a direct role in the production process. They are unable to provide leadership to any social group, neither do they strive for change. Their interest is in maintaining the status-quo so that they can continue with their existence and privileges.

The categorigation of intellectuals on the basis of location, Gramsci feels, is important as it facilitates the analysis of regional culture forms. But more significant and fundamental is their demarcation on functional basis. An analysis of American society shows that it is growing steadily as it has no residue shows that is traditional intellectuals or parasitic classes who project themselves on the leading class of the changed system in order to preserve the status-quo. The European civilization being old there are vestiges of traditional intellectual who just live off society. In a way, these classes are the cultural dregs of the past and play a prominant role in building up of a society and in perpetuating values that are beneficial for their existence. In America, on the other hand, the society does not have such dregs of the past and as such can continue to prosper unhindered by any traditional values. However, in its development process, America is creating a new category of parasites—the womenfolk of rich groups who fritter away the wealth of the society and generate hypocricy. But, as yet this malady has not reached that stage of menacing proportions as to threaten those values of the society on which the free development of capitalist production is based.[1]

Needless to say that these categories of intellectuals have different roles in the different modes of production. All societies do not witness the same process of activities of their intellectuals. It is true that all intellectuals are born on the terrain of production relation, but the mode and pattern of

1. See Gramsci, *Selections From Prison Notebooks*, pp. 297-8 and 306.

their birth and development differ from society to society. Thus, the intellectuals of today are radically different from the intellectuals of the past societies. Again, the organic intellectual of the proletariat is historically determined to make revolution and it is radically different from the organic intellectual of the capitalist. Gramsci declares: "Industry has introduced a new type of intellectual; the techical organizer, the specialist in applied science. In the societies where the economic forces have developed in a capitalist direction,...it is this type of intellectual which has prevailed..."[1]

It is significant to note here that the Gramscian stress on placing the formation of intellectuals within the arena of structure is altogether different from other theories. Other theories place intellectuals on the field of superstructure alone, and thus the confusion regarding the 'above-class' nature of the concept arises. The Gramscian study is also unique in the sense that it highlights the relationship of intellectuals to the class of their origin and to other classes, As the function of an organic intellectual is to provide cohesion to its class it becomes imperative for the proletariat class to build its organic intellectual in order to organize their class and to win over traditional intellectuals to its way of thinking. Gramsci is emphatic in his assertion that the position of intellectuals is not determined by any internal criterion of intellectual activity, Rather the intellectuals must be located in the process of production. He says: "Treated on the basis of their social being, their position in the relations of production, intellectuals are located in a certain division of labour, and perform definite functions."[2]

As mentioned above[3] any change in society that is of a fundamental nature, is marked by an intellectual and moral reform—a change in the consciousness of men. The traditional

---

1. Gramsci, *Selections From Political Writings*, vol. 2, pp. 454-55.
2. Gramsci, quoted in Glucksmann, *Gramsci and The State*, p. 29.
3. See Chapter III.

intellectuals are so conditioned to attach themselves to the group in power that they are not even aware of the transition whereby the new classes try to achieve control of the state. As organic intellectuals operating on the terrian of sturcture intensify the struggle, the ruling classes try to diffuse this situation by changing the contours of superstructure and try to absorb limited views of antagonistic groups in order to project their universal character. The struggle, thus, is carried on the terrain of superstructure which is the domain of intellectuals and the intentions of traditional intellectuals in perpetuating a system become obvious. As the intellectual is also identified on the basis of relations of production (and not functions alone), the intellectual of proleteriat is characterised as the organiser and political intellectual while the preceding categories of intellectual ecclesiastics of aristocracy etc. were identified not by their place in production but by the level of their consciousness and ideological functions.

In fact, the popular misconception about the autonomy of intellectuals is based on the belief that they are the originators of ideas and philosophy and it was exactly this that became the hall-mark of bourgeois concept of intellectuals. And the concept of autonomous intellectuals has brought forth various concepts regarding function of intellectuals, for example Croce's 'intellectual' leaders.[1] But Gramsci finds that traditional intellectuals are not the only ones in any society and the other class of organic intellectuals plays an important role in its striving for change. What distinguishes

---

1. Regarding intellectuals as superior to masses Croce said, "We must trust the class called the intellectuals: as Hegel acknowledged by calling them the 'universal class' or the 'unclassed'. Their function is to leaven the other parties... and suiting the action to the perceived needs and conditions of the time with a watchful eye to the future" whereas the masses "who can never be induced to think scientifically and critically only want "some myth which flatters their feelings" and not any concern for truth Intellectuals are thus custodians of moral forces of human history which is ethico-political. See, Croce, *My Philosophy*, pp. 90-91.

these organic intellectuals of workers from previous categories of intellectuals is their consciousness of the process of relations of production, their place in this process as well as a programme to change this process in order to bring about a society where their own worldview prevails. It is clear, then, that intellectuals of all classes represent their class interests but there is a difference in the degree of their involvement in political process. Tne intellectual of bourrgeoisie directly performed this function in the feudal system which they overthrew, as it (feudal system) did not have a strong apparatus of hegemony to perpetuate their rule whereas capitalist hegemony suppresses any group that may threaten it from emerging. The intellectual of bourgeoisie, then, made their class hegemonic by playing a direct role in the class's constitution but the intellectual of protetariat, on their own, cannot enable their class to become leading. They play an essential role in the political organization of their class within a wide political terrain—in dialectical way, organised in a political party.

In the complex dialectics between intellectual and masses of working class, intellectuals individually cannot do much. The proletarian intellectuals require a political party, 'collective intellectual' to overthrow the burgeois oppression. This requirement also determines their relationship to the proletariat masses. In other words, it becomes imperative for proletarian intellectuals to evolve a cohesive consciousness and also an alternative culture in order to overthrow the hegemony of the capitalist. The proletariat mass cannot become conscious of its rights automatically or by itself. This is the task of the collective intellectuals. Exhorting this point, Gramsci says "The formation of a unitary collective consciousness requires various initiatives and conditions. The diffusion of a homogeneous mode of thinking and acting on the basis of a homogeneous leadership, is its principal condition, though it cannot be the only one. A very widespread error is the belief that every social stratum develops its specific consciousness and culture in the same manner and with the same methods, i.e. with the methods of the professional intellectuals."[1]

The need, then is to counter bourgeois institutional control and establish alternative system of production. This does not, in any way, reduce the necessity of class struggle. On the contrary, it tries to wage class struggle on all fronts. The ultimate success or failure of the class struggles depends on the psychological attitude of intellectual towards fundamental classes. Gramsci asks : "Do they have a 'paternalistic attitude towards the instrumental classes ? Or do they think they are an organic expression of them ? Do they have a 'servile' attitude towards ruling classes or do they think that they themselves are leaders, an integral part of the ruling class ?[2]

Gramsci envisages three levels in the formation of the intellectuals of a elass. These three levels—leadership, intermediate stage and the 'base'—are revealing to understand the functioning of leaders and the party. The division of semi-intellectuals and intellectuals in a factory though rooted in the role in production process, has its repercussions on the movement also. The intellectuals "give concrete expression to the work project as laid down in broad terms by the leadership", the semi-intellectuals have the task of "technica and administrative supervision over the correct execution of the works."[3]

It can be compared to the hierarchy of the armed forces viz. leadership, intermediate level and soldiers. The levels of consciousness characterize this distinction between intellectuals, semi-intellectuals and the base. This also illustrates the extent of involvement of these categories with the class of their origin. However, this classification of intelllectuatls at various levels does not mean a rigid hierarchy in Gramsci's schema nor does it contradict with Gramsci's postulates that

---

1. Gramsci, Notebook-I. 431, quoted in Glucksmann, *Gramsci and The State*, p. 32.
2. Gramsci, *Selection From Prison Notebooks*, p. 97.
3. Glucksmann *Gramsci, and The State*, p. 33.

identify intellectuals on their social function and not on "any criterion internal to intellectual activities"[1] because the degrees of consciousness have corresponding functions. The intellectuals are distinguished by their historic perspective and use of hegemonic tools in a way that serves the interests of their classes best. The difference between these levels of intellectuals is highlighted by Gramsci : "The professional or technical philosopher does not only 'think' with greater logical vigour, with greater coherence, with more systematic sense than do other men, but he knows the entire history of thought."[2] Thus it is not as Glucksmann suggests on "internal criterion for specifying external criteria of social function"[3] that distinguishes these levels of intellectual activity but its organic content that identifies these levels. This distinction leads to the need for a study of relation between state and society and role of intellectuals at various levels. Since all intellectuals perform function of countering or reinforcing hegemony, they are involved in direct political action. *They are "organizers" and 'mediators' of 'consent'.*[4]

The above analysis of the origin and situation of intellectuals in society makes it clear that the intellectuals (of the proletariat and others classes) act as organizers of society ; and at the same time, they educate their own ranks. The subordinate classes are influenced by the ideas of the ruling classes. In a capitalist system the middle classes, especially the rural, are influenced by the bourgeoisie.

Analysing this phenomenon further Gramsci finds that the rural intellectual is mostly 'traditional' and brings into contact the peasant masses with the local and state administration...(they) represent a social model for the peasant to look to in his aspiration to improve his condition...One can understand nothing of the collective life of peasantry...if one does not take into consideration this effective subordination

1. *Ibid.*
2. Gramsci, *Selections From Prison Notebooks*, p. 347.
3. Glucksmann, *Gramsci and The State*, p. 35.
4. *Ibid.* (Emphasis added).

to the intellectuals. Every organic development of peasant masses, upto a certain point, is linked to and depends on movements among intellectuals".[1] The intellectuals provide a kind of automatic consent of the masses to the system, so much so that it appears voluntary. This, in fact, is the function of hegemony.[2] It entails that all the organic intellectuals must be able to comprehend and articulate the interests of the social group to which they belong. As the ruling classes also use their intellectuals, the subordinate classes have to throw away their influences and build an alternative system. Since this cannot be done all at once, a select number of intellectuals (of leadership) must be able to mobilize and coordinate together members of the group. Besides one more important function of this elite is the ability to create conditions for producing more organic intellectuals and weld them into a forum to achieve their hegemony. These specialised members serve as representatives of their class in the process of reformulating processes and factors that effect the economic structure, but are external to it.

A scanning of the capitalist system brings out the fact that the bourgeoisie always tried to impose their organizations on the masses and also sought to make them conformist to their way of thinking, irrespective of the class affliations. This means that the chief characteristic "of any group that is developing towards dominance is to struggle to assimilate and to conquer 'ideologically' the traditional intellectuals, but the assimilation is made quicker...the more the group in question succeeds in simultaneously elaborating its own organic intellectuals".[3] This suggests another important function of intellectuals of the proletariat—education of the masses. And this is not an easy task. Because to affect a change in views of people it is necessary to change those very social institutions that had integrated masses in the system. As intellectuals of the bourgeoisie themselves organised the

---

1. Gramsci, *Selection from Prison Notebooks*, pp. 14-15.
2. See chapter VI.
3. Gramsci, *Selections from Prison Notebooks*, p. 10.

society (and also explained it) the whole system seemed logical and rational fusion of the contradictions. But this 'rational' fusion excludes class struggle and fails to perceive that proletariat is historically progressive. However, the all pervasive hegemony of the bourgeois infiltrates all the institutions of society—schools, culture and political institutions, etc.—and it is an uphill task for proletariat to break it. The bourgeois organic intellectuals never faced this type of difficulty. In the absence of all pervasive hegemony in feudal system, the transition from feudalism to capitalism was easy at the time when the economic conditions for such transitions were ripe. This is not the case today. Even when the socio-economic conditions are fast deteriorating, there is exploitation, the bourgeois hegemonic apparatus is able to defer the revolution. Gramsci, therefore, vouchsafes for injecting subjective will into the objective situation.

In no stage of social development, does the human volitions play such a crucial role as in the case of establishing a proletariat system. This gigantic task, however, cannot be performed by intellectuals alone. It requires the skill of a party of the proletariat to mount a sustained attack on all fronts—hegemonic economic, cultural educational etc.—in order to intensify struggle and bring revolution to fruition. This is implict in Gramsci's declarations in the "Southern Question". He says : We are interested in the mass of intellectuals and not just in individuals...it is also important and useful for a break to occur in the mass of intellectuals ; a break of an organic kind, historically characterized."[1] As the essential task is assigned to political party of proletariat, it was necessary to shatter the myth of greatness of intellectuals and looking down upon masses. Gramsci gives a sharp rebuff to these intellectuals who "believe they are the salt of the earth and see the workers as the material instrument of social transformation rather than as the conscious and intellegent protagonist of revolution."[2] The party, by welding masses and

1. Gramsci, *Selections fro n Political Writings*, vol. 2, p. 456.
2. Gramsci quoted in Glucksmann, *Gramsci and The State*, p. 29.

intellectuals in an organic whole, welds the elements of spontaneous outbreaks and consciousness or of 'felt' and 'knowing' elements of a revolution. In other words, the intellectuals are only 'stimulants', and not the sole agent. The subaltern classes in capitalist system are not 'awakened' by the 'inspiring' intellectuals who function essentially on the level of superstructure. The economic as well as hegemonic battle is fought, and cannot but be the onus of political party in the exploitative capitalist system. As intellectuals are the deputies of the dominant group 'exercising' the subaltern function of social hegemony and political government, it is necessary, to assess the function of intellectuals on this terrain.

The intellectuals acquir consciousness in a manner that is not necessarily enumerated by the masses. Gramsci contends that the essential task of the proletariat is the formation of "a unitary collective consciousness" and intellectuals perform the principal task of achieving it, that of 'diffusion of a homogeneous mode of thinking and acting, on the basis of a homogeneous leadership."[1] This postulates that in the ultimate relationship all members of political party are intellectuals. Prior to its achievement, intellectuals try to evolve more organic intellectuals, win over the intellectuals of other classes, and educate the masses in revolutionary situation and thereby strengthen the party. The intellectuals of capitalist system secure the consent of the masses in a climate where this seems spontaneous and voluntary, hiding the coeysive apparatus of the state. Gramsci observes : "Every revolution has been preceded by an intense labour of criticism, by the diffusion of culture and the spread of ideas amongst masses of men who are at first resistant, and think only of solving their own immediate economic and political problems themselves, who have no ties of solidarity with others, in the same condition."[2] This cultural battle is a long battle of the intellectuals and requires a critique of all the past philosophies that exercise domination over society. Gramsci, therefore,

---

1. Gramsci, quoted, *Ibid.*, p. 32.
2. Gramsci, *Selections from Political Writings 1910-1920*, pp. 12-13.

carries out a critique of Croce, the greatest liberal philosopher whose philosophy produced "gastric juices"[1] to digest upheavals in society. Gramsci, also focused on the misconception of mechanists like Bukharin who concentrated on popular common sense to counter with it anti Marxist. Bukharin appears to shy away from higher philosophy of great intellectuals' and thereby is unable to win over the masses. To undermine the superstructure, it is necessary to counter even the most refined from of ideologies. Bukharin's attempts seem "of someone who cannot sleep for the moonlight" and, "struggles to massacre fireflies" in the hope of making "brightness lessen or disappear"[2] and cannot resolve question facing the proletarian movement.

The other task of evolving its own organic intellectuals can be fulfilled by a multi-thronged effort to educate and organise the masses. The cultural struggle entails, among other things, a study of the role of language, literature and education. The developed societies have witnessed a crisis of intellectuals in various extremist movements. The popular literature was distant from people and intellectuals failed to involve masses in their works. The need is to produce revolutionary literature since the "struggle for a new culture is the struggie for a new way of life."[3] The first step is to abolish the barrier between cultures of 'popular' and 'cultured' men. Gramsci himself waged a battle through *L'Ordine Nuovo* and tried to apprise the workers of the development in society, analysing these on Marxian principles. A study of educational appratus is necessary in order to evolve organic intellectual. Gramsci explains : In modern civilization, all practical activities have become so complex, and the sciences so interwoven with everyday life that each practical activity tends to create a new type of school for its own executives and specialists."[4] This complexity was not therein old systems

1. Gramsci, in a letter to Tania, in Gramsci, *Letters from Prison*, p. 244.
2. Gramsci, *Selections from Prison Notebooks*, p. 433.
3. Gramsci, quoted by Glucksmann, *Gramsci and The State*, p. 42.
4. Gramsci. *Selections from Prison Notebooks*, p. 26.

where the classical schools produced intellectuals and vocational ones enrolled masses. Now-a-days, specialized schools have elbowed out other 'disinterested', philosophical vocations by highlighting the immediate function in the world of production. These divisions of education into specialized branches have consequently catapulted into prominence the bureaucracy, that coordinate all these schools. The middle classes occupy prominent place in this bureaucracy. The "traditional" leaders of the system are raw without specialized skill and are losing their hold over political processes. As a result an 'expert' government is emerging. But it is clear that this system also perpetuates division. As the functions of society can be classified into ruling or subordinate functions, corresponding schools produce similar specialized training, thereby perpetrating old social divisions giving, at the same time, a semblance of democratic education accessible to all. The need, therefore, is to expose this modern educational stratification and try to give highest education to masses in order to destroy all barriers between rulers and ruled classes.

In order to evolve alternative appratus of hegemony intellectuals need to penetrate all the institutions of civil society and organise themselves in a party whose primary aim would be "the intellectual and moral reform of the masses." It needs to win over intellectuals of other classes.[1]

The intellectuals are leaders and organizers of all the activities and functions inherent in the development of an integral society. These functions are locatred in the terrain of civil society.[2] As the intellectual born on the economic terrian of structural divisions, function at the level of superstructure, it is necessary to analyse the relationship between base and superstructure as postulated by Gramsci.

II

The Gramscian analysis attributes three meaning to dialectics —"At its simplest it means the reciprocal interaction of one

---

1. *Ibid.*
2. See chapter VI.

thing on another",[1] in another aspect, it is viewed as the synthesing of contradictions; and lastly it "explains the relation between the "structure and the superstructure."[2] As intellectuals are born on the terrain of structure and function at the level of superstructure, it is vital to understand the relationship between the base and the superstructure.

Gramsci has been called the "theoretician of superstructure"[3] on account of his stress on the element of subjective will in the process of history. He firmly believed that revolution can only be made with a change in the consciousness of the masses. In other words, he wanted "to leave more room for the influence of ideas and indeed of individual men in the process of history.[4] Man is the maker of history and a reflection of structural determinant. "Historical materialism can incorporate a crucial role for consciousness without losing, in the process, the essential economic core that constitutes its uniqueness. It was Gramsci's achievement to fashion just such a synthesis.[5] It is in the context that the question of human will is to be understood by grasping the notion of consciousness.

As is clear, Marx never substituted 'matter' for 'idea' in Hegelian dialection. Marx has stressed the reciprocity between men and objective world. The Italian Marxists too, (for example Labriola, Gramsci et al) had emphasised this dialectics of reciprocity. This is the core of praxis theory. The attempts of Bukharin[6] to establish a reducible relationship between base and superstructure—where superstructure is a mere image of means of production—is not only simplistic, but also fails to grasp the essence of historical materialism. Gramsci categorically says that "man is a process of his

---

1. James Joll, *Gramsci*, Fontana/Collins, Glasgow, 1977, pp. 81-82.
2. *Ibid.*, p. 82,
3. D. McLellan, *Marxism After Marx*, MacMillan Press Ltd. London, 1979, p. 180.
4. James Joll, *Gramsci*, p. 82.
5. Femia, *Gramsci's Political Thought*, p. 5.
6. Bukharin's *Historical Materialism* (1921) was criticised by Gramsci for its economistic tendencies. See also chapter II.

actions"[1] and Marx firmly believes in "the ensemble of social relations."[2] Both these statements make it crystal clear that by gauging the limits of mass relation/domination over nature, the difference between the past and the present can be perceived. In other words, "The existence of objective conditions, of possibilities or of freedom is not yet enough : it is nccessary to 'know' them, and know how to use them. And to want to use them. Man, in this sense, is concrete will, that is, the effective application of the abstract will or vital impulse to the concrete means which realise such a will."[3]

Superstructure is evolved on the basis of structure. Gramsci comments: "A class is formed on the basis of its function in the mode of production : development, and the struggle for power, for the conservation of power, creates superstructures that determine the formation of a special material structure (of the superstructure)."[4] This effectively exposes the vulgar marxists, who think that the superstructure is directly and only conditioned by the economic system. It is true that the base is the ultimate determinant of social change but ideological factors, also play a vital rolc as they provide the consciousness of contraditctions existing between the base and the superstructure.

Marxists believe "that consciousness is a product of the prolonged evolution of matter. But having taken shape on the basis of matter it actively influences the latters development."[5] With a consciousness of contradiction, masses can feel the need for change and tro to strive for it. One can, therefore, concur with Lenin : "Man's consciousness not only reflects the objctive world, but creates it."[6]

---

1. Gramsci, *Selections from Prison Notebooks*, p. 351.
2. Marx, "6th Thesis on Feuerbach". Marx Engels, *Selected Works*, p. 29 (Emphasis added).
3. Gramsci, *Selections from Prison Notebooks*, p. 360.
4. *Ibid.*
5. V. Afanasyev, *Scientific Communism* Progress Publications, Moscow, 1967, p. 212.
6. Lenin, *Setected Works*, Progress Publications, Moscow, 1977.

In fact, the Hegelian theory of dialectical development from quantity to quality is explaind only on the basis of the active intervention of subjective forces. Dialectics is not an irrational confrontation of opposing forces : it is a process in which man actively participates and tries to mould it according to one's beliefs. The Marxian proclaimation[1] about revolutionary changes and his stress that, "a distinction should always be made between material transformation of the economic conditions and the legal political philosophic—in short, ideological forms in which men become conscious of this conflict and fight it out"[2] is noteworthy. There is no truth in the Crocean assertion[3] that in Marxism, idea is replaced by matter and the dialectics is the same 'noumenon' of change. This is a fallacy as the Hegelian idea has been resolved both in structure and superstructure. Marxism changes the whole way of conceiving philosophy. Philosophy has now been "historicised" and all factors that directly or indirectly effect the process of change are taken account of. The subjectivist theories of Croce are useful to expose the transcendental theories; but it is still required to be studied in depth as to why and how a conception is born; and more meaningfully, how the conception initially emerges and grasped only by some intellectuals in the beginning, and later on spread among the masses through the mediation of inteliectuals.

As is evident, new social groups emerge with a change in the mode of productions. Its complimentary values are articulated by a group of intellectuals who gradually strive for hegemony. When the balance of forces favours the establishment of hegemony and the structural changes also permit alternation. The new values are imbibed by all and when such conditions arise a revolution takes place and is successful. Now in this

---

1. "Thesis on Feuerbach "The philosophers have only *interpreted* the world invarious ways; the point, however, is to *change* it". See Marx, Engles *Selected Works*, p. 30.
2. Marx, Preface to *Critique of Political Economy*. quoted in Marx, Engels, *Selected Works*, p. 182.
3. See chapter II.

schema of things, it is impossible to establish any precise relationship between the base and the superstructure or between the economic circumstances and the intellectual development. Gramsci contends; "In this conception of history, intellectuals are the purveyors of consciousness but the form and content of this consciousness must be rooted in the world of production."[1]

Gramsci riduculed the simplistic logic of mechanists who tried to establish a cause and effect relationship between the base and the superstructure. He asserted : "The claim presented as an essential postulate of historical materialism, that every fluctuation of politics and ideology can be presented as an immediate expression of the structure must be contested in theory as primitive infantilism, and combated in practice with the authentic testimony of Marx, the author of concrete political and historical works."[2]

There is a need to understand the relation of forces in any society that chart out the course of its development. A cursary glance on the history of a various nations reveals the fact that despite various struggles to establish equality and franternity in different sections, the minority dissent always remains intact and these minority revolutionary groups strive to hasten the revolutions. As the system is based on exploitation of one closs by another, there is bound to be a change in the relations of productions with the change in modes of production. The antagonistic classes try to maintain and impose their own system on society. This struggle is carried out in all areas of society. The subordinate groups try to exploit the crisis of society to hasten the revolution.

In such situations, a society faces two types of crisis— First, organic crises, it has its root in fundamental contradiction and anomalies in the system; and second, a conjunctural crisis which is rooted in immediate, short term struggle. "The conjuncture is a set of immediate and

---

1. Gramsci, Glucksmann, *Gramsci and The State*, p. 47.
2. Gramsci, *Selections from Prison Notebooks*. p. 407.

ephemeral characteristics of the economic situation",[1] it is dependent on orgonic phenomena that "give rise to socio-historical criticism".[2]

The hegemony is eflective to avoid only the latter type of crisis, the former type of crisis at the most can be postponed. The tast of subordinate groups is to bring these organic moments of crisis, to a head in order to annhilate the hegemony of rulers. If the correct relationship between organic and conjunctural crisis is established, it can hasten the process of revolution. But if the nature of crisis is not perceived clearly it may lead to disastrous results. An emphasis on "causes as immediately operative which in fact only operate indirectly,"[3] tends to encourage 'economism' and mechanistic tendencies. If emphasis is on "immediate cause's" as "the only effective ones,"[4] it leads to voluntarism. Economism leaves out a whole terrain of socio-political historical reasons of crisis and the activities of superstructure are ignored. Thus, economism in marxist theory has resulted in a separation between economic struggle of workers and political activity of political party.

There is a strong belief in an ideology as the harbinger of change, which could be effective even without mobilising the masses. Again there is an Utopian belief that objective conditions would automatically appear to follow a given course. This viewpoint fails to conceive the organic relationship between economics and politics and thereby the far reaching impact of economics is missed altogether. Gramsci, making this point clear, says : "For there is no understanding of the fact that mass ideological factors always lag behind mass economic phenomena and therefore, at certain moments, the automatic thrust due to the economic factor is slowed down, obstructed or even momentarily broken down by traditional ideological elements—hence that there must be a

1. *Ibid.*, p. 177.
2. *Ibid.*, p. 178.
3. *Ibid.*
4. *Ibid.*

conscious, planned struggle to ensure that the exigencies of the economic position of the masses, which may conflict with the traditional leadership's policies, are understood."[1]

The discussion on the relationship between structural and conjunctural moments, leads to the concept of 'historic bloc'. According to Gramsci : "Base and superstructures form a 'historic bloc', i.e. the complex and contradictory set of superstructure is the reflention of the sets of social relation of production.[2] As Joll explains, Gramsci was "trying to describe the moment when both objective and subjective forces combine to produce a situation of revolutionary change, the moment when the economic structure of the old order was collapsing but when there also were people with the will determination had historical insight to take advantage of this."[3]

This means that a historic bloc is formed when an equilibrium between the base and superstructure exists. In other words, when a given class succeeds in maintaining hegemony over society through both direction and domination or pursuation and force. The historic bloc, to a large extent depends on economic conditions and any neglect of this perspective is liable to lead to either excessive voluntarism, or excessive domination. It may be maintained. that the placing of conflict in social totality—where relations of forces may or may not be precarious—is vital for the concept of historic bloc; the moment the balance of forces is tilted either way the historic bloc is broken. It is in this perspective that Gramsci exhorts that "material forces are the content and ideologies are the form."[4] Gramsci tries to prove that ideological facts have the same impact as material forces in the process of change. This is what makes the classification of intellectuals in 'traditional' and 'organic' categories important. The transition from traditional to organic intellectuals is only possible

---

1. *Ibid.*, p. 178.
2. *Ibid.*, p. 366.
3. James Joll, *Gramsci*, p. 86.
4. Gramsci, *Selections from Prison Notebooks*, p. 377.

with an imminent change in the mode of production. A class expands on the basis of its role in production as well as in superstructural fields. The need therefore is "to stimulate theformation of homogeneous, compact blocs."[1]

Superstructure, an essential field of hegemony is dialectically related to the base. The intellectuals as functionaries of superstructure assume vital importance. Gramsci's contention is that the hegemony of capitalist surpasses all the systems and Fordism[2] (a tool of capitalist) also becomes a form of exploitation. It seeks to mechanise men as well as regulate his social and moral life. This means imposition of such cultural values that perpetrate the enslavement to bourgeoisie.

In fact, the nature of culture is vital to understand superstrucural activities. Culture is inculcated in the masses through hegemonic apparatus and if the intellectuals of workers are able to carry a critique of past cultures and capitalist development, it may succeed in striving towards formation of a unitary culture consciousness. An important point to note here is that a mere cultural reform cannot bring about the hegemony of proletariat. A critique of the past is necessary, it cannot even be ignored if the workers intend to carry on the struggle in the superstructrure. Says Gramsci : "If the task of the intellectuals is to determine and to organize the cultural revolution in other words, to make culture and practical function coincide, it is clear that 'crystallized' intellectuals are reactionaries".[3] Intellectuals play a crucial role in changing the cultural consciousness of men. This also stipulates an organic link between the intellectuals and the masses. The *L'Ordine Nuovo*, with a primacy of cultural issues, sought to raise the consciousness of masses. Without arousing consciousness of the masses it is practically impossible to throw away the shackles of bourgeoisie hegemony.

---

1. *Ibid.*
2. See chapter VI.
3. Gramsci, *Selections from Prison Notebooks*, p. 377.

To understand the function of historic bloc and its role at the moment of crisis, it is necessary to conceive the implications of superstructure and to isolate factors that formulate it. State power or political control cannot be simplistically identified with the superstructures. More often than not, it (superstructure) is misunderstood to mean political power on account of the stress on attacks on the institutions of state control, and such organisms that covertly or overtly reinforce political system. The state being an apparatus containing both civil society and political society, ideologies play a vital role in securing the consent of the civil society for the prevalling political society. The civil society is the organ of consent and functions at the level of ideas and provides personnel to perpetuate political power. This relationship does not in the least imply a fixed system of ideas for a particular system nor does it mean a mechanical development of ideas to correspond to a particular system of production. This had been the main thrust of Bukharin's ideas.[1] He misconceived the material character of superstructures or rather failed to see it altogether. Gramsci criticised Bukharin for identifying certain activities as belonging to superstructure and others to the structure. In a ridiculing tone, Gramsci says "If one starts from this baroque way of thinking a whole series of baroque questions are thrown up. For example, are libraries structure or superstructure"?[2] It is foolish to identify ideological instrument of society apart from technological ones. In Gramsci's words : "There are superstructures that have a material structure but their character remains superstructural. Their development cannot be explained by the immanent development of their particular material structure, but only by the material structure of society."[3] Bukharin's analysis confuses "material infrastructure and instruments of production, making artistic development depend simply on the

---

1. Far Bukharin's ideas, see chtaper II.
2. Gramsci, *Selections from Prison Notebooks*, p. 461.
3. Gramsci, quoted in Glucksmann, *Gramsci and The State*, p. 257.

material instruments of production or reproduction."[1] We cannot say that artistic development is directly related to production or vice-versa. The interaction between base and superstructure is too complicated to be rduced in a direct causal relationship. All this leads Gramsci to declare that even though superstucture is geared to cope with problems posed by the structure, the essential terrain or path of superstructure is to impose hegemony of one class over another. Some superstructures have a material base but the development cannot be comprehended only by an analysis of this base. They function on a separate level. Moreover certain superstructures create changes in material base by generating a demand for their material apparatus and encouraging industries that meet their essential tools of operation. In fact "Scientific thought is a superstructure which creates scientific instrument".[2]

An Important deduction from the above is that superstructure and structure have a relationship that suggest priorities. In the ultimate analysis, the superstructures are rooted in material structure and infrastructures are evolved to perpetuate the ideological form suitable for this structure or the material forces now try to preserve the apparatus of superstrucure. In this complex dialectics, it is fallacious to search for direct relationships and reductionist model. In this relationspip, it is politics that permeates both structure and superstructure and is decisive. This allows ample role for the interplay of objective and subjective factors in the process of history. The balance of forces is thus modified and altered by the active role of politics. This reasoning once again focuses on the 'historic bloc' of socio historic forces in the context of affecting change in the society.

The Gramscian analysis thus finds the hegemony factor as the distinguishing mark of modern capitalist state. It it this factor that demarcates modern state from the past societies. Fordism is a culmination of this all pervasive

---

1. *Ibid.*
2. *Ibid.*

dominance of the capitalist hegemony. Past societies did not have such an elaborate apparatus of hegemony. Military reasons, social needs joined together various forces to form a state. This was, in fact, a mechanistic state where classes maintained their specific and separate institutions and there was no centralization of social values. In direct contrast to it, a modern 'integral state' is much more complex because it is hegemonic and as such the proletariat have an uphill task in altering the capitalist state system. Theirs is an 'organic bloc' and not the old type of the 'mechanical bloc'. Against this backdrop, the institution of proletariat tries to become viable through the trade unions, cultural parties etc., so that it could give expression to aims and aspirations of those subordinate classes, who are effectively diffused in the capitalist hegemonic state. To succeed, the proletariat need to form a 'historic bloc' with other sub-ordinate classes in the society (viz. the peasants etc.) so that they could present an alternative system of hegemony capable of replacing the bourgeoiste.

A significant point to mention here is that this historic bloc of subordinate forces is not to the confused with the system of alliance or the 'class front' whose sole aim is to wage immediate political battles in pursuance of some short gains. The concept of 'class front' envisages a type of political struggle and to gain control over state institutions. It looks for an alliance with other parties to achieve success in short-term, goal-oriented movements; it has no long-term hegemonic designs. Henemony, as discussed ın the following chapters, entails a cultural leadership over allied classes.

Again, there is a difference between the worker-peasant bloc and historic bloc. A 'historic bloc' is based on a complex relationship between "knowing" of intellectual, "feeling" of masses and the understanding of 'historic necessities".[1] The organic relation of intellectuals to their class, is an essential postulate of the 'historic bloc.' It is also vastly different from class alliances in that it requires an integral state based on an organic relationship between the ruler and

1. Gramsci, *Selections from Prison Noteboaks*, p. 418.

the led. As such, this concept envisages the primacy of politics over economics, even while economics is determinant in the last instance.

The creation of 'historic bloc'—by effecting an equilibrium between structure and superstructure—assigns an important role to intellectual who carry out a critique of the past philosophies. This is transmitted to the consciousness of the masses via a critique of common sense. A cultural struggle is the inevitable concommitant of historic bloc. The philosophy of praxis thus seeks to provide an alternative to the capitalist hegemony. The struggle for 'historic bloc' in the ultimate analysis involves a struggle for the state and this provides a crucial role to political initiative. As this concept is dealt with again in the study of state, hegemony and civil society,[1] it is suffice to mention here, that the intellectuals play a vital role in forming the historic bloc and their activities are essentially focussed on the terrain of superstructure.

To conclude, the capitalist hegemony of the modern state could be demolished only when a proletariat hegemony is established through the formation of a proletarian 'historic bloc': and this is the function of the organic intellectuals of the proletariat. They need to be organized in a political party and function as the 'Collective Will' of the masses in theri bid to change the society.

---

1. See chapter VI.

5

Gramsci's Views of Politics

The relationship between base and superstructure reveals a complex interplay of conjunctural and organic crises. In this complex interplay, it is necessary to understand how intellectuals, individual men and parties can participate in order to change the balance in this favour and to establish the worldview of the workers and peasants. This is the area of political activity. Before taking up Gramsci, a glance on popular sense of the term politics would not be out of the way.

The term 'politics' was used by Aristotle to explain the phenomena of state. It is derived from the Greek word 'polis' meaning 'state'. Its modern usage has considerably changed. Gilchrist says : "politics now-a-days refers to the current problems of government".[1] But, in the common parlance it has acquired altogether a different connotation. It has come to be associated with opportunism, factionalism, or with the actual practices of men striving to attain their goal by every type of machination and strategy. Even practitioners of political strategies denigrate the term 'politics'. In academic parlance, too, the term is no longer confined to the study of

---

1. R.N. Gilchrist, *Principles of Political Science*, p. 16.

the state. Now, it not only includes practices of government, but also the practice of those institutions and organisations of human activity that fall totally outside the purview of the state or the government. The pursuance of international relations and its complications also form the subject matter of politics. If an analysis of the definitions of the term, provided by various dictionaries and statesmen, is undertaken, certain common factors may be isolated.

According to *Encyclopaedia of Religion and Ethics*, the word 'politics' is used to refer both to administration or legislation and to the study of this department of human activity."[1] Another dictionary defines politics as "the art or science of government: manoeuvring and intriguing".[2] In fact, the broad meaning attributed to the term covers almost every activity. According to T. Parker, "Politics is the science of exigencies."[3] For D.D. Eisenhower, it "is a profession; a serious, complicated and, in its true sense, a noble one."[4] All these definitions revolve round a basic theme—the activities of men primarily in the context of the state and its machinery, but also in the context of the entire social system. The derogatory connotation provided is similar to the denigration of Machiavelli's rating as a politician.

Machiavelli exercised a great influence on practices of states and rulers; yet, almost all systems denounce Machiavellian practices as diabolic, opportunist, manipulative. However, there is no denying the fact that Machiavelli was the first Itallian to suggest in an embryonic form the concept of an Italian nation. He wrote *The Prince* to outline the requirements

---

1. *Encyclopaedia of Religion and Ethies*, Vol. X, p. 98.
2. *Chambers Twentieth Century Dictionary*, Allied Publishers Pvt. Ltd., Bombay, 1972, p. 1036.
3. *Quoted in The New Dictionary of Thought*, (originally compiled by Tryon Edwards, revised and enlarged by C.N. Catrevas. Jonathan Edwards Ralph Emerson Browns) Standard Book Company, New York, 1966, p. 494.
4. *Ibid.*, p. 492.

of a ruler in order to consolidate, expand and perpetuate the rule of a monarch. This treatise was not so much concerned with the moral and ethical issues as with the actual political practices—e.g. the motivation behind political practices, the extent to which a ruler could go to adopt hard and cruel and appeasing tactics, etc. It is a classic example that succinctly reveals how rulers adopt both force and populist methods with the sole aim of retaining power. The end of *Price* of Machiavelli is to maintain the power of the ruler and expand it with all the possible means. This revelation of actual practices has led political scientists to accuse Machiavelli of being an opportunist, and an apostle of power seekers. A new phrase 'Machiavellian politics' is coined to characterize all politics devoid of morality and based solely on opportunism.

However, in contradistinction to the above view, Gramsci first endeavoured to put Machiavelli in a historical perspective and then tried to analyse his theories and contributions. Before him, Croce had already perceived the cardinal values of Machiavellian ideas and had analysed his writings. This factor also contributed in making Gramsci veer towards the notions of the sixteenth century Italian thinker.

Gramsci's comments on the nature of the Italian politics start with an analysis of Machiavelli's ideas and their relevance today. According to him, *The Prince* outlines the rational, logical assets of the collective will of the masses; masses repose all authority in the Prince particularly because he posseses special qualities to reach near the goal. The Prince combines in himself "political ideology and political science in the dramatic form of a 'Myth".[1] He is a Centaur—half animal,

1. Explaining the terms 'political ideology' and 'political science', Gramsci further says: "Before machiavelli, political science had taken the form either of the utopia or of scholarly treatise. Machiavelli, combining the two, gave imaginative and artistic form to his conceptions." He clarifies that in Machiavelli, political ideology is expressed "neither in the form of a cold utopia nor as learned theorising, but rather by a creation of concrete phantasy which acts on a dispersed and shattered people to arouse and organise its collective will". See Gramsci, *Selection from Prison Notebooks*, pp. 125-26.

half human. The most significant fact in Gramsci's analysis of Machiavelli's Prince is that he renders him (the Prince) no historical existence. But through him the Italian politics is analysed and a solution is suggested. The study of Machiavelli enabled Gramsci to perceive 'politics' as an autonomous science, it is autonomous of religion and morality, having its own laws. Machiavellianism, in fact, as the true practice of politics, was in existence even before the Middle Ages, his (Machiavelli's) exposition only paved the way for teaching those 'who are not in the know' of political practices i.e. the revolutionary class of the time.

To be exact, Machiavelli theorized a practice to enlighten those who are unaware of political practices. Gramsci contends that although Machiavelli had realized the importance of political science yet he was not a scientist relevant for all times. By this contention he means to say that Machiavelli's views of State may be relevant today, but not his analysis of various social forces that form these institutions, because the social forces are entirely different today. It is in this sense that Gramsci says : "Machiavelli is a man wholly of his period, his political science represents the philosophy of the time."[1] He championed the cause of the progressive forces of his day. Peasants and citizens were advised to form militias that could successfully repulse the attack of mercenaries aided and abetted by the feudal lords. Thus Machiavelli's chief concern was with politics, and his *Art of War* had the purpose of knowing how the military could help the cause of politics.

Thus, according to Gramsci, Machiavelli was the champion of the 'have-nots' of society; and to credit him with more than this was transgressing the truth. He had a vision of the world where mrsses could hope to improve their lot by reposing their faith in Prince, embodying the collective will. The masses could check the powers of the Prince through republican means. This is the essence of Machiavelli.

The all ecompassing activity of politics, Machiavelli felt, might use military for furthering its aim. As such, he conducted a study of military tactics within a political

---

2. *Ibid.*, p. 140.

framework. There is no denying the fact that at times Machiavelli erred in the analysis of military arrangements; but this only goes to prove that he envisaged of military tactics as subsidiary to the political programme of the Prince. In fact, Gramsci thought that the importance of machiavelli could be throughly assessed by analysing the behaviour of the so-called anti-Machiavellians,[1] who had based their formulations merely on the exigencies of their times.

Analysing Machiavelli's views on politics as an autonomous science, Croce developed his own ideas about 'politics' through his formula of 'dialectics of distincts'. Indetifying various sciences, Croce has mentioned only Asthetics, Logic, Economics and Ethics, and has ignored politics altogether. All these sciences he believed, were immanent in philosophy. Politics to him, is merely a 'passion'. But, says Gramsci, this conception denies any "permanent passion which is the condition for orgasm and spasm."[2] The Crocean conception also fails to provide for 'war' wnich is characterised as a moral duty. It is also a passion and therefore it can not rationalise standing armies. Croce's politics as passion and interest is dissolved in political sicence by explaining this theoretically. In Croce, Gramsci feels, political science becomes a "medicine of passions."[3] Croce, "thus theorized that political action stems from the need to remove injustices" and is a "defensive political activity",[4] providing no way to improve the lot of masses. This is a logical critical formulation of Croce's positions as Gramsci understood them. Croce tried to exclude political parties from politics on the basis of an assertion that parties differ at times of organic crises from parties prior to crises. There may be some factual validity of argument, but Gramsci asserts that

---

1. G ramsci calls Jesuits, Pasquale Villari, B. Spaventa et. al., anti-Machiavellians.
2. Gramsci, *Selections from Prison Notebooks*, p. 138.
3. Gramsci, *Quadernidel Carcere*, vol. I, p. 1307.
4. M.A. Finocchiaro, "Gramsci's Crocean Marxism", *Telos*, 41, p. 31.

there is no fundamental difference between the two stages of party. For him, two stages are merely a process of logical change. War, a passion, can not have a long time programme or plan of action as party has.

Croce's formulations seem to be distortions of reality avoiding such issues as might endanger his framework. The theory of politics as 'passion' results from accepting politics as a spontaneous action, and this, according to Gramsci, is a totally unfounded conception. True to the idealist tradition, Croce denigraded politics and heightened the role of 'idea' believing in the supremacy of thought. For Croce, history was the movement of 'liberty' and 'man' was the centre of history. However, his 'man' is a metaphysical, universal man, and not one grounded in concrete historical reality. This excludes objective situations and contradictions from his formulations; it also excludes the effect of time in the process of history. By identifying history as liberty, Croce strives to show the rationality of existing systems. Moreover, liberty by becoming a process in the unfolding of history, justifies all the stages of history. This conception also effectively eliminates the importance and role of political struggles and strengthens the conservative forces. The exclusion or overlooking of political activity from the process of change allows Croce to diffuse the revolutionary element of change altogether.

For Gramsci, on the other hand, historicism is the consciousnesss of the role of history as an instrument of action and political mobilization of the masses. As such, he accuses Croce for not making his historicism absolute. Absolute histricism necessarily leads to politics. Adopting a Crocean method to criticise Croce, Gramsci asserts that Croce's historiography is "noting but a form of political moderatism, which proposes as the only method political action, the one in which the historical development and progress result from the dialectic of conservation and innovation."[1]

---

1. Gramsci quoted in M.A. Finocchiaro, "Gramsci's Crocean Marxism" *Tetos*, p. 29.

Gramsci asserts that Marxism alone is a philosophy that suggests methods for implementing the theories in concrete situation. It is a new practice. Croce resort to a wilful distortion of Marxism when he refers to structure as the 'hidden God' of Marxism and superstructure as mere appearance Dialectical materialism never credits structure alone with the process of change nor is the supersturcture directly reducible to economic structure. Gramsci's definition of history of philosophy as the history of conflicts among antagonistic classes leads to the assertion that philosophy is politics. Political science aims to solve social conflicts and philosophy must become political to continue to be a philosophy otherwise it is redundant. Philosophy of praxis alone has understood the unity of theory and practice and tries to end social contradictions.

Gramsci's writings on politics examine these. He concurs with Lenin : "Politics means a struggle between classes; means the relations of the proletariat in its struggle for its emancipation, against the world bourgeosie."[1] The Marxian stress "to change the world" for Gramsci, is the key to an understanding of politics. he credited both Machiavelli and Marx as being "the theorists of militant politics, of action."[2] What Gramsci has written in his *Prison Notebooks* could be aptly applied to him, he says "A man of politics writes about philosophy : it could be that his 'true' philosophy should be looked for rather in his writings on politics".[3]

This statement clearly reveals that in Gramsci's view there is an inseparable connection between politics and philosophy. The philosophy of praxis is a unity of theory and praxis. Philosophy to be real must be 'political'. It is also clear that Gramsci, attributes a general meaning to the term politics. For him all activities directly or indirectly related to the formulation of one or many conceptions of the world

---

1. Lenin, *Selected Works* Progress Publications, Moscow, 1977, p. 623.
2. Gramsci, *Selections from Prison Notebooks*, p. 123.
3. *Ibid.*, p. 403.

and equally a participation in one or many conceptions come under the term 'politics'. As has been said, Gramsci takes up the critique of economism to analyse relationship between base and superstructure and to understand the impact of politics. The Leninist views on politics also reveal these concerns, particularly where Lenin suggests a denunciation of economism and positivism, crediting the proletariat with undertaking a political initiative in a dialectical relationship between class and class consciousness. Both Lenin and Gramsci draw their conclusions on the basis of the practical activity or political leadership.

All the writings of Gramsci on politics are guided by and rooted in the philosophy of Marxism, which is the philosophy of praxis. It "*is a philosophy which is also politics and a politics which is also philosophy*."[1] As all men are political, politics in a general sense means all activities directly and indirectly related to formulation of one or many conceptions of the world and equally a participation in one or many of them. The philosophy of praxis aims to propound "the general conception of life able to wage a struggle against the dominate ideologies, and the creation of an educational apparatus with its programme, method of teaching and type of personnel."[2] And, this is also the aim of politics.

A question now arises as to whether politics is "a mere reflection of ongoing infrastructural processes or whether it plays an autonomous role in the socialist practice?"[3] To understand this, it is necessary to analyse the relationship between politics, philosophy and economics.

In fact there are three constituent elements of Marxism—philosophy, politics and economics. The contradictions between man and matter are dialectically related. The three constituents are united in a dialectical development. Philosophy is an approach to understand the relationship between human

---

1. *Ibid.*, p. 395 (Emphasis added).
2. Gramsci quoted in Glucksmann *Gramsci and The State*, p. 389.
3. Salamini, *A Sociology of Political Praxis*, Routledge and Kegen Paul, London, 1981, p. 27.

will and economic condition. In other words, philosophy is point of unity between structure and superstructure. In economics the relationship between workers and industrial productive forces is governed by value; in politics the relationship between state and society provides the equilibrium. These three elements have a translatibility. Each of these is implicit in other elements. The philosophy of each man is contained both in his professed views and actual practices. "Politics in fact is at any given time the reflection of the tendencies of development in the structure, but it is not necessarily the case that these tendencies must be realised."[1] This is due to interaction between the tree elements. Influences of any philosophy may hasten or delay the process of change. The assertion of Marx that "No social order ever perishes before all the productive forces for which there is room in it have developed; and new, higher relations of production never appear before the material conditions their existence have matured in the womb of old society itself"[2] is important to understand the extent of role of politics in social change.

The fundamental assertion of Gramsci is that politics must be based on the fact that there are two categories in society—the rulers and the ruled, or the leaders and the led. "The entire science and art of politics are based on this primordial and (given, certain general conditions) irredubible fact."[3] The question now arises—what is the object of practice? Is it to perpetuate this division or to transform it? The rulers and the ruled division is based on class dichotomy; but that of the leaders and the led may also refer to such relations within a homogeneous group. This relation (of the leaders and the led) brings into relief the responsibility of politcal practice of leaders and their relationship with the large masses. Political acts, if inspired by leaders (as is only logical in a party, may be based on an erroneous judgement of

---

1. Gramsci, *Selections from Prison Notebooks*, p. 408.
2. Marx, 'Preface' to *A Contribution to the Critique of Political Economy Selected Works*, p. 182.
3. Framsci, *Selections from Prison Notebooks*, p. 144.

the situation, and for this also the responsibility is that of the leaders.

The positivist approach to problems can be suicidal here. The positivists aver that society can be judged or understood by the methods of natural sciences. If adopting the laws of natural sciences, we act according to the law of statics—i.e. by basing ourselves on the study of various data—we may do 'irreparable harm' to the movement. It, in fact, generates a shallow understanding of the society and suggests a type of political lethargy. By aiming to arouse masses to change the society, politics abandons these very laws of averages and large numbers. If follows that relationship between the leaders and the led is based on a dialectical interaction. Leaders act and base their politics according to the preparedness and consciousness of the masses.

The natural corollary of division of society between the rulers and the ruled is the existence of leaders. In this age, parties are the most effective way of projecting leaders. In other words, parties are distinguished because of their role in developing leaders. The individualists who claimed to be leaders are not necessarily so as the fascist example reveals.[1] Representing organic movements, parties as a matter of fact deny petty—individualism and apoliticism. They represent contiunity or 'State Spirit'.

In the Hegelian theory also the concept of the State Spirit' creeps in, but it is entirely different from the Gramscian formulation. In Hegel, State Spirit[2] is the awareness of being part of a process of development, having links with the past and a responsibility to work with these unknown forces. In this concept, the State spirit has no links with infinity; rather, it has links with past and future that is contained within a specific, measurable limit. The Gramscian conclusion, on the other hand, is "that party spirit is the basic component of

---

1. See *Ibid.*, p. 146.

2. Hegel in *Philosophy of History* uses the term to distinguish between 'particular spirit' of a people and nations's consciousness or 'Spirit of the State.'

'State spirit'".[1] The links with an ideology and a certain goal postulate a contiunity in the party spirit as a form of the state spirit.

The evolution of parties is the reflection of division of society into two antagonistic classes of the exploiters and the exploited. The political party is an expression of a social group. In order to understand the organisation of political forces in a society it is necessary to note the Gramscian concept of class. Gramsci prefers the use of the term 'social group, in place of a class. A social group may share various worldviews that are not necessarily consistent with its role in the system of production. The stress here is not on socio-economic terms but on ideas viz., the worldview. This is because of a complicated relationship that exists between the base and the superstructure. There are only two fundamental classes in society, antagonistic to each other due to their position in the relations of productions. This is the basic Marxist tenet. The ruling classes achieve a unity in the State; but in contrast to it, the subaltern classes are not unified either culturally of politically to achieve their interests. They can achieve their goal only when they become a 'State'.

There are various moments of politics. Various subaltern groups are born on the terrian of economic production. In this economic-corporate phase these groups do not have a conception of their own and are diffused in pre-existing social groups: and, for the time being they also adopt the mentality, ideolgy and aims of these other groups. Gradually these groups, having similar role in the production relations, being to align themselves in search for a common political and social identity. These potentially hegemonic groups thus attain the political phase. This phase leads to a trade-union consciousness and class solidarity is formed. This is seen by Gramsci as a reformist stage in which the goal is not to gain the control of

1. Gramsci's 'State spirit' reveals that (a) it is present in every moment "which is not arbtiary" (b) it presupposes that every act is a moment in a complex process, with not abstract but organic limits. See *Ibid.*. pp. 146-7.

the State, but only to question (by these subaltern classes) the techniques of state control. A class then attains solidarity and tries to gain hegemony—and this is the phase when a political party is born. Each class, according to Gramsci, is potentially hegemonic; and when many groups in society thus become conscious and politically hegemonic, they enter the arena of intense political struggle. The truly hegemonic class tries to converge its interests with the general interests of subaltern groups.

It is in this phase that a historic bloc[1] is created. Classes evolve their specific worldview in this stage of political consciousness, and, in fact, the worldview now becomes the criterion for deciding the nature of a class and its party. Therefore, classses are not defined in terms of their ideological independence and separation, but according to the level of production. It is not classes that create structures, but as Marx says : "Material conditions are the supports for determinate social relations".[2] The intellectuals of a class provide it with a worldview. There are, in fact, only two fundamental classes but a multitude of political parties. This can be understood in terms of the nature of movement and programmes of parties. In the modern age of specialisations, various, parties emerge representing only certain immediate interests; but at times of crises there is a clear alignment of forces and marginal currents are absorbed into the mainstream of their respective class movements. Every class, to be specific, contains only one party; other parties represent its partial problems, being reformist in character.

This detailed analysis of class character is necessary to understand the relationship between elements of Marxism. The economists, by ignoring the element of political consciousness,

---

1. 'Historic bloc' is formed, according to Gramsci, when an equilibrium exists between civil society and political society; that is to say, when a given class succeeds in maintaining hegemony over society through persuation and direction.
2. Marx, *Capital* quoted in Glucksmann, *Gramsci and The State*, p. 74.

overlook the role of intellectuals and the masses in the political praxis. Lenin has denounced this type of reductionist approach, and has characterized it as the fundamental political tendency of economism that believes in saying—"Let the workers carry on the economic struggle and let the Marxist intelligentia merge with the liberals for the political struggle.[1] The reductionist approch, as Gramsci perceived it, is encouraged by the compulsions of the capitalist civilization which mistakenly believes in the separation of politics from economics. Gramsci insists on the dialectical unity between the two discplines of politics and economics. Politics, by means of attacking structure and superstructure simultaneously, in fact attacks both the economic and the political system. Politics is directed towards changing the basis economic (exploitative) order. Lenin's anti-economism and 'concentrated economics'[2] are conciliatory. Not all action is directly derived from economics nor the political action devoid of economic objectives. This essential postulate is everywhere evident in the writings of Marx and Lenin.

Revolutionary Marxism is a philosophy that is also politics. In the contemporary stage of capitalism, Gramsci finds the bourgeois state gradually shouldering greater responsibility of production—process. This implied that ruling classes were gradually losing their hold on economic system and were relying on political, coercive apparatus to maintain its status-quo. Fascism is a case in point; Gramsci views it as the culmination of state-capitalism. It reaffirms the basic theme of Gramsci. He assets : "*Politics and economics, milieu and social organism, always make a single whole and it is one of Marx's* greatest merits to have maintained this unity".[3]

---

1. Lenin, "What is to be Done ? *Against Revisionism*, Progress Publishers, Moscow, 1972, p. 48.
2. 'Anti-economism' of Lenin provides for primacy of politics whereas 'concentrated economics' stressed on formation of 'Soviets' as a new form of power founded on the structure.
3. Gramsci, quoted by Glucksmann, *Gramsci and The State*, p. 133 (Emphasis added).

The analysis of economism led Gramsci to a realisation that there is a need to be 'more political' in the countries of advanced capitalism. The need is "to combat economism not only in historiography but in the theory and practice of politics."[1] Politics, as he understood it, "*is above all a practice designed to transform a given balance of forces by the application of political initiative* to the enemy's week point, a point that euables one to attack his 'centre of gravity."[2]

If Politics "is...a practice...to transform a given balance of forces", it may be linked with the concept of Jacobinism. Gramsci called Machiavelli a 'precocious Jacobin'. Machiavelli's Jacobinism first sets a goal for society, and then strives to achieve it; that is, it has a definite aim and also a will to act.

Even if in Gramsci's formulation Jacobinism is concerned with politics, it is clear that his concept of politics does not emphasise on the political activity alone. He has emply clarified his stand in the context of referring to Jame's theory of pragmatism. For the Marxists, 'practical' means political, and 'politcal' is the action of organised masses. For the Jamesian—type pragmatist, 'practical' refers to "the control that the individual exercise over theories by being able to check them against immediate experience".[3] The pragmatists are concerned with immediate practice. The idealists and German thinkers are related tc practice in a mediated way. A minute analysis reveals that the latter category of philiosophers is in reality more practical as it has a higher aim of raising the cultural level of the masses or part of them. Pragmatists, on the other hand, have a short term, often populist aims that tend to dilute the intensity of social contradictions, thus contributing to reactionary forces. Gramsci's definition of politics emphasises on its long term goals. Let him speak for himself : "Politics imagines man such

---

1. Gramsci, *Selections from Prison Notebooks*, p. 165.
2. Glucksmann, *Gramsci and The State*, p. 237 (Emphasis added).
3. Lawner (Ed.) Introduction, *Letters from Prison*, p. 48.

as he is, and at the same time such as he should be, in order to attain a determinate goal."[1]

Gramsci's contention is that just as pragmatists try to revert the revolutionary practice through reformist movement, similarly economist theories hamper the cultural expansion of the philosophy of praxis. An example of this contamination of Marxist theory by economist concept is historical-economism. Gramsci describes such contaminated theoreticians as those who "do not intend to overtax their brains, but still wish to appear to know everything."[2] They, in fact, fail to understand that philosophy of praxis postulates political initiative or the role of will as vital in the development of society. This again is the logic of art of prediction and perception. Prediction means seeing the present and the past clearly as a movement. The objective factors and permanent elements of the process can be pinpointed, but the programme or the possible outcome of circumstances depends on voluntary elements or the human will. A conception of the world is hidden in every prediction.

The pregmatists emphasis on the situation is 'therefore' not the approach of a politician. The political scientist has to keep within the bound of effective reality in so far as he is merely a scientist"[3], but an active politician is partisan and has a conception of world. "The real philosopher is and cannot be other than the politician, the active man who modifies the environment understanding by environment the ensemble of relations whicn each of us enters to take part in".[4] Thus, the active politician, like a scientist, bases himself on effective reality, a relation of forces continually mobile and subject to change. This change is envisaged on a conscious pattern. What ought to be is a prespective and therefore concrete, realistic, historical interpretation of reality. The intervention of subjective elements is based on an analysis of

1. Gramsci, *Letteratura Vita nazionale* Einaudi, Turin, 1966, p. 13.
2. Gramsci, *Selections from Prison, Notebooks*, p. 164.
3. *Ibid.*, p. 172.
4. *Ibid.*, p. 352.

relations of forces. Gramsci assests that relation of force explain "science and art of politics" which can be understood as a body of practical rules for research and of detailed observations useful for awakening an interest in effective reality and for stimulating more rigorous and more vigourous political insights."[1] This is a dynamic praxis, and the method of its study is historical materialism. A critique of positivism is necessary at this juncture to eliminate any controversy over the understanding of the process of change.

Bukharin, the main architect of positivist theory, believed that economic processes operate independently of human volition and are outside history. He analysed social phenomena in terms of certain objective and necessary causalities. This is a purely mechanistic conception. In his *Popular Manual*, Bukharin said that "Marxism is philosophical materialism and philosophy of praxis is a sociology". In this conception, Bukharin has totally ignored the cultural and philosophical factors. In his quest for a scientific methodology, he merely borrowed the method of natural sciences and split marxism into two—a sociology or a doctrine of history and politics and a philosophy of dialectical materialism. He could not comprehend that dialectics is not only a methodology of science, but it itself is, and must be scientific. For mechanists, Gramsci upholds, philosophy is simply a general methodology divorced from class struggle. Another current of vulgar marxism is 'idealism'. Materialistic Marxists put emphasis on economics over philosophy and idealist marxists give primacy to philosophy over economics. Both are divorced from the social-economic context and create a caste like concept of knowledge. Lenin had already condemned these two currents through the mediation of praxis. He envisaged a dialectical relationship between economic structure and ideological superstructure. In fact, the economic moment of consciousness constitutes a negative phase; i.e. the realm of necessity in the historical ascendency of subaltern classes towards hegemony. This is replaced by the positive phase of the realm of freedom. The

---

3. *Ibid.*, pp. 175-76.

mechanists fail to provide for the possibility of error in politics. This could only be possible in a philosophy of praxis that accounts for the role of subjective factors. Gramsci feels that the evolutionist method of Bukharin is more harmful for marxism than the liberal philosophies of Croce, etc.; because the later provides, even if for a limited number of intellectuals, a cultural and ideological consciousness. Bukharian's marxism tends to leave the masses in the condtions of cultural backwardness.

In reality philosophy is itself a part of politics and history. Marxist philosophy accelerates the historical process and makes practic more homogeneous. Practice, on its part, raises new questions for theory. The unity of theory and practice is a critical act involving various concrete steps and an uneven development that the hegemony and political practice of vanguard party must be able to overcome. Marxism can be a basis of science of political practice. Philosophical objects like matter, dialectics etc. are not 'objects of philosophy'. He says : It is essential to be more politcal, to know how to use the political element and have less fear of doing so".[1] Politics is not merely a reflection of infrastructure.

The conclusion, then is : "The fact that economic interests play a decisive role *does not in the least imply* that the economic struggle is of prime importance; for the most essential, the 'decisive' interests of classes can be satisfied *only* by radical *political* changes in general".[2]

Political science being the study of State, it deals with the whole gamut of practical and theoretical activities with which the ruling class establishes, maintains and consolidates its control over those whom it rules. Gramsci maintains that the rise of sociology is due to the deline of the concept of political science and of the art of politics as a result of positivism. His critique of sociology as philosophy of non-philosophers and its "attempt to derive 'experimentally' the

---

1. Gramsci to Athos Lisa in prison conversations quoted in Glucksmann, *Gramsci and The State*, p 237.
2. Lenin, *Collected Works*, vol. 5, p. 390.

laws of evolution of human society in such a way as to "predict" that the oak tree will develop out of the acorn",[1] is actually a criticism of positivist sociology. Sociology adopts laws of large numbers and statistics and is a mere compilation of facts, devoid of critical consciousness.

Political activity goes much beyond; it requires some kind of programme and planning. The parties act as vanguard of their respective classes. The party of masses in this stage of capitalism is communist party. Though its planning it replaces naturalistic 'spontaneity' with human awareness. Party, thus, becomes a 'collective man'. The philosophy of praxis aims to propound a general conception of the world able to counter other dominant ideologies and the creation of an educational apparatus with its programme and method of teaching and transforming society. This is the objective of politics and entails its (politics) interaction with culture.

The relationship between politics and culture covers a wide field. The correct method of the proletariat political struggle is a struggle for hegemony, and in a struggle for hegemony, culture and politics are dialectically related. The politician, active-man-in-the-mass, tries, to achieve his goal of establishing a worldview by adopting such tactics as may hasten organic crises in the system and simulataneously prepare the masses to take over the state apparatus. Since the whole of state apparatus is designed to perpetuate the rule of capitalists, it is vital to understand its various organs in order to destroy them. According to Gramsci, bureaucracy and army, legel institutions, civil society, all organs of state perpetuate the system in the name of defending the constitution or "the legel form of the State, together with its related institutions."[2]

Gramsci contends, State, "is an instrument of rationalization", of a particular structure and its corresponding superstructure. "Law is an instrument of the state to encourage certain modes of behaviour and eliminate certain

1. Gramsci, *Selections from Prison Notebooks*, p. 426.
2. *Ibid.*, p. 212.

customs and attitudes. As such it is primarily the repressive and negative aspect of the entire positive civilizing activity undertaken by the State."[1] Law comes under the purview of 'politics' which is the art of governing men. This understanding is the contribution of Machiavelli. He realized that Italian medieval bourgeois could not pass from the corporate to political phase, because Pope prevented the formation of a strong Italian State and excluded religion from the domain of state policy. The absence of autonomous State, and its conmitant constitutional law, thus, hampered the full evolution of bourgeoisie.

The art of politics also takes into accouct the element of 'intuition'. Intuition in politics is not something superior or outside comprehension. It is expressed by political leaders. The skill a leader displays in connecting 'seemingly disparate' elements and link various apparently different occurances and then in guaging the reaction of the masses towards his plan of action and ultimately in preparing them to accept a desired policy—all this comes under the scope of intuition. Political party is the collective organism that displays political intuition in an extraordinary way.

In the present day systems, the role of legislator is important in political process. Legislator is the person who is empowered by the law to enact laws, he not only creates instruments by means of which the directive becomes the norm of conduct for others, but also indicates how to implement the norms. Bureaucrats and other functionaries of State also have their contribution in this process. Gramsci opines that in a broad sense all men are legislators, because at one level or the other they contribute in the formation of a norm of conduct. Private organisations, pressure groups, etc. are also, in this sense legislators. All these are the pillars of the State. Therefore, to make a revolution, it is necessary to have a thorough understanding of all these pillars before undermining their validity.

---

1. *Ibid.*, p. 247.

An early as 1916 Gramsci perceived an imperative necessity to prepare Italy for a revolution. He exhorts : "Every revolution has been Preceded by an intense labour of criticism, of cultural penetration, of permeation of ideas through groups of men initially refractory and engrossed with solving day-by-day, their own political and economic problem."[1] He found the present day situation on a surface level, a bit deceiving. In fact the 1930s had witnessed an increase in unproductive labour along with a rise in consumption. Gramsci queried : "What is the excess of consumption to be attributed to ? Can one prove that the working masses have raised their living standards to such an extent that it can be seen as an excess of consumption ?"[2] Inspite of these deceptions, then the worker remained exploited. The rise in unemployment creates a vast social group haveing no link with the production system. Such group lives, off the various schemes of society. And, these new dependent classes not only change the formation of classes but also influence the structure of the society.

The American system is a case in point. Its analysis reveals that these masses have a direct relationship with the state. The organization of the American society has changed in such a way that the working people share in the process of production by depositing their savings in various shares and debenture schemes. America, thus, is a classic example of the hegemonic role of the state. Gramsci contends that within this system of hegemonic capitalism parasitic forces are being generated in the form of female dependents of ruling classes. Their luxurious life-style leads to a new alignment, resulting in a cast like crystallization of forces. Thus, a new type of exploitation and mechanisation of workers is taking place in the name of 'work-ethics'. The workers are asked to conform to an austere, moralist life and the preachers of this morality

---

1. Gramsci, 'Il Grido del Popolo' quoted McInnes, "Antonio Gramsci", *Survey*, October 1964, No. 53, p. 7.
2. Gramsci, *Quaderni del Carcere*, quoted in Glucksmann, *Gramsci and The State*, p. 27.

practice hypoceisy. The culture and conditions of work, providing socio-economic benefits to workers, force the workers to voluntarily adopt a regulated life-style in which they contribute more and more to production, but themselves remain exploited, in a concealed manner.

The American state structure, thus, remains elilist, despite the participation of masses in economic production. Politics to longer remains a superstructure pnenomena; it becomes the mediation betwean structure and superstructure. It has two repercusions. First, the productivity of the masses becomes political productivity on account of direct participation in the State, giving rise to a kind of the labour aristocracy and second, the relationship between masses and the state takes a non-contradictory appearance and leads to a diffusion of politics.

This analysis of Americanism, according to Gramsci, reveals the new form capitalism has taken in order to sustain its exploitative character. He, therefore, giving a clarion call the proletariat to break the capitalist hegemony and transform the exploitative social order. To achieve this, the structure of the complex capitalist hegemonic State has to be understood and the revolutionary tactics have to be sharpened so that the capitalist-state-structure could be struck at the right place when the time is ripe. In short, the need of the time is to replace the capitalist hegemony by a proletariat hegemony.

The above analysis makes 'politics' an organic, developing discipline ever facing new challenges. Politics as such is contained in the philosophy of praxis in which its three constituent elements—Philosophy, Politics and Economics—are all rolled into one. It logically follows that politics has to get itself attuned to the changes in the 'structure', its aim being the recomposition of society.

In this context, Lenin's perception of proletariat's political struggle is significant inasmuch as he saw the necessities of fanning the class-consciousness amidst the poleteriat from outside the phase of economic struggle also. The sphere from where it could be generated is the sphere of interrelations between classes. To bring political knowledge to the workers 'the social Democrats' must go among all classes of population. The agent of bringing about this awareness is the proletarian party and other organisations (trade unions, etc.) which view political consciousness as 'primary basis for bringing change'.

Since in Gramsci's formulations politics has to be attuned to the changes in the structure for the sake of social reconstruction, it is but natural that he veers towards Lenin's concept of the party. It is the party—the organic intellectual—which according to Gramsci, caters to the demands of the times and instils political consciousness in the masses in order to establish the proletarian hegemony.

II

'Political party', as has been indicated, has assumed a pivotal role in the Marxist theory of revolution. How a party comes into existence, what are its characterstics, its constituent, elements, its functions etc.—all these facets are to be understood in order to effectively appreciate the role of party in bringing abuut a revolution. Gramsci has blended thoughts of Machavelli, Marx and Lenin[1] to evolve his concept of the party. Before Gramsci, theories of Pareto, Michels and Mosca[2] were much in circulation in Italy. As a result, the traditional Marxist concept was subjected to various interpretations. From amongst a medly of concepts, Gramsci manufactured his own viewpoint. Various organisms that covertly or overtly perform political function come under the purview of Gramscian study of the party. This type of broad analysis enables him to distinguish precisely a political party from other organisms. A brief account of Machiavelli and Sorel is given in order to highlight the position of references in Gramsci's thought.

Machiavelli's Prince expresses a myth that seeks to stir the imagination with the thoughts of moral courage, needed for a revolutionary change. The Prince "*represents the process*

---

1. References to Marx and Lenin's Concepts are given along with Gramsci's philosophy. For general introduction see chapter II.
2. See chapter II for Elite theories.

whereby a given collective will devoted towards a given political objective is formed."[1] The theoritical abstraction or the myth of Prince gradually merges with the people. The Prince, or a Jacohin as Gramsci calls him, establishes a theoretical pattern for society; and then uses all his force to create this pattern. The absolutism of Prince is an instrument designed for the success of revolution. As the bourgeoisie of that time had not become politically conscious, and the city states were going through the economic-corporate phase, the Prince, according to Gramsci, represented the superstructure of political society, necessarily required for the organic development of the structure.

Sorel used the myth of the General Strike to evoke the unconsciousness of the masses in order to bring the revolution. However, Sorel's General Strike cannot be the logical culmination of a myth as proved by Gramsci. It is because the 'General Strike' is a negative activity and does not intend to build up institutions of socialism. Sorel had failed to comprehend the revolutionary nature of the political party; he remained content with trade unionism. He forgot that trade unionism is conerned with mere immediate economic benefits and is incapable of proposing, leave alone securing, the long-term socio-econmic changes that help to transform the structure of a society.

Sorel rejected the concept of the party, perhaps because the success as a party depends on 'preparedness'; and as such it altogether rules out the role of 'spontaneity' in which he (Sorel) had great faith. But, in such a reliance on an irrational element, there is always a danger of slipping into futile opportunism and recalcitrance. Again, Sorel's concept of myth is also defective, in *the sense that it* (*myth*) *is* supposed to be realized in the collective will operative in trade unions; but, in the absence of proper education and leadership this type of collective will becomes vague and as such cannot continue to exist after the negative phase is over.

---

2. Gramsci, *Selections from Prison Notebooks*, p. 125 (Emphasis added).

The Marxist concept of party rests on the assumption that the capitalist society is divided into two antagonistic classes of exploiters and exploited. In the beginning masses are not aware of their exploitation by the ruling class, and have no class-consciousness. But, gradually they attain consciousness of their common interests, and step into the economic-corporate stage. In the next stage workers organise themselves in trade-unions and try to gain a better deal within the framework of the bourgeois system. Even in this stage they do not realize the fundamental characteristic of class division—an antagonism born out of the desire of rulers and its consequent implementation in society to control the means of production and appropriate all wealth. The institutions of State are directed towards this end. The State, thus is a tool in the hand of the ruling class to perpetuate their economic domination and there is a dialectual relationship between the economic base and the social-political superstructure. Workers can spontaneously achieve only trade-union level of consciousness to act within the capitalist framework. The third stage of consciousness is reached when the subordinate groups become conscious of the class-characteristic of exploitation and try to achieve an alternative balance of forces where there is no exploitation; in other words where there is hegemony of these subordinate classes. The stage of hegemonic designs requires political orientation; and this orientation is provided by political party. In sum, when contradictions at the level of structure occure, these are organised leading to a unity or homogeneity of various social groups. The subjective elements take congnizance of objective elements and try to intervence in the process of history.

It is at this point that the party is formed. In the words of Gramsci : When the conditions for its 'triumph' and for its inevitable progress to state power are, at least, in the process of formation, and allow their future evolution—all things going normally—to be foreseen",[1] then a party becomes 'historically necessary'.

---

1. Gramsci, *Selections from Prison Notebooks*, p 152.

The question now arises : "Is political action (in the strict sense) necessary for one to be able to speak of a 'political party'.[1] Gramsci asserts that over political function is not necessary for a party. Various parties or forces emerge by the expediency of situation to manifest diverse facets of socio-political life. These group perform political tasks of effecting the cultural consciousness of masses, or, like newspapers, preach their views ostensibly from a political point of view. Again, there are instances of various parties that deny having any immediate political objective. Anarchist parties claim to have no political programme at all; in fact, they denounce any such programme. Yet by propounding explicitly their educative, moral, cultural activities, they proclaim their worldview. The 'cultural' parties of elites also come in this category. Their explicit aim is to propound certain ideas and provide indirect leadership to various parties and groups which adhere to their ideology. These are actually hegemonic functions of a party. The Fascist party, too, does not ostensibly have a political function. The masses seem to follow their leader, a charismatic figure, in the quest for a new model-society; and this also is a political advice to conquer power. Since the party is born out of a consciousness of power-relations generated by the system, its determinate aim is to found a new State. All the groups that strive towards this goal are performing a political function.[2]

Every party is the expression of a single class although it may represent the interests of the allied classes also. It may form alliance with other groups in order to secure the interest of their own class. These groups may "exercise a balancing and arbitrating function between the interest of their group and those of other groups." Thus, for Gramsci, party is a nomenclature for a class. The multitude of parties does not necessarily imply the existence of as many classes. Many parties are the result of reformative tendencies of a movement. They represent only partial interest of their class

---

1. *Ibid* , p. 148.
2. *Ibid.*, p. 151.

and at times of crises merge with the party that truly represents interests of their class. These marginal movements are on the periphery of real revolutionary process. In other words, the history of a party reveals the history of social group whose representative the party is.

In the words of Gramsci : The history of any given party can only emerge from the complex portyal of the totality of society and State (often with international ramifications too).

There are parties of ruling class and subordinate groups. The former try to maintain a status-quo or continuation of favourable conditions for their continued supermacy, and the latter try to achieve hegemony. In the present system of production, the party of the proletariat (of the working class) is potential 'State' and is representative of subordinate groups. "Parties come into existence, and constitute themselves as organisations, in order to influence the situation at moments which are historically vital for their class; but they are not always capable of adapting themselves to new tasks and to new epochs, nor of evolving *pari passu* with the overall relations of force (and hence the relative position of their class) in the country in question, or in the international field.[1] The party of the proletariat[2] is the chief instrument in Gramscian theory to affect change in society and bring a communist revolution. It is the 'Modern Prince' on the model of the mythical 'Prince' of Machiavelli. It is also referred as the collective will of the masses. Therefore, to understand the birth of political party the need is to analyse the collective will and its relevance for the revolution. Gramsci takes up a problem—"how can dispersed wills manage to unify themselves, ideologically speaking?"[3] The historical conditions, no doubt, are a requisite for formation of the national-popular collective will; but when actually do the

---

1. *Ibid.*, p. 211.
2. Henceforth only party (otherwise specifically mentioned).
3. Glucksmann, *Gramsci and The State*, p. 354.

conditions warrant the development of a collective will? It is ascertained on the basis of "historical (economic) analysis of the social structure of the given country."[1] The national-popular collective will can be formed only with the active participation of all the classes and strata of society, notably the peasants. The rudimentary collective will based on class antagonism will, however, remain scattered with the destruction of classes; but it is not allowed to reconstruct the society. The truely collective will, unified in a party, has a concrete programme of action, and is capable of reconstructing the society.

This suggests that the task of social-reconstruction cannot be performed by a single individual particulary within the framework of the present socio-economic system. Machiavelli's Prince undertakes this function alone in a very different socio-economic conditions. But to day the myth Prince "can only be on organism, a complex element of society in which a collective will, which has already been recognised and has to some extent cesserted itself in action, begins to take concrete form. History has already provided this organism, and it is the political party—the first cell in which there come together germs of a collective will tending to become universal.[2] The party does not organise this will out of nothing; these wills already exist in the society. The modern prince or the party only channelizes them to form a national will. The Marxian proposition is : "No social order ever perishes before all the productive forces for which there is room in it have developed ; and new, higher relations of production never appear before the material conditions of their existence have matured in the womb of old society itself. Therefore mankind always sets itself only such tasks as it can solve".[3] This (Marxian proposition) is applicable to the formation of the collective will as well.

---

1. Gramsci, *Selections from Prison Notebooks*, p. 130.
2. *Ibid.*, p. 129.
3. Marx, 'Preface' to *A Contribution to the Critique of Political Economy*, in Marx, Engels. *Selected Works*, Progress Publishers, Moscow, 1977, p. 182.

The 'collective will', after being transformed into 'national-popular', seeks to establish a new social order where the subordinate classes enjoy freedom. The modern day progressive force—the proletariat—seeks to establish a classless state through its organ—the party; neglect of this aspect, Gramsci contends, would only lead to a supereficial analysis of parties and their behaviour. The collective will, properly so called when formed on a permanent basis, will have both longterm objectives as well as immediate steps to strengthen itself. Any sudden birth of an active selective will is not a part of the dialectical development. It may only mean a negative and a destructive grouping of dispered wills. It cannot represent the true aspirations of masses that are evolved over a period of time in an organic relation to the structure.

The political party as an agent cf 'intellectual and moral reform' struggles to form a 'national-popular' will in an assiduous way. There is a dialectical unity between political organisation and ideology in the formation of the collective will. The political party, on the basis of scientific study, evolves a worldview of the proletariat that aims to establish a new order where the interests of this class could be preserved. Since it entails the abolition of antagonistic classes by ending the class of exploiters, and also by creating an apparatus for the equal distribution of the means of production, it requires a clear illustration of its wants. Gramsci, therefore, asserts : "Wants which form clusters called morality exists in their own right, all on the one level. The first question to ask about them is whose they are, whether they are demands of isolated Utopians or the morality of a great mass movements. If latter, they will need coherent exposition by organic intellectuals of the movement. *Above all they will need a Leninist Party which will exercise the specialised function of directing spontaneity*".[1]

Gramsci felt the necessity of a Leninist type party after

---

1. Gramsci, *Passato e Presente*, Einaudi, Turin, 1966, pp. 65-66. (Emphasis added.)

studying and participating in the Factory Councils Movement. It is true that though influenced by the Russian revolution, Gramsci had an insufficient knowledge of its progress. He had heard of the Soviets; and had envisaged the Factory Council as equivalent bodies and as tools for mobilizing masses for change and for preparing them to attain communism. He tried to develop a body parallel to the Soviets however, the circumstances to establish Soviet type of organization were not yet ripe in Italy. In Russia also they had outlived their utility. And it is exactly because of this factor that a hiatus occurred in Gramsci's concept of the party—the dividing line being the year 1921.

At this juncture, the need arises to analyse the Factory Council Movement, its functions and relations with the party. The Factory Councils movement evolved on the model of Soviets of Russia had organised a large number of worker in different units; and Internal Commissions were its apex bodies coordinating issues within a factory as well as with other factories. These economic organisations of workers were utilized to impart them not only technical skill and managing productivity but also to educate them culturally. The Councils, as they arose on the terrian of necessary productive relations, were in fact public institution of the workers. The membership of Councils entailed participation in the essential function of production.

The trade unions essential function, on the other hand, is of securing better conditions for workers. And, this function is performed within the framework of the bourgeois production-relations. Trade Unions are, thus, essentially reformative, and not revolutionary bodies. Gramsci reiterates that the ideology of trade unions is bourgeois ideology; whereas workers need a socialist ideology to control the State. Gramsci's denunciation of trade unions was in fact the denunciation of the Confederation of Labour (C.G.L.), the dominant trade-union organisation of Italian workers. The limited role assigned to the party is also in effect a realisation of the inefficacy of the Italian Socialist Party

(PSI).[1]

Factory Councils were in fact, reflections of the aspirations and struggle of the masses. They represented the working classes as the conscious protagonist of history. The socialist state, Gramsci thought, had existed potentially in these Factory Councils. Thc membership of the party and trade unions being voluntary, it was felt that they may take a long time to enlist the support as the masses and organise them. Councils, on the other hand, had the advantage of an automatic membership of all the workers; the councils also educated workers both in productive processes and in raising their cultural consciouness. They prepared the workers by imparting revolutionary education to them.[2] Besides, these councils constantly attacked the legality of bourgeois production system.

Thus, the main tasks of councils were : first, to organise workers, second, to involve them in decision-making, and, third, to expose the bureaucratic nature of the trade unions. As the unions, alienated from masses, were totally unaware of the simmering discontent of the masses, it was feared that the discontent might explode at any moment, depleting the energy of the workers. Councils were expected to expose this reality and perform political and military functions against capitalism. Incipient reappropriation of works and products within the Factory made the working-class realise that it was the fundamental productive class which had been imprisoned

---

1. The process of Factory Council movement proved the validity of this assesment of CGL and PSI. Both these bodies by a pact in 1918 segregated political and economic strikes as the respective exclusive activities of PSI and CGL. This bankruptcy of ideology and perception harmed the proletarian movement incalculably. It also created an elite leadership of workers in trade unions and alienated the masses from the party. The PSI failed to understand the urge of masses for change and harness it.
2. Gramsci himself participated in educational function through the agency of '*L'Ordine Nuovo*. This newspaper played a pivotal role during 1919-20 Gramsci *Tasca and Togliatti* were the main force behind *L'Ordine Nuovo*.

by the capitalist relations of production. It also suggested that the greatest liberation of forces of production was possible with the maximum speed of revolution and a new model-order could be established, which in its turn could be an architect of future classless society.[1] Workers were, thus, trained in the task of acquisition of state-power.

Gramsci's views on Factory Councils were accused of being "'syndicalist' and 'voluntarist' by his opponents whom he regarded as Blanquists"[2] This was due to his reliance on Councils as the agent of revolution and his emphasis on attack on economic structure alone with less emphasis on the superstructures. Rejecting this charge, Gramsci countered : "Is the Councils movement a form of Syndicalism, Italian syndicalism? The Italian practice of pseudo-revolutionary syndicalism is negated by the Turin movement of workers' delegates. *It is the beginning of a great historical process, a process in which the working masses will acquire consciousness of their indissoluble unity based on production and on concrete activity of labour and will provide this consciousness with an organic form, by building up their own leadership, so that they will be, as it were the conscious expression of a precise goal to be* accomplished.[3] Syndicalism, on the other hand, has never expressed such a resolution, it has only created a 'Utopia'.

With the formation of the PCI, Gramsci enthusiatically worked to make it the organ of 'workers' revolution. His stress on the party, does not, however, imply a break in his thought process, nor his silence on Factory Councils implied the abandonment of ihe concept. The Factory Councils, as a means to by-pass the trade unions were beneficial for the movement. Trade union, representing the spontaneous striving of working class led to its subordination to the bourgeois ideology. The councils, on the other hand, functioned

---

1. Views of Andersion in "Introduction to Gramsci." New Left Review 51, pp. 22-25.
2. McInnes, "Antonio Gramsci", *Survey* No. 53, p. 5.
3. Gramsci, *Selections from Political Writings*, Vol. I, p. 112. (Emphasis added.)

outside the framework of the bourgeois ideology. More importantly, the Councils endeavoured to spread the ideology of Marxism. Moreover to attain its objective, the councils were supposed to educate the workers, to acquire cohesion, unity and organisation. They tried to accomplish a unity of economics and politics in the factory itself ; although it was an elementary stage of unity.

In fact, the failure of the Councils movements hammered into Gramsci's mend that Factory Councils are unable to make the transition to Socialist State, because they performed no direct political activity. The political party, on the other hand, being rooted in the contradictory relations of production, can become an external political agent to arouse and mobilize the masses. Party can also intervene in the revolutionary dialectics to win over other subordinate classes to the cause of workers revolution. Since workers alone cannot replace the all-pervasive capitalist system, they need allies which the party can cultivate and, the utility of the councils for the party cannot be minimised.

Gramsci, thus, realized that although the councils were necessary to prepare workers for the take-over after the revolution, but the revolution itself could be brought about only and only through the agency of the political party. He categorically said : "A class cannot remain itself, cannot develop itself to the point of seizing power, unless it possesses a party and an organisation which embraces the best, the most conscious part of itself".[1]

Gramsci thus, clearly perceived that the Councils performed the function of organising the majority of the masses who had not yet attained the communist consciousness. They not only provided the Communist party (PCI) a mass-base to carry out the revolution, but also laid foundations of the dialectics,—both the dialectics of spontaneity and leadership and of economics and politics—vital for Marxism.

1. Gramsci, speech in Parliament, 16 May, 1925; quoted in Fiori, *Antonio Gramsci, Life of A Revolutionary*, New Left Books, London 1970, p. 194.

Gramsci also realized that the working class can spontaneously achieve only trade-union consciousness; it is the party which provides a worldview, a political dimension to the struggle; it is the party, again, that intervenes to make the revolution.

Needless to emphasis that Gramsci acquired this perception (about the party) with the formation of the Italian Communist Party (PCI) which, unlike the maximalist PSI, strove to become political and proletariat in the true sense of the term. He asserted : "The party must acquire a precise and distinctive image : from being a party-bourgeois parliamentary party it must become the part of the revolutionary proletariat which is struggling for the coming of a communist society by means of the workers' state a homogeneous party with its own doctrine, its own tactics...a rigid and implacable discipline...The leadership, remaining always in contact with the sections, must become the motive force for proletarian action in all its developments. The sections must promote in all the factories, in the unions, in the co-operatives, in the barracks the formation of communist groups who incessently spread among the masses the ideas and tactics of the Party, which will organize the creation of Factory Councils for the exercise of control over industrial and agricultural production which will put out the necessary propaganda to achieve an organic conquest of the unions, the Chambers of Labour and the General Confederation of labour, to become the elements of confidence to which the masses will delegate authority for the formation of political Soviets and for the exercise of the dictatorship of the proletariat.[1]

Gramsci's silence about the Councils in his *Prison Notebooks* and later writings, led many commentators to regard it as a break in his thought process. During the Councils movement Gramsci had emphasised that even after the revolution, the Councils would continue to exist whereas in his *Prison Notes*, the party is seen as the central vehicles of revolution and it is stated that the party would cease to

---

1. Gramsci, *L'Ordine Nuovo*, 8 May, 1920, pp. 121-122; also quoted in Joll, *Gramsci*, pp. 38-39.

exist when there is no class conflict. A close examination reveals that this transitory nature of party does not in any way diminish its role as compared with the Councils. Firstly, the class struggle would not cease simply with an overthrow of bourgeois yoke and the party would continue to exercise a dominating role even after the revolution. Then, the Councils are the stage of class struggle based chiefly on production and to control forms of production. The party, on the other hand, "comes to be identified with the historical consciousness of the mass of the people, and it governs their spontaneous, irresistable movement".[1] They party, then, welds economics and politics as well as masses and leadership. The Councils and party are thus in no way opposed to each other. The crucial role that councils played in educating masses and raising their cultural level, is continued by the party. As the political party, too, is based on the economic reality, it is an essential instrument to enable the class whose representative it is, to attain political consciousness.

The essential functions of education and cultural upliftment are regarded as crucial factors of revolution throughout his writings. Gramsci has always recognised the need of guiding spontaneous movement of the masses, and has stressed the necessity of harnessing these outbursts for a revolution. Workers are always to be educated and prepared for the takeover of State. In all these issues, the thread of his thought is consistent. He may not have used the precise notion of Council in the prison, or may have simply concentrated on the means to attain the State power through his definition of the party as a potential State, and as such may have focused his attention on the party—but, all these factors in no way show a break in his thought—process. Instead, we find a thread linking Councils to the party in a dialectical way. It simply implies the realisation by Gramsci of other crucial factors i.e. question of superstructure, political issues etc.—in the process of revolution. One cannot, therefore, minimise the importance of Councils. The need is to blend

---

1. Gramsci, quoted in Glucksmann, *Gramsci and The State*, p. 168.

it as a subordinate organ of workers, useful for party in propagating consciousness among workers. Gramsci's view in the regard are worthquoting. He says "The establishment of the Councils is only valuable if it is conceived as the beginning of a revolutionary process. The exercise of control (in the factories) has a significance only if it is stage in this process".[1]

As has been said, the political party is born on the terrain of economic struggle but it has wide ranging goals, and it represents the interests of a class. It has also been noticed that the working class can reach only a trade union level of consciousness on its own. Political Party is the external agent of a particular class interests. It is against this backdrop that the question of the relation of party to the class of its origin becomes important. We have also seen[2] that the organic intellectuals articulate the interests of the class of their origin and provide their class leadership. It is particularly at this point that Gramsci, on the one hand, decries the claim of anarchist that masses alone are capable of making revolution and there is no need of a party or a programme and, on the other hand, highlights the role of the modern Prince.

The question of collective will is at the core of Machiavelli's Prince. The Prince understands what is good for masses and acts accordingly. Masses, too, have faith in Prince even when they cannot always fathom the rationality of Prince's working. The Prince acts for the 'moral reform' of his people, i.e. a constructive plan of action. All these ingradients of the Prince form the essential spirit and the backbone of Gramsci's Modern Prince' or the political party. Gramsci reiterated time and again that the masses cannot achieve class consciousness on their own as Sorel believed. A spontaneous development, according to him, cannot envisage a political programme of action. Class consciousness has to be nurtured carefully. In his own words : "To expect that a

---

1. Gramsci, 'Controllo di classe' 3 Jan. 1920. quoted in Joll, *Gramsci*, p. 42.
2. See, chapter IV.

mass reduced to such conditions of physical and spiritual slavery could embody a spontaneous historical development, to expect that it would spontaneously being and continue an act of revolutionary creation is an illusion of ideologists : to rely on the unique creative capacity of such a mass and not work systematically to organise a great army of disciplined and conscious militants, ready for every sacrifice, educated to put their slogans into practice simultaneously, ready to assume effective responsibility for its revolution, ready to be agents of revolution not to do this is the real betrayal of the working class and an unconscious counter-revolution in advance."[1] Sorel and anarchists thus betray the revolutionary class in their impatience and illogical aversion to organisation and intellectuals. The orgrnic intllectuals provide the class consciousness via the organism of party. Party is the conscious vanguard of the class of its origin.

Here, the relationship of party with the class of its origin becomes a moot point. A question arises : since the party is an external agent, how far does it align itself and identify itself with the class of its origin? In this context, a brief survey of Bordiga's view becomes necessary.

Bordiga assigned to the party a role distinct and separate from the class. He called party an organ of the working class. Party is a leader, an organizer of the working class; but it does not concern itself with the day-to-day struggle of the class, nor does it believe in preparing the masses for revolution. It intends to train a cadre of dedicated leadership who issue a call to masses to join them when the revolutionary moment is ripe. The essential function of Bordiga's party thus, is to prepare dadres—and not the masses for revolution. This view originated due to the fact that in Italy working class was in a minority, and there was a danger of infiltration of party by the members of the other classes. But, Bordiga's conception of doctrinaire purity of the party required a pure working class

1. Gramsci, "Discorso agli anarchici", *L'Ordine Nuovo*, pp. 400-401, also quoted in Joil, *Gramscl*, p. 53.

having a closeknit and disciplined party. The 'abstentionism'[1] of PSI and Bordiga are a symptom of this misunderstanding of relation of party to the masses. It is manifest that this view is in contravention to the Marxist-Leninist concept of the party

Party, Gramsci explains, is a 'part' of the working class, concerned with its daily struggles and objective situations. The party cannot remain passive to the daily struggles while striving for national and higher goals. This ultra-leftism given to the party by Bordiga, Gramsci feels, "is like the right wing tendencies, the expression of a scepticism concering the possibility for the working-class masses to organize, from within themselves, a class party capable of leading the broad masses and at the same time striving to keep them bound to it at all times."[2] For Gramsci, the proletarian party is a mass party; it is international in character and is concerned with matters having repercussions of international development. Proletariat the class of the exploited, will be free in the real sense of the term only, when the entire world is free from exploitation.

The question now arises as to what are the stages through which the party arrives to becomes a homogeneous, cohesive party with itsd own doctrine and tactics and a rigid and impeccable discipline.

When the mass of any group is not coscious of its aims and goals and when its wants are not yet articulated, its organic intellectuals form an elite party. This party is born on the terrain of economic contradictions, being aware of the class antagonism, it comes into existence to organize the interest of its class. It tries to arouse the consciousness of the masses about their interest; and thus, it gradually becomes a mass party by admitting in its fold a large section of the masses. The initial elitist stage of the party is comparable to

---

1. 'Absentionism' of PSI and Bordiga favoured *non-participation in election* where masses have to be woed. It favoured isolated activity of the party. See chapter I, for details.
2. Gramsci, *Selection from Political Writings*, Vol. 2, p. 361.

the concept of elitist party enonciated by Michels and Pareto. However the elite of Gramsci are born out of historic and socio-economic conditions, and are organically linked to the class of their origin. They are not chosen solely on the basis of merit or of aristocratic lineage. They are the conscious representatives of their class. Moreover, even in the Gramscian concept of the so-called elitist stage of the development of the party, there is no linkage with the concept of the 'circulation of elites' to continue the system as suggested by Pareto and Michels. The Gramscian party aims at mobilizing and organising the masses. It strives to lose its elitist nature gradually by involving greater and greater section of the masses. The sole aim of the party is the attainment of hegemony. And, when hegemony is achieved, the party having completed its historic assignment, becomes redundant. In other words, the political party in its active and historic role, envisages a worldview of its own on the basis of historical facts and tries to foresee the state of future progressive society; it seeks to change the order of the society—its economic system and production relations.[1]

Gramsci has elaborately dealt with the nature of the elitist party and the mass party. So long as the masses do not attain the requisite consciousness, the party has to maintain its elitist nature. But even then masses are not at the mercy of the apex body of law makers. The democratic centralism and rigid discipline keeps the interests of the working class active and supreme. Even at times of repression, the party is forced to become a close knit, elite organization, maintaining secrecy and finghting repressions effectively, because of the exigencies of the circumstances.

In fact, in this elitist stage the party retains its mass character through democratic centralism. The concept of democratic centralism is a contribution of Marxist-Leninist thought. It envisages a system in which decisions are democratically arived at and then implimented centrally. Its chief characteristic is organic centralism. There are, according

---

1. See chapter I.

to Gramsci, two types of organic centralism. One which conceals the "programme of predominance" of one part "over the whole".[1] In such a case, it may lead to bureaucratic centralism. Gramsci says : "If the constitutive element of an organism is posed in a rigorously and rigidly doctrinaire system, there is a caste-like, priest type of relationship". In such cases : "Formula will be recited from memory without changing a single syllable, but real activity will be something else.[2] In direct contrast to imposition from above is 'real' organic centralism—the hallmark of democratic centralism. It is according to Gramsci, characterised by "centralism' in movement—i.e. continual adaptation of organization to the real movement, a matching of thrusts from below with orders from above, a continuous insertion of elements thrown up from the depths of ranks and file into the solid framework of the leadership apparatus which ensures continuity and regular accumulation of experience.[3]

The party by fusing, together 'spontaneous acts' and 'conscious leadership' ensures the transition of theory into practice. The party mediates through its function of education. It is the collective intellectual embodying the "collective will" of the masses. The party is a vanguard and leads the progressive forces towards revolution. It is a vanguard primarily because it leads other allied and subordinate classes towards the revolution.

It is against this background that Gramsci insists that the economistic view that a proletarian party is historically inevitable must be shown to be devoid of scientific analysis. The party, according to him, is born only when subjective factors (i.e. its constituent elements) are present and subjective condition are ripe. The relationship between subjective and objective factors for the birth of a party are complex and dialectical. The subjective political factors correspond to the levels of the consciousness of masses.

---

1. Gramsci, *Selections from Prison Notebooks*, p. 188.
2. Gramsci, *Quadernidel Carcere*, p. 337.
3. Gramsci, *Selections from Prison Notebooks*, pp. 188-189.

Party, being the nomenclature for a social group, its constituent elements (or subjective factors) are three in number. In fact, Gramsci illustrates the three elements of the party through a military description. These are the faithful soldiers, the corporals and the Captains. The disciplined soldiers obey the command of the leadership. They are those faithful soldiers of their party who have faith in their ideology, but who lack any creative spirit or organizational skill.

The second element, the corporals are placed in between the faithful soldiers and captains, and they are the "principal cohesive element" who transmit the views of the captains and coordinate all acts and channelise all the forces of their class. Even if the leaders command the movement they must involve the masses in the struggle. Any neglect of masses is fatal. Illustrating this Gramsci emphasises that even though "in every political situation the active part a minority...if this minority when it is followed by the multitudes does not organise this following in a lasting way, and it (the multitude) becomes dispirited through whatever circumstances which, is propituous to the adverse minority, the whole apparatus will break up and a new one be found in which the old multitude no longer count and no longer move or have any effect. What is called mass has been pulverised in many atoms without will and orientation."[1]

The third element, comprising of the captains, "articulates the first element with the second and maintains contact between them, not only physically but also morally and intellectually."[2]

Gramsci always maintained that there was a dialectical relationship between the leaders and the masses. As such there is no predominent role of any one element of the party. All elements are balanced according to the stage of the ongoing dialectics between the objective and the subjective factors. Any emphasis on the one element to the detriment or neglect of the other, makes the party illequipped for revolution. In fact,

---

1. Gamsci, *Quadernidel Carcere*, p. 1787.
2. Gramsci, *Selections from Prison Notebooks*, p. 153.

the second element (of leadership) is born in the beginning to articulate the demands and aspiration of their class. The leadership is born on the terrain of objective conditions. Each social group brings into existence, together with itself, its organic intellectuals, and these very intellectuals are the leaders of political party when they consciously try to establish their hegemony.

When all the three elements exist and their existence is inevitable, and when the level of cosciousness of the masses is organised and linked by intermediatry levels in such a fashion that all understand the need of this relationship, then the party cannot be annhilated defeated by normal means.

Now reverting to the problem of relations between the party and the class of its origin, it can be said that this refers to the problem of balance between the three elements of the party. The party can be mass party only by raising the level of the masses. The PSI by relying on the dictets of the masses failed to seize the revolutionary moment. The party, to be successful, cannot wait to secure the consent of the masses without raising their intellectual level, nor can it wait for the task of revolution to begin whan the masses have become conscious. Gramsci's clear contention is that if the party fails to seize every point of struggle on this pretext it has to be unequivocably condemned. The leaders, he exharts, "base themselves on the 'masses' that is they seek a preventive consensus on action, moving to consulation in forms and at a time which they chose themselves."[1] The revolutionary moment can only be founded on the proletarian vanguard and has to be conducted without prior consulation and without the apparatus of representative assemblies. "Revolution is like a war." He asserted that the task of revolutionary vanguard is to keep "the revolutionary spirit permamently alive in the masses to create the conditions in which the masses respond instantly to revolutionary orders".[2] Political party in the

1. Gramsci, "Capacita Politica", translated in *New Edinburgh Review*, 1974 II, p. 110.
2. *Ibid.*, pp. 110-111.

process of becoming mass party is a vanguard of the proletariat. The element of leadership has to be the most organised and it provides the thrust of the party. Leaders or intellectuals perform the task of political party when all the members of class are as yet not ready to participate in the movement; though in the ultimate analysis masses' contribution is the decisive factor.

The party is a vanguard and leads other progressive forces and organisations. But what safeguard does this vanguard party haveagainst the arbitrariness of its leaders? The basic difference between workers party and elitist party of non-proletarian process is that of the intent of leaders. The non-proletarian forces have the interest to prolong the forces of division. The proletarian leaders understand the difference between the rulers and the ruled and try to creat conditions where no such differences exist.

In fact, Sorel's critique of party as an elite organisation, and various other conservative elite concepts (like that of Pareto Mosca and Michel) made Gramsci acutely aware of the relationship between the political party and the masses. Sorel finds masses as the ridding force of any revolution; as such the party becomes redundant to him for the proletarian revolution. Diametrically opposed is Lenin's view that the masses alone can attain only trade union consciousness and cannot arrive at class consciousness by themselves. Political consciousness and a programme of action is brought to the working class through the external agency of the party. Gramsci's concept is much more complex, because he operated in a complex society where the capitalist system was all pervasive. Gramsci, therefore, though assigns a major role to the masses in his concept of party, yet does not praise the spontaneity of masses as was done by Sorel. He does not also make the party as the sole creator of revolution. For him, there is an organic, dialectical relationship between the leaders and the masses. The leaders are aware of the contradiction that is existing in society; therefore, they are able to perceive the role of bourgeois state. The party of the proletariat, or of its intellectuals has a clear understanding of the system; as such it is in a vintage position to analyse the moments of crises. The masses, on the other hand, fell the injustices of system, are conscious of daily struggle and their outburst is voluntary. To organise these two elements, to reconcile the spontaneity of masses and directive role of leadership, a dialectical unity of 'knowing' and 'feeling', between party and masses is necessary.

Gramsci ruled out that there is any such thing as 'pure' spontaneity. Spontaneity is the halmark of such subordinate groups that have not attained the level of class consciousness. "The fact that every spontaneous movement contains rudimentary element of conscious leadership, of discipline, is indirectly demonstrated by the fact that there exist tendencies and groups who extol spontaneity as a method ".[1] Apart from these spontaneous movements any activity on the part of masses based on diffused worldview or on common sense can be called spontaneous. There is only a quantitative difference of political awareness between this spontaneity and conscious leadership and hence, there cannot be an exposition between the two. The party must guide such movements as Lenin also has envisaged. The spontaneity is based on common sense pereception. The conscious leadership provides it direction by educating the masses and making their worldview critical.

In fact, party has to perform a double task—organizational and political. First, the organizational task. Since the proletariat is in a minority in the society, Gramsci finds that the party's primary task is to win allies for the attainment of its revolutionary aim. In every society besides the tow fundamental classes of the exploited and the exploiters, there exists large category of other secondary classes. On the basis of their participation in the relations of production, these can broadly be classified as dominant classes and subordinate classes.

The constant effort of the dominant classes to win over allies of other classes by providing them fringed benefits and thereby assimilating them, compounds the problem of the alignment of the social forces. The subordinate classes that

---

1. Gramsci, *Selections from Prison Notebooks*, p. 197.

are the most exploited are peasants and workers. The relations of production are such that the alliance of these two classes is necessary to bring about the revolution. But the peasants are not conscious of their role; and even when they are, they cannot successfully carry out a revolution. The need is to identify the role of various classes in the field or production and their consequential status in the superstructure.

The study to locate different classes in the field of production entails a separate account of rural and urban societies. In rural societies, two major classes exist—traditional intellectuals and feudal lords comprise one and poor peasants the other. There is a great chasm between the proletariat of urban and rural areas. The rural proletariat—peasantry is the historically ally of workers but is reactionary by its role in production processes. The aim of peasantry is always to posses land. It is connected with state apparatus through the mediation of great intellectuals and bureaucracy, it also has petty-bourgeois aspirations to join the civil services. Another group exercising great influence over peasants is of religions leaders who generate possivity and fatalism in peasantry. They try to dominate struggles of peasants in order to diffuse their revolutionary favour. The agricultural peasants, in Italy, remain landless. Gramsci also realised that there was no agricultural industry in Italy and hence the labourers remain stagnant. They, therefore, cannot form a party of their own. The peasants and rural proletariat at best, generate a 'tendency' to organise themselves but a lack of consciousness results in absence of party of rural proletariat. The attempts of rural proletariat to form Fasci dei Lavoratori[1] in Italy in order to forcibly occupy land were crushed by government.

The urban proletariat, on the other hand, is an essential component of industry. It is directly involved in class

---

1. Fasci dei Lavoratori were formed in Sicilya in 1892-93 for redistribution of land. These were crushed by Crispi's government during the economic crisis of 1893-94.

struggle and conscious of its role in production process. It could act in such a way as to further the interests of peasants also. Thus the rural and urban proletariat have different characteristics. The chasm is exploited by rulers. Indeed in Italy, rural proletariat was used to suppress urban workers' uprisings.[1]

The petty bourgeois, despite being different at rural and urban levels—join together through national bureaucracy, services, armed forces etc., and acquire a national character. They influence peasantry to support ruling classes. The need, therefore, is to make urban proletariat conscious of its historic role of leader. It should make the cause of rural proletariat its own, in order to win them over to their common goal. It should strive to make peasantry aware of its proletariat character and the goal of changing the exploitative order.

This analysis suggests that the role of middle classes in advanced capitalist societies is vital; and many a times it is decisive. The bourgeoisie maintain their control over society through alliance with one or the other class of petty-bourgeoise. The construction of society is such that proletariat alone or capitalists alone are not capable of controlling the society single handedly. They need allies. As such, it becomes imperative for the working class to win over peasantry and other subordinate groups to achieve hegemony.[2]

The political party is the collective intellectual necessary to hasten the revolution. The dialectical relationship between its leading element and mass element ensures the implementation of the task of education and cultural upliftment of the

---

1. In the 1917 Turin insurrection, the Sassari Brigade, largely of soldiers of South with peasant origins, was used by government, against workers'. The members of Brigade regarded workers as 'white-collared' gentry, as exploiters, Later on, when the Brigade was convinced of revolutionary character of Turin workers, it was shifted out within a year. See Gramsci, *Selections from Political Writings*, Vol. 2, p. 447.
2. The United Front Tactics of International were aimed at winning allies for workers.

masses. The party leadership (or intellectual) is always aware of the fact that since consciousness tends to lag behind economic realities it becomes the primary task of the party to lessen this gap and arouse the revolutionary consciousness of the masses. However, in an advanced capitalist society this political task of the party becomes difficult because of the capitalist-hegemonic control. The level of cultural consciousness is apparently high in such societies in contrast to the backward. condition of Lenin's Russia. In Russia, the party used the period of dictatorship to educate the masses after the revolution; whereas in the advanced countries of the West, revolution has to be preceded by the cultural consciousness among masses in order to break the hegemony of the bourgeoisie. For this reason, the party has two roles to play—first it is the vanguard of the proletariat; and second, it is the collective intellectual on the pattern of the Prince of Machiavelli A query may arise here. If party is collective intellectual, are all its members intellectual? The claim that "all members of a political party should be regarded as intellectual is an affiirmation that can easily lend itself to mockery and caricature. But if one thinks about it nothing could be more exact. There are of course distinctions of level to be made. A party might have a greater or lesser proportion of members in the higher grades or in the lower but this is not the point. What matters is the function, which is directive and organisational, i.e. educative, i.e. intellectual."[1]

The aim of the party is, thus, to produce its own intellectuals, organise them and win over the intellectuals of other classes. The intellectuals also provide leadership to allied classes. The most important ally of workers, as we have seen above, are peasants; but traditionally they have been controlled either by the bourgeois or by the clergy. On its own the peasantry remains an undirected discountent and a disparate lot. In Gramsci's words : "What does a poor peasant obtain by invading an uncultivated piece of land ? Without machines, what can a poor peasant expect from seizing the land ? It

1. Gramsci, *Selections from Prison Notebooks*, p. 16.

satisfies for the first moment his primitive greed for land but at the next moment when he realizes that his own arms are not enough to break up the soil...he realizes his own impotence his isolation, his disperate condition and becomes a brigand not a revolutionary, becomes an assassin of the 'gentry', and not a fighter for 'worker' and peasants' communism."[1] This situation of the peasantry can improve, if their revolutionary zeal is harnessed; and this is the task of the party. Despite being in a minority, the workers must lead the allied classes in their struggle.

In short, the organizational task of the party is to produce intellectuals to form a well-knit disciplined party based on principles of democratict centralism; its political functions include, educating the masses, improving their cultural level and winning over the intellectuals of the other classes. In fact, political party is a potential state and strives to achieve hegemony. It its active, historic role the political party envisages a worldview of its own on the basis of historical facts and tries to foresee the state of future progressive society.

A brief comparative analysis of Lenin's and Gramsci's concept of party may be undertaken here. There are differences of opinion as to whether Gramsci is a developer of Lenin, or he has evolved an entirely new concept of the party having shades of syndicalism and fascist totalitraianism. In fact, Gramsci and Lenin both assign a vanguard role to the party. However, the difference appears when they discussed the strategy and the stages of the party. Gramsci's stress on a period of education of the masses, his concept of party as a moral force and his belief that the party is not concerned with what to do and how but with what ought to be done in order to bring about a revolution all these are regarded as non-Marxist views. But, if we, pause and analyse the different socio-historical perspective against the backdrop of which the two thinkers proposed their views, it becomes clear that the difference in their views is because of the different realities of their times. Lenin operate in a backward society where the

---

1. Gramsci, quoted in Joll, *Gramsci*, p. 69.

institutions of civil society where practically non-existant; there was only the coersive authority of the States. In the absence of any ideological hegemony, the party's stress was only on overturning the state-apparatus and then to organise workers for the dictatorship of the proletariate, ultimately leading to a communist society. In the West, where Gramsci functioned, the ideological control or hegemony of the capitalist class was so powerful that class-conflicts were ruccessfully sougth to be diffused. The tasks of the party, under the circumstances, was to prepare a revolutionary condition by making the masses aware of the class conflicts. Thus the party in the West was required to build a counter-hegemonic consciousness prior to the revolution. In Russia, Lenin's party had to take this task after the revolution. The comparative analysis suggests that the role of the party is dependent on the nature of the State.

III

The study of Gramsci's views on politics reveals his fundamental marxian thesis that although 'economics' is determinant in last instance, yet 'politics' has primacy over economics in the process of chage. The political party is the instrument of the proletariat through which change is affected; and, fulfils its historic task by its endeavours to replace the bourgeois hegemony by the proletariat hegemony. And, this necessitates an examination of the nature of the State and Society. All these—the role of hegemony, the nature of the State and Sociey—are precisely the chief concern of the next chapter which is based on the above analysis of politics as an autonomous science.

6

Views on State and Civil Society

The political party strives to establish its worldview and to create a new state that would adequately reflect its weltanschauung. In fact, the founding of a new state is equal to the creation of a weltanschauung. Gramsci's concept of state can be better understood against the backdrop of an analysis of the prevalent idealist, neo-idealist, Marxist and positivist concepts of the state. Yet another major influence on Gramsci is that of Machiavelli; and his observations on state has also to be recollected before embarking on Gramscian concept of state.

Niccolo Machiavelli may be regarded as the precursor of the concept of the modern nation state. He discarded the idea of state as Divine, and regarded 'politics' as autonomous of religion and other transcendent rules. He was also the first Italian who demanded a united state. He laid down the foundation of a national State. He declared : "The Middle Ages have given us anarchy; we must, therefore, establish a new power, a real and living one, the State. The State, having in itself its ends and its means, has no need of any theological investiture, it is."[1] He advocated formation of militia to

---

1. Machiavelli quoted in Sforza, *Contemporary Italy—Its Intellectual and Moral Origins* (trans, by DD. Kay), Fredrick Muller Ltd. London, 1946, p. 9.

include peasant masses into political process. But, Machiavelli was too much ahead of his Times and his call went unheeded.

There were many new and divergent concepts of the State floating in the air in the nineteenth and the early twentieth century. There were Hegelians and neo-Hegelians; there were Marxists, neo-marxists and socialists; there were liberals, and democrats; and, the Fascist tendencies were struggling to be born.

Hegal starts with the conviction that history is not an arbitrary and accidental revelation. History reveals a meaningful pattern, not in any way affected by theological premiss. The whole of history reveals the progress of the idea or the Spirit. The only reality in the universe is this Idea, and other rational phenomena are its manifestations. The 'Idea' or 'Spirit' progresses towards self-realization. History is nothing else but the 'strife of the finite self-consciousness with the absolute self-consciousness."[1] The development of Spirit is dialectical in a spiral process and is applicable to all social, political and ethical changes.

Social institutions are based on family that rests on love, dependence and mutual self-sacrifice. A number of families when interact create a society where competition is the guiding principle. The next stage is creation of the State. The State is essentially transcendental in origin. Hegel discounted theories of pre-political societies forming state on contract basis; and consequently for him, there were no natural rights of man to be safeguarded by the state. Hegel regards man as essentially a social and political being on account of the movement of Absolute Spirit in human beings. The Spirit took the form of State through a process of evolution through various stages. As such, the 'State is the divine will as a present spirit, which unfolds itself in the actual shape of an organized world."[2] The individual is subordinate to the State.

---

1. Hegel, *Lectures on the History of Philosophy*, p. 551.
2. Hegel, *Philosophy of Right*, (Trans. T.M. Knox), Oxford, Univ. Press, 1942, p. 260.

"The state is the objective spirit and the individual has his truth, his real existence and ethical status only in being a member of it."[1] The state is an end in itself; it is the "actualization of Freedom."[2] Freedom means attainment of World Spirit. The spirit is attained in three stages—(a) the will as immediate (the state of formal right) (b) the will reflected (subjective Morality) (c) and, social ethics or *sittlichkeit. Sittlichkeit* is divided into three moments of family, civil society and the state.

The individual at the stage of family is selfless and sacrificial, but in society competitiveness pervades one's relations. These feelings are transcended in the State in the feeling of universality and total allegiance to state. Analysing these three moments, Hegel finds that an individual maintaining his family, acquires property in order to get recognition and respect from others. It is not a materialistic desire, but a very limited relationship with the idea.

In this way Hegel advocates private property as a means to establish one's personality. At this juncture of attaining individuality, a man enters into family life in order to experience "self-consciousness of one's individuality within this unity as the absolute essence of oneself...as a member."[3] This stage of objective unity is a transitory stage and numerous families lead towards Civil Society.

Civil Society "is the achievement of the modern world which has for the first time given all determinations of the Idea their due."[4] This stage of interdependence, provides for associations, legel system and other functions that are normally associated with the state. It is "external state" based on understanding; but the ends are particular, not universal. Paradoxical it may seem, but it is a fact that "civil society, though it precedes the state in the logical order, is ultimately

---

1. *Ibid.*, p. 240.
2. *Ibid.*, p. 244.
3. *Ibid.*, p. 158.
4. *Ibid.*, p. 182.

dependent upon the state for its very existence and preservations."[1] It is a society based on needs that are mediated through labour. As self-interest and self-assertion are motives of civil society, men produce in order to exchange. The state of dependence on others results in the generation of static spirit. Hegel explains that "by a dialectical advance, subjective self-seeking turns into the mediation of the particular through the universal, with the result that each man in earning, producing and enjoying on his own account, is '*eo ipso* producing and earning for the enjoyment of everyone else."[2] Gradually, the activities of civil society increase and a new class of civil servants, vested with universality, emerges. In order to adjust the contradictory and particular interests, the representation of public is sought in the process of governing. This is done through the media of corporations and estates. Hegel claims : "The real significance of the Estates lies in the fact that it is through them that the state enters the subjective consciousness of the people and that the people begin to participate in the state."[3] In this way, civil society covers a whole spectrum of relations that "lie outside the absolutely universal interests of the state proper."[4] The efforts of civil society are to regulate relations between men and economic and legel affairs in such a way that 'reason' comes to occupy a guiding role. In civil society, autonomous bodies balance each other.

Religion is also inferior to the state in Hegel's schema. Religion is a necessary moment of self-consciousness. Religion strives for absolute truths but in particular ways. The confinement to limited people of specific characteristics religion is subservient to the State which is a 'Universality of thought'. A mature and strong state adopts liberal and tolerant attitude towards religion.

Civil society is superseded by the state. The state of

1. *Ibid* , p. 182.
2. *Ibid.*, p. 199.
3. *Ibid.*, p. 301.
4. *Ibid* , p. 288.

Hegel does not refer to any existing state but to the idea of state of which all existing states are an aproximation. "The state is the actuality of the ethical Idea."[1] It is the result of a historical development. In the rational state, particularity of society and individuality of person are transcended in universality. Various forms of state represent the level of rationality attained by it in the course of development towards freedom. A modern, rational state is characterized by the rule of law, a constitutional government and an organic interdependence among its various organs. Thus the ethical state is also an 'integral' state. The Hegelian state-concept is restricted to 'national' state only.

The Hegelian conception of state influenced schools of thought as diverse as Marxism, neo-Idealism and totalitarianism.

In Italy neo-Hegelians influenced a whole generation. The most prominent neo-Hegelians Gentile and Croce represented two different elements of Hegel to formulate divergent views.[2]

For Giovanni Gentile, the ethical state was a real divinity and above the individual. Every philosophical conception is philosophy. The state strives towards ethico-political moment when a new culture would be established and it would ensure the education of the whole man. The 'abstract' freedom of liberalism has no place in Gentile's Absolute state which provides a 'concrete' freedom. The state authority pervades all areas of life of men in society or in ethical community. In this context. Gentile carried out a critique of Marx. He identified 'praxis' as the hall-mark of Marxist philosophy. He averred that Marx applied praxis to materialism which is in effect a mediation between 'men and nature'. Gentile finds a contradiction between materialism and its realism—praxis. For Gentile "Praxis is absorbed in the reality of the Spirit which is Action."[3] Thus Gentile

---

1. *Ibid*., p. 257.
2. See, Chapter II.
3. Gentile, quoted in Glucksmann, *Gramsci and The State*, p. 299.

absolves Hegelianism of its material aspects and reduces it to historical and historicised spiritualism. Praxis, in Gentile, becomes identity of theory and spirit.

Gramsci claimed that 'Marxist philosophy is "neither idealist monism nor materialist monism, but historical materialism."'[1] The reformist Hegelianism of Gentile, according to Gramsci, identifies state and government; it identifies ethical state and dictatorship (or Fascism). For Gentile, Hegel perceived an ethical state as a completely spiritual creation where it (state) is the ethical means for achieving Freedom. Gramsci accused Gentile of depriving Hegelianism of its dielectics and reducing it (Hegelianism) to history of the Spirit that is actualized in the State.

Croce, on the other hand, had a liberal, philosophical concept with emphasis on division between economics and politics, and a dominance of ethical moment over these two. In Croce, a distinction is made between civil society and political society. Croce's distinction between masses and intellectuals leads him to make the latter the sole repository of knowledge and wisdom to rule. The intellectuals, therefore, dominate civil society and obtain the consent of the masses for the system. The history is ethico-political, and not merely the history of state; and, therefore for Croce, the state is of a spiritual category not confined to the mere fact. Croce also rejected any specific Marxist philosophy. The judicial regulation of economics indeed requires a state, and that, Croce believed, could be identified with government. There are then, for Croce, two forces—material force and true human force governing the society. These forces are represented in moments of 'force' and 'consent' in the state. Thus, the ethical moment arrives when authority and freedom are transcended. Croce, therefore, asserts primacy of intellectuals and absence of contradictions in the state.

The common points in Croce and Gentile are stress on strong, powerful state and absence of democracy. Both have no place for masses. If Croce tried to diffuse contradiction

---

3. Gramsci, quoted in Glucksmann, *Gramsci and The State*, p. 300.

and perpetuate intellectual domination, Gentile perceived of a fascist model in the separate visions of Hegelian state.

The Marxian thought is also evolved out of a critique of Hegel's ideas. Croce, acknowledging Hegel's contribution in giving a new dimension to the-then prevalent ideas and breaking from the past, rightly says: "Political thought...abondoned the eighteenth century faith in intellectualism, rationalism, enlightenment and Jacobin radicalism, so that the new revolutionary movement which was adumbrated as socialism or communism aspired to scientific status by adopting...the historical method of Hegel."[1] Marx constructed his philosophy of materialism out of the critique of Hegelian system. He exhorted : "Hegel turns the moments of the idea of the state into a subject and makes the old political arrangements into a predicate, while in historical reality things operate always the other way round: the idea of the state is always a predicate of these arrangements. Thus Hegel only expresses the general political climate of the period, its political theology."[2] Explaining his own method, Marx said that dialectics was standing on its head with Hegel and Marx turned it "right side up again."[3]

In Marxist parliance, state is a tools of exploitation. According to Lenin : "The state is manifestation of the irreconcilablity of class-antagonisms. The state arises where, when and in so for as class antagonisms objectively cannot be reconciled. And conversely, the existence of the state proves that the class antagonisms are irreconciliable."[4] This can be traced back to Marx. According to Marx, a "superstitious belief in the state has passed from philosophy into the general consciousness of the bourgeoisie and even of many workers. According to the philosophical conception, the state is the 'realization of the idea' or the kingdom of God on earth,

1. Croce, *My Philosophy*, p. 13.
2. Marx, quoted in Avineri. *The Social and Political Thought of Karl Marx*, (University Press, Cambridge, 1968, p. 32.
3. Marx and Engels, *Selected Works*, p. 609.
4. Lenin, *Collected Works*, p. 266.

translated into philosophical term, the sphere in which eternal truth and justice are or should be realized."[1] In reality, the state is "by no means a power forced on society from without; just as little is it 'the reality of the ethical idea', 'the image and reality of reason', as Hegel maintains. Rather, is a product of society at a certain-stage of development; it is the admission that this society has become entangled in an insoluble contradiction with itself, that is has split into irreconcilable antagonisms which it is powerless to dispel. But in order that these antagonisms and classes with conflicting economic interests might not consume themselves and society in fruitless struggle, it became necessary to have a power seemingly standing above society that would alleviate conflict and keep it within the bounds of 'order'; and this power arisen out of society but placing itself above it, and alierating itself more and more from it, is the state."[2] The state, then has not existed from eternity, and in future a stage would come where the existence of classes would hamper production and then, these classes would fall inevitably. The proletariat is the historically most progressive class and the moment it seizes power, it turns the means of production into state property and strives to abolish classes from society. The state gradually withers away. "Between capitalist and communist society lies the period of the revolutionary transformation of the one into the other."[3] Corresponding to this is "a political transition period in which the state can be nothing but the *revolutionary dictatorship of the proletariat*."[4] This theorem does not rule out conflict with the bourgeois state in the vain hope of its inevitable dissolution.

Marx also clarified that "by the word 'state' is meant the government machine, or the state in so for as it forms a social organism separated from society through division of

---

1. Marx & Engels, *Selected Works*, p. 258.
2. Engel, "Origin of Family, Private property and The State", *Ibid.*, p. 576.
3 Marx, "Critique of the Gotha Programme", in *Ibid.*, p. 327.
4. *Ibid.*

labour,"[1]—a fact not properly understood by the Hegelians. He assailed Hegel for regarding state as a higher form of civil society and making it an incarnation of the Absolute Reason. He asserted that "neither legal relations nor political froms could be comprehended whether by themselves or on the basis of so-called general development of the human mind, but that on the contrary they originate in the material conditions of life, the totality or which Hegel embraces within the term 'civil society'.[2] The civil society is based on economic structure of society. But it is not directly reducible to the economic basis. Mark held that consciousness of men is formed as a social being; and the social being is formulated in the dialectric of men, production relations and mode of production. The civil society emerged with the bourgeois class. Marx explains the relation between civil society and state and its institutions : "Since the state is the form in which the individuals of a ruling class assert their common interests, and in which the whole civil society of an epoch is epitomised, it follows that all common institutions are set up with the help of the state and are given a political from".[3]

This was the core of Marxist theory of the state. But during the Second International many mechanistic and positivist trends led to distortions of Marxist concepts. The positivists favoured adoption of methods of natural science to explain the process of development. The mechanists, on the other hand, believed in the ultimate demise of state due to the accentuation in class conflict. The ideas of these currents were adequately refuted by Gramsci, who was geatly influenced by the ideas of Hegel, Croce and Lenin regarding the state.

Lenin had rightly percieved in *Marxism and the State* that the question of state implied "tasks of proletarian revolution in relation to the state. The state, for Lenin, is "an

---

1. *Ibid.*, p. 328.
2. Marx, "Preface" to *A Contribution to the Critique of Political Economy*, Progress Publishers, 1978, p. 20
3. Marx and Engels, *The German Ideology*, Progress Publishers, Moscow, 1976, p. 99.

organ of the rule of a definite class which *cannot* be reconciled with its antipode (the class opposite to it)".[1] The proletariat must strive to overthrow this. As far back as 1899, Lenin had clearly perceived the aims of proletariat. He said : "The proletariat must strive to form independent political parties, the main aim of which must be the capture of political power by the proletariat for the purpose of organising socialist society".[5] This capture can only succeed by engineering a voilent revolution. The state even after the overthrow of bourgeois, continues to exist under proletariat. It is "a centralised organisation of force, an organisation of the exploiters and to *lead* the enormous mass of population—the peasants, the petty bourgeoisie and semi-proletarians—in the work of organising a socialist economy".[3] He carried a critique of economists who tried to limit the struggle to the sphere of economics and who tried to exclude political struggle. The positiveists also came under his scathing attacks. He discounted theories that predicted the inevitable collapse of capitalism. Lenin also provided for different techniquies of revolution in different countries with emphasis on systematic, planned preparation under a political party. He never said that enemy can "be overthrown only by a regular seige or by organised assault. Such a view would be absurd and doctrinaire".[4] A long, prolonged struggle is required before the establishment of a socialist. Gramsci almost echoed a similar idea in an article in 1920. He said : "The battle has only to commence. We have to destroy the spirit of class collaboration and reformism, and formulate exactly and precisely what it is we mean by the state."[5] Gramaci's concept of state involves a two pronged analysis of political and philosophical factors in the formation of a state.

1. Lenin, *State and Revolution*, in *Selected Works*, p. 267.
2. Lenin, *Against Revisionism*, p. 31.
3. Lenin *State and Revolntion*, *Selected Works*, pp. 279 80.
4. Lenin, "Where to Begin" ?, *Selected Works* p. 43.
5. Gramsci, quoted in Glucksmann, *Gramsci's and The State*, p. 125.

Gramsci starts from where Lenin has left. In fact, Gramsci's initiation in political thought via the philosophy of Croce led him to perceive the errors of positivist and mechanistic Marxism. Moreover, the Italian tradition and the Italian state apparatus from the times of Risorgimento to Fascism was also quite different from other European systems and from Russia. Naturally its (Italian State) analysis would also be different. However, the cardinal point of Gramsci's writings was his historical perspective and capacity to understand the dialectical relationship between theory and practice.

As a political activist, Gramsci had perceived that the "Italian state has never been democratic, but rather despotic and a police state (one sole power, the government, with the parliament as a consultative body); it has always been a dictatorship exercised by the industrialists against the working class and the peasant masses."[1] Even this industrial strata was incapable of effecting the dictatorship on its own, and recruited and absorbed rural petty-bourgeoisie and intellectuals with the help of the state apparatus. This was evident by the domination of these supporting groups in bureaucracy, judiciary and other forumis; they directly or indirectly thrived on such government patronage as press, media, etc. This central theme is disseminated in "Notes on Southern Question" in order to perceive the foundations of state.

Gramsci starts his study of state by undertaking a histarical analysis of the Italian state since its very inception as a unified nation. He had a firm conviction that the "historical unity of the ruling classes is realised in the State, and their history is essentially the history of States..."[2] Thus, Gramsci's problematic not only deals with the formation of Italian state but also studies the role of various forces in the making a new state.

Gramsci's perception was that the city states of Italy remained autonomous primarily because the bourgeoisie failed there to unite aationally. Despite Machiavelli's appeal to

---

1. Gramsci, *Ordine Nuovo*, Einaudi' Turin, p. 71.
2. Gramsci, *Selections from Prison Notebooks*, p. 52.

make 'Italy what France was' Italy had remained fragmented till as late as the last quarter of the nineteenth century. At that time even its unification and the formation of Risorgimento was achieved under two different ideologies. Garibaldi conquered Sicily and Naples, and the rest of Italy was mobilized by Cavour and Mazzini.[1] Mazzini attempted revolutionary movements with the French help in the regions of Po, Moderna and Parma, and not by mobilizing Italian peasantry. This failure of perception in Mazzini made Cavour the sole voice of nationalists who were in favour of bestowing constitutional sovereignty to the parliament. The Garibaldi brigade, on the other hand, supported monarchy. In the end, no force could become decisive, and both royalists and nationalists joined under the banner of constitutional monarchy. Since both these groups had failed to mobilize the rural masses, the Italian unification remained only 'mechanical'. Even after the formation of Risorgimento, no outstanding personality or group emerged and mediocrity prevailed. The hiatus between rural and urban areas areated further rifts between the prosperous North and the impoverished South. The intellectuals of bourgeois under Cavour tried to absorb active elements of allied classes as well as of antagonistic classes but failed to hold a decisive away. As a result, the other classes were also deprived of leadership. Since the absorption was not on the basis of any specific ideological content, nationalist parties were formed in order to ensure mere existence of the government.

Gramsci also perceived that the Italian unification was more a result of international ramifications rather than of rnational urges. Bourgeois groups in Italy were not economically strong; and even the analysis of Risorgimento literature

---

2. Mazzini (1805-72 founded an organization Young Italy for establishment of a free nation and under his leadership a republic was founded in Rome in 1848 driving cut the pope. Garibaldi (1807-82) had helped him but the Republic fell with the fall of forces of Garibaldi against French forces. This ronvinced Cavour (1810-61) that foreign help is necessary to drive out Austrians and unite Italy. The North under victor Emmanuel II was united with the able guidance of Cavour and South under forces of Garibaldi.

reveals is as a sign of "inconsistancy and gelantinousness" of the movement itself. Most of the interpretations of Risorgimento, Gramsci felt, were "immediate and ideological" rather than "historical".[1] For example, for Croce Risorgimento was a "mere parenthesis' in the history of liberal Italy."[2]

The analysis of Italian state in the past revealed to Gramsci that the "conception of the State according to the productive function of the social classes cannot be applied mechanically to the interpretation of Italian and European history." He felt that although for the "fundamental productive classes", state is "only conceivable as the concrete form of a specific economic world", yet there is no causal reductionist relationship between the state and the system of production. Gramsci insisted that when developed states (advance countries) provide impetus to progress and "transmit their ideological currents" which are "born on the basis of the productive development", then the "group which is the bearer of new ideas is not the economic group but the intellectual stratum."[3] It follows then, that the state is not only an instrument of exploitation but it is "*the entire complex of practical and theoritical activities with which the ruling class not only justifies and maintains its dominance, but manages to win the active consent of those* over whom it rules."[4]

Incorporating the Hegelian notion of civil socity Gramsci formulates the equation thus : "State = political society + civil society, in other words hegemony protected by the armour of coercion."[5] This makes abundanlly clear the orientations of any enquiry into Gramsci's concept of state. The two elements

---

1. Gramsci, quoted in Cammett, "Two Recent Polemics on the character of the Risorgimento", *Science and Society*, No. XXVII, 1962, p. 443.
2. *Ibid.*
3. All quotes from Gramsci, *Selections from Prison Notebooks*, pp. 116-17.
4. *Ibid.*, p. 244. (Emphasis added.)
5. *Ibid.*, p. 263.

of the state can be understood by the extent of participation of intellectuals in various processes. Let Gramsci speak : "What we can do, for the moment, is to fix two major superstructural 'levels' : the one that can be called 'civil society', that is, the ensemble of organisms commonly called 'private' and that of 'political society' or the 'State'. These two levels correspond on the one hand to the function of 'hegemony' which the dominant group exercises throughout society and, on the other hand, to that of 'direct domination' or command exercised through the State and 'juridicial' government".[1] The function characterising political sociey demonstrates that it is to be used to restore the balance of forces in such a way as to make continuance of state unhindered. The state being constituted of two levels of political and civil society, Gramsci makes a comparative analysis of the ancient (and even the medieval states) and the modern states on this point and says : "The State was, in a certain sense, a mechanical bloc of sociai groups, often of different race : within the circle of political-military compression, which was only exercised harshly at certian moments the subaltern groups had a life of their own."[2] The modern state, on the other hand, "substitutes for the mechanical bloc of social groups their subordination to the active hegemony of the directive and dominant group".[3] It follows that the functions of political society are essentially coercive; it exercises domination over antagonistic classes in an attempt to annihilate these classes. However, at the same time, the ruling class tries to win over allied classes to their own way of thinking; and, this function is performed in the terrain of the civil society.

The Hegelians attributed merely economic functions to civil society and tried to keep it outside the purview of state activities. This was manifested in various doctrines of state that gave only the function of law and order to state and thereby sought to explain social and ideological relations as

---

1. *Ibid.*, p. 12.
2. *Ibid.*, f.n. p. 54.
3. *Ibid.*

independent of it. We shall take up these types of state later, now to civil society.

Gramsci conceives 'civil society' as the private apparatus of hegemony which is an element of State, therefore in order to carry the examination of the Gramscian State any further, it isimperative to have a clear perception of the concept of hegemony, the chief characteristic of the modern integral state.

A conceptual vagueness exists regarding 'hegemony' in so far as it has been used as a catchward to distinguish Gramsci's thinking from other Marxist without clearly understanding its nauances. Different interpretations has been put forth to explain his philosophy of hegemony, and this renders the concept vague. However, there is not much disareement in the brord definition/meaning of the term. For Femia, the supermacy of a social group or class manifests itself in two different ways—domination or coercion and iatellectual and moral leadership. The latter is hegemony". To be specific the social control takes two forms—"external influence punishment etc. and internally moulding personal convictions into a replica of prevailing norms or hegemony".[1] For Roger Simons : "Hegemony is a relation, not of political and ideological leadership. It is the organisation of consent".[2] For Bates, it means political leadership based on the consent of the led, a consent which is secured by the "diffusion and popularization of the worldveiw of the ruling classes".[3]

In the traditional sense the term 'hegemony' implied domination of a nation. Later on it was used denoting domination of any sort. In Marxist literature, Russian revolutionaires used it during the social Democratic movement. Gramsci credited Bolsheviks to be the "first movement in the

---

1. Femia, *Gramsci's Political Thought—Hegemony, Consciousness and Revolutionary Process*, Clarendon Press, Oxford, 1981, p. 23.
2. Simon, *Gramsci's Political Thought*, Lawrence and Wishart, London 1982, p. 21.
3. Bates, "Gramsci and the theory of Hegemony," *Journal of History of Ideas*, XXXVI, p. 352.

international history of class struggle to have posed in practice the chief problems of the revolution that Marx presented in theory.[1] Plekeanov[2] did not use 'gegemonia' and stuck to 'domination' for political power as such.

Axelrod,[3] used it first. Lenin used the term in 'What is to be done'? in 1902. In fact, both Mensheviks and Bolsheviks used it in their dispute over the question of spontaneity. Lenin further developed the idea of hegemony in Two Tactics; it was further developed by his experience of bourgeois revolution of 1905.,[4] Lenin was clear in mind that Russian bourgeosi was incapable politically to lead a bourgeois-democratic revolution to completion. The economists descounted it on the plea that spontaniety is more important than the vanguard leadership. Lenin believed "that proletariat needs to grab all chances to strike a blow at enemy and tries to provide ideological leadership so that theory can be put into practice."[5] It may be claimed that for Lenin, hegemony meant a class leadership, specifically leadership of the proletariat organized under a vanguard party and an alliance with allied classes having long term common interests. The hegemony is won in the course a long struggle which is both ideological and political. Simply stated it reveals three aspects—first, it is the leadership of a class, second, it is the leadership of a class in order to come out as an independent political power; and third, to maintain an independent political power it requires a vanguard party. The class leadership postulate alliances. Lenin was emphatic when he says : "To preach to workers that what they need is not hegemony, but a 'class party' means to betray the cause of

---

1. Gramsci, quoted in Glucksmann, *Gramsci and The State*, p. 177.
2. Plekhanov (1857-1918), one of the founders of Russian Social Democratic Movement, dealt with many theoritical problems of Socialism.
3. Axelrod (1849 1928) was an important member of Social Democratic Party in Russia.
4. Russian Revolution of 1905, also called bourgeois democratic revolution, was the first stage towards Socialist revolution and was led by the proletariat.
5. Lenin, *Collected Works*, vol. 8, p. 80.

proletariat to the liberals".[1] This view makes hegemony as equal to dictatorship of the proletariat. It is significant to note that no place is given to cultural element in his schema. Lenin, in fact, rearranged his schema after the R(volution. He stressed that hegemony provides ideological and political leadership of proletariat over whole of society. But since the class in power is not capable of exercising power, the vanguard performs it. Both hegemony and dictatorship stand in dialectical relation. Hegemony in a socialist state is a function of the whole class and is distinct from the state. For Lenin, Gramsci perceived, hegemony is linked to leadership of the proletariat and qualifies its expansive character. Commenting on Lenin's contribution, Gramsci asserted : "The idea of the hegemony of the proletariat, because it was conceived historically and concretely, involved the requirement of seeking an ally for the working class in the poor peasants".[2] Gramsci credited Lenin for having "advanced philosophy as philosophy in so far as he had advanced political doctrine and practice. The realisation of a hegemonic apparatus, in so far as it creates a new ideological terrain. determines a reform of consciousness and of methods of knowledge : it is a fact of knowledge, a philosophical fact. In Crocean terms : "when one succeeds in introducing a new morality in conformity with a new conception of the world, one finishes by introducing the conception as well; in other words, one determines a reform of the whole of philosophy."[3]

Coming to the Gramscian usage of the term hegemony, it is interesting to note that in the early stages of his career, Gramsci used the term in the traditional sense of a system of domination. But, his political practices reveal an intution of hegemony. The efforts of *L'Ordine Nuovo* at educating the workers for the creation of a new state, to train workers in the techniques of government through factory councils, etc.,

---

1. Lenin, quoted in Anderson, "Antinomies of Antonio Gramsci", *New Left Review*, 100, p. 16.
2. Gramsci, quoted in Glucksmann, *Gramsci and The State*, p. 177.
3. Gramsci, *Selections from Prison Notebooks*, pp. 365-66.

in fact highlight his perception of the role of consciousness in the process of revolution. When he says "The workers state, in Lenin's vigorous definition, is a bourgeois state without bourgeoisie",[1] he acknowledges the continution of state after revolution as some of the contradictions are not yet overcome. The dictatorship of proletariat is required to train workers in the art of governing. For this the state apparatus with its coercive characteristics is required. Even at this early stage, Gramsci perceived the dialectics between economics and politics. But, by then he had not made it a precondition for hegemonistic state. Then, the prime requirement for Gramsci was to guide spontaneity and a consciousness of the obligations of class striving towards state control. The Gramscian formulations on hegemony, thus, can be traced back in embryonic form to his early political practices and formulations.

The Factory Council movement had brought forth the various problems—the problem of the method for combating the existing state; the issue of revolution; and the problem of establishment of socialist state. Thus, Gramsci's chief concern, at that time, was "to destroy the spirit of class collaboration and reformism and formulate exactly and precisely what it is, we mean by the state";[2] and he used the term 'hegemony' in the sense of domination. But, he also fore-saw the need for a new state "as a national consensus around the initiatives and actions of, the working power",[3] and thus reveals Gramsci understanding of the relationship between class and state and the theme of consensus as the basic of state. Also evident at this stage is Gramsci's stress of involve peasants in the revolutionary process.

In the "Southern Question" Gramsci has mentioned 'hegemony' as the alternative strategy for the proletariat. Thus, like Lenin, till 1926 his concept suggeted hegemony as a class leadership which workers ought to evolve as an independent

---

1. Gramsci, quoted in Glucksmann, *Gramsci and The State*, p. 154.
2. Gramsci quoted in *Ibid.*, p. 125.
3. *Ibid.*

political entity. The workers could achieve this level after having a consciousness of their class interests. They could also win over subordinate classes (such as peasantry) and broaden their mass base. The struggle for hegemony was conceived to be both political and ideological. "Hegemony' then for Gramsci, as for Lenin, was a method of providing leadership over allied classes, and was a function of the class in power. It was a function of the whole class, but till the time the class was unable to attain this level, it was to be exercised by the vanguard in the phase of dictatorship, it entailed domination over bourgeois and allied classes.

In the prison writings, however, the concept underwent a change and was amply elaborated. Now, Gramsci regards 'hegemony' as moral and intellectuals leadership of a group in its manifestation of supermacy. The other manifestation of supremacy in its coercive form is domination. Gramsci takes pains to explain this dual aspect of supremacy with the help of the Greek myth of Centaur—half animal (representing coercion) and half-human (representing hegemony) creative. The basic dictum of Marx that "the ruling ideas of each epoch have ever been the ideas of its ruling classes,"[1] suggested to Gramsci his concept of hegemony. He pinpointed that the "foundation of a ruling class is equivalent to the creation of a *weltanschauung*."[2] *Weltanschauung*, in fact, is the core of hegemony; it suggests that the way a class can and ought to become hegemonic in order to win over the state. This problematic also involves an analysis of the bourgeois hegemony (the basis of their state power) that has to be countered, so that the class aspiring for hegemony develops its own organization.

As has been referred earlier,[3] there are three phases in the development of a class—economic, corporate, and hegemonic (or political phase), aspirations and aims of these stages too are different—of trade unions, of seeking limited

---

1. Marx, and Engels, *The German Ideology*, Progress Publishers, Moscow, 1976, p. 67.
2. Gramsci, *Il Materialismo storico e la Filosofia di B. Croce*, p. 75.
3. See Chapter V.

benefits of political nature for the class like interest groups, and in the third stage—the ruling class is challenged by the class aspiring for hegemony through the agency of political party and programmes. Thus, hegemony is the leadership and domination of a group over its allies; it postulates absorption of intellectuals of other classes and secures consent for the system. It is, thus, much more than ideology. Hegemony is not and cannot be a consensus, over the whole of society, it is consensus over allied classes. Walter aptly comments : "In many an important sense, Gramsci had not one but two concepts of hegemony, a point which eluded nearly all of his interpreters". Moreover, he continues, "Gramsci will sometimes define a pair of concept with respect to one another, then offer a historical generalization about their usage, and then, finally incorporate that generalization into the definitions. Finally, sets of Gramscian conceptual double stars sometimes from a 'constellation'. Consent (as opposed to force) hegemony (as opposed to domination)".[1]

The above discussion makes it clear that Gramsci has used hegemony in two senses in its first sense it denotes a tactic of the proletariat, and in its other sense it is a part of the state. This concept also makes it clear that the 'state' is not an institution of pure force or coercion. The study of state with its two elements of hegemony and coercion highlights the relevance of relations of forces and the role of auxilliary classes in the class-struggle. The concept also makes amply clear the organic relationship between the civil society and the political society. Gramsci emphasises that the division between these two elements is never definitive and these are inter penetrated in the state. The integral state, for him, is "the entire complex of political and theoretical activity by which the ruling classes not only justify and maintain their domination but also succeed in obtaining the active consent of the governed."[2] The chief task of hegemony, according to this

1. Walter Adamson, *Hegemony and Revolution—A Study of Gramsci's Political and Cultural Theory*, Berkeley, Press, California, 1986, p. 10.
2. Gramsci quoted in Femia, *Gramsci' Political Thought*, p. 28.

definition, is to secure consent for the ruling group. The group aspiring to be ruling, the proletariat in Gramsci's case, has to create a crisis in bourgeois for attaining success. To do this, it must analyse the broad base of state in other words the historic bloc.

The relations of force effect the characteristics of a state. Every state, Gramsci affirms, must undergo an economic corporate stage. The struggle for political hegemony, thus, is aimed at establishing a new economic order. At the level of attaining cultural hegemony, the starting point is negative—that of criticising past philosophies, but, the second stage is positive, that of creating a new superstructure.

The economists, without understanding these moments, explain all changes according to the base alone. There has been an ideological debate over the issue of materialism vs. idealism. The materialists stress the primacy of economics over philosophy. They rxplain the process of evolution in a positivist manner where history develops according to scientific predictable laws. These schools not only fail to comprehend the relations of force but also are unable to perceive the role of superstructures in social changes. Lenin had clearly established the primacy of politics over philosophy and economics and had also established a relationship—dialectical and historic—between the economic infrastructure and its superstructure. Gramsci explains that in the political phase of relations of force, there occurs "the decisive passage from the structure to the sphere of the complex superstructure; it is the phase in which previously germinated ideologies become 'party', come into confronation and conflict, until only one of them, or at least a single combination of them, tends to prevail, to gain the upperhand, to propagate itself throughout society".[1] This is because of the "formation of the historic bloc".[2]

The historic bloc is formed with a leading class striving towards domination over antagonistic classes and hegemony

---

1. Gramsci, *Selections from Prison Notebooks*, p. 18.
2. See also Chapter IV.

over allied classes. This bloc is vital for state power being a unity of base and superstructure and intellectuals play a vital role in its constitution. As the modern state is an organic bloc of social forces where leading group exercises hegemony, it can be claimed that the leading classes are unified in a state. The Gramscian notion: "Structure and superstructure form a historic bloc",[1] has wide ramifications for hegemony.

The historic bloc not only postulates a homogeneity between base and superstructure, it is also "an organic adhesion between intellectuals and the people".[2] It reveals that at the level of superstructure, two blocs are constantly striving—one to maintain the status-quo, and the other to form an alternative historic bloc of antagonistic classes (as the historic bloc is formed of allied groups only). The concept of historic bloc exposes mechanist Marxists as well as those thinkers who present a hiatus between the intellectuals and the masses. The historic bloc can only be created through the exercise of hegemony, it can never be externally or mechanically imposed. A study of various forms of state reveals that the formation of historic bloc explains various relationship of intellectuals, masses, state apparatus, etc. It also highlights the fact that politics has primacy over economics in the struggle for state.

The hegemony of a class is exercised over allied groups only and leaves ample scope for antagonistic classes to organize in an autonomous political force. The hegemonic class must have control over various apparatuses of hegemony or to have full control over superstructure. The active consent of masses is the hallmark of hegemony in the progressive historical stage and in this phase the ruling class has universalist aims. When its aim begins to serve only its specific class interests, the regressive phase alternately initiates a crisis of hegemony. This is because hegemony, too, in the last instance, is determined by class struggle and relations of production. In the absence of an active consent and when

---

1. Gramsci, *Selections from Prison Notebooks*, p. 366.
2. Gramsci, Notebook, 4, 33 *Ouaderni del Carcere*.

only the leadership of allied as well as antagonistic classes is absorbed, the revolution remains passive. If hegemonic apparatuses are ignored, it (the hegemony) is reduced to mere ideological domination. The economic condtions, need for change in production relations, are necessary for hegemony. The state institutions, other apparatuses all embody these requirements. Besides hegemony is political, cultural as well as educational relationship in the terrain of civil sciety. There are various forms of state that try to present a break between these two moments of state, that is, political society and civil society, in order to perpetrate their hegemony in civil society, at the same time, maintaining the facade of an 'above class' state.

First, a look at the liberal concept of state. Liberals regard state as a custodian of law and order, leaving the domain of civil society to the free initiative of individual men. This ideology distregards the fact that state power is class 'power. Gramsci, however, realized that the liberal ideas were quite revolutionary for their times and have accentuated the class struggle. Liberalism discusses only the coercive moment of the state power. The Free Trade policies of liberals denoted the requirement of nascent bourgeoisie and assigned economic activity to civil society, ostensibly outside the purview of state control. The initiative for change, therefore, is left with civil society in liberal philosophy. A parliamentary democracy is the manifestation of the form most suited to the liberals. The liberals identify state and government, "an identification', which according to Gramsci, is precisely a "representation of the economic corporate form, in other words of the confusion between civil society and political society."[1]

Naturally in a liberal state, the ruling class does not wish to change the system that suits its programme and that has helped it to become the ruling. However, the moral aspect of liberalism appealed to Gramsci; he says : "liberalism

---

1. Gramsci, *Selections from Prison Notebooks*, p. 262.

at the level of morality is an ideal and historical presupposition for socialism".[1] He felt that the liberal ideas contained, the seeds of ethical state. In his own words : "As a border-line idea, the liberal programme creates the ethical state, i.e. a state which, in the sphere of ideas, holds itself above class competition."[2]

It is clear, then, that a liberal state acts as a unifying power; it unifies bourgeoisie. Lenin had also dimly perceived this, as he says : "Liberals are prepared to recognise the class struggle in the sphere of politics, too, but on one condition—that the organization of state power should not enter into that sphere".[3] Thus the liberals, ignored dialectical unity of economics and politics. This cleverly concealed the hold of liberals over the civil society. It also reveals that bourgeoisie are not unified outside the state and are chiefly concerned with economic function of state. They use state to solve the class struggle under the garb of a judicial settlement. After this initial unification under state, bourgeoisie gradually strengthen their class base in civil society. The hallmark of liberal ideology is separation between economics and politics.

The syndicalists too are characterized by this division between economics and politics. It confined itself to the management of trade and adopted anti-state stance, and this strengthened the capitalist civilization. Syndicalism according to Gramsci, is an expression of a subaltern group that is unable to establish its hegemony, and thus it altogether abondons the plans of achieving domination. Gramsci felt that syndicalism propounded on Utopian idea of "leaping from class society directly into a society of perfect equality with a syndicalist economy."[4] Such an 'economism' believes hegemony to be merely ethico-political and not emanating from economic necessity. In fact the two manifestations of

---

1. Gramsci, *Scritti Giovanni*, p. 225.
2. Quoted in Glucksmann, *Gramsci and The State*, p. 128
3. Lenin; *Collected Works*, vol 9, p. 122.
4. Gramsci. *Selections from Prison Notebooks*, p. 161.

economism—liberalism and syndicalism—ignored the organic requirement of hegemony. Gramsci, therefore, exhorts: "Undoubtedly, the fact of hegemony presupposes account be taken of the interests and the tendencies of the groups over which hegemony is to be exercised, and that a certain compromise equilibrium should be formed—in other words, that the leading group should make sacrifices of an economic-corporate kind. But there is no doubt that such sacrifices and such a compromise cannot touch the essential; for though hegemony is ethical-political, it must also be economic, as in economics the leading class has decisive function."[1]

Scanning the Italian history, Gramsci found that the Italian state was not based on an equilibrium, because the Italian bourgoisie could not effect a revolution in the hegemonic apparatuses. The Italian bourgeoisie came to the forefront when the bourgeoisie revolution had already been accomplished in the rest of Europe and it could achieve unification of the nation on the strength of external factors. Thus, it remained economically weak on account of the lack of proper national mobilization. The unifying factor for Italian bourgeois was not its hegemony as it could not exercise leadership. This was done by the state. The bureaucracy also sought to unify different forces in the nation and acted as a link between the state and the civil society. The dominance of bureaucracy brought the petty-bourgeois element—the main forces comprising bureaucracy—into prominence and made it the only 'territorially' national class. Thus, the unification of Italy was a passive revolution in the absence of an active consent for the bourgeois system. Behind the democratic-liberal form of state, it was essentially a despotic state. At the time of any crisis, the despotic character came out in bold relief.

A crisis may occur in the relations of forces. The Crises are of two types—conjunctural and organic. Conjunectural crisis seems accidental and transient. It also depends on organic movement to be sure" but it is different from it in as much as it does not "have any very far-reaching historical

---

1. *Ibid.*

significance"[1] and may be confied to mere governmental issues. Gramsci explains : "At a certain point in their historical lives, social classes become detached from their traditional parties. In other words, the traditional parties in that particular organizational form, with the particular men who constitute, represent and lead them, are no longer recognised by their class (or fraction of a class) as its expression. When such crisis occur, the immediate situation becomes delicate and dangerous, because the field is open for violent solutions, for the activities of unknown forces, represented by charismatic 'men of destiny.[2] The economic crisis is first manifest as a crisis of leadership; it is a crisis between "represented and representatives". As such it is actually "the crisis of the ruling class's hegemony, which occurs either because the ruling class has failed in some major political undertaking for which it has requested, or forcibly extracted the consent of broad mases", or because "huge masses have passed suddenly from a state of political passivity to certain activity."[3] In other words, it is a crisis of base manifest in superstructure or the crisis of historic bloc. When the consent is withdrawn, an organic crisis occurs. If an organic solution, the coming to power of an alternate historic bloc (in this case of proletariat) is not possible, the field is open for various options—of despotic rule, of charismatic rule or solution of 'transformismo'.[4]

It is interesting to note how organic crises are sought to be resolved. The proletariat has to understand the mechanisms whereby ruling classes try to diffuse the crisis of the base. One example is shift in favour of political society in Italy in 1920s at the time of economic crisis after the War. Gramsci, clearly perceiving the nature of crisis said : "The present phase of the

---

1. *Ibid* , p. 177.
2. *Ibid.*, p. 210.
3. *Ibid.*
4. 'Transformismo' is specific Italian characteristic whereby left and right forces born of Risorgimento tended to converge on the basis of programmes, ultimately leading to more or less diffusion of their views.

class struggle in Italy is the phase that precedes either the conquest of political power on the part the revolutionary proletariat...or a tremendous reaction on the part of the propertied classes and governing caste."[1] Needless to suggest that in such crisis, both structure and superstructure play an important role to mould new forces. If the civil society is strong, it can resist the crisis of base to a large extent. It is against this perspective that Gramsci analysed the phenomenon of fascism in Italy.

The organic crisis of Italian society manifested in the crisis of leadership, or the crisis 'at the top; because even prior to the crisis the Italian bourgeoisie was not very strong. The masses that erupted in a movement revealed the movement of forces at the base. They lacked proper leadership to form an alternative historic bloc with allied (peasantry) forces These masses were, as Gramsci perceived them, "still weakly organised, and abondoned by their own political leadership." They intervene in a chaotic and disordered movement, without leadership and without a "precise and collective political will."[2] In such a situation, the petty bourgeois—the middle strata who had enjoyed the function of command and responsibility during the War—intervened actively. These forces were not necessarily counter-revolutionary. As they had no hopes from the proletariat, the interests of both dominant classes and middle bourgois coincided, and they immediately joined to prevent the proletariat to organise itself. The equiliburium of historic bloc, even after the jolt, did not shift in favour of the antagonistic forces. The crisis was solved by a recourse to an extreme from of political society. The means adopted were extreme repression of workers, and strengthening of state apparatus and of organizing of economic resistance; the fascists had taken control of the state and society both. In order to strengthen its (state's) new power base of bureaucracy, petty-bourgeois received impetus from international forces of imperialism. The fascist state

---

1. Gramsci, *Selections from Political Writings* 1910-1920, p. 191.
2. Gramsci, Notebook 7, *Quaderni del Carcere.*

was based on coerion and there was a total absence of consent. It was a sort passive revolution.

Initially in *Prison Notes*, Gramsci had used 'passive revolution' to explain the process of revolution without any revolutionary activity; it was conceived to be a situation where the active hegemony is missing in the new balance of forces. Such a crisis-situation leads to solution in the form of the emergence of a charismatic leader, who may try to restore the historic bloc to an equilibrium in which the antagonistic forces are almost equally poised. This form of 'Caesarism' or 'Bonapartism' has two facets—regressive and progressive. Fascism is an example of regressive Caesarism. The phenomenon of fascism is the product of the clash between economic forces. It is a manifestation in an advanced capitalist country where proletariat forces are strong enough to disrupt the balance, but are not organised to form a historic bloc. The failure of hegemony, thus, results in the emergence of military, Caesarist solutions.

The question now arises in what ways can antagonistic forces strive towards hegemony ? To be more specific, what tactics should the proletariat adopt to bring about a socialist state ?

As has already been said, hegemony for Gramsci, prior to his arrest, suggested a strategy for dictatorship of the proletariat. In this sense the essential requirements of the proletariat is a vanguard party and an alliance with the subordinate classes. Such an alliance has to be based on long-term organic interests, even though the interests are used as the immediate basis of the alliance. This postulates a political as well as an ideological struggle. As the party acts in the capacity of the collective consciousness of the masses, and masses themselves have not yet attained a clear perception of their class interest, the hegemonic function can be exercised only under the dictatorship of the proletariat which is expansive unlike the repressive dictatorship of the capitalists. The party seeks to realise full hegemony through various proletarian organs, chiefly the Soviets. The dialectical relationship between the party and the masses ensures that the class is organically linked to the leadership. A significant feature of

this hegemony is the necessity to "wield political hegemony before even coming to government."[1] Gramsci later developed this concept in the fascist prison.

There are two ways of achieving hegemony and the conquest of power—by a direct frontal attack, or by a prolonged struggle in civil society. The former is termed in military parlance as 'war of manoevre' and the latter is 'war of position'. Taking the example of Russia, Gramsci found that in Russia, coercive element of state dominated and civil society was weak. In such a situation the proletariat demolished the existing rulers by direct, frontal assault; even without having established its political hegemony over subaltern class. This function was sought to be performed in the stage of dictatorship of proletariat.

The Comintern guidelines[2] at its Fourth Congress to adopt United Front tactics were theoretically explaind by Gramsci thus : "It seems to me that Ilitch understood that a change was necessary from the war of manoeuvre applied victoriously in the East in 1917, to a war of position which was the only form possible in the West—where...the social structures were of themselves still capable of becoming heavily armed fortification. This is what the formula of the 'United Front' seems to me to mean."[3] The function of hegemony in Russia was to be achieved after the revolution. But, in the West the bourgeois had a strong hegemonic apparatus and even after a frontal assault on state, the workers would have failed in the absence of their hegemony. As such the strategy had to be different in the West in view of struggle. This long-drawn struggle to establish the proletariat hegemony is termed by Gramsci as the war of position, it is a struggle for hegemony prior to the conquest.

The hegemonic class always has an universalist aim. The concept of establishing hegemony means struggle at all the levels—cultural, political, educational, etc. Gramsci

---

1. Gramsci quoted in Glucksmann, *Gramsci and The State*, p. 184.
2. See chapter I.
3. Gramsci, *Selections from Prison Notebooks*, pp. 237-8.

clarifies : "In politics, war of position is the concept of hegemony."[1] In developed countries, as civil society is so strong that it appears independent of state, a long drawn struggle is required. Elaborating further, Gramsci says : "The massive structures of the modern democracies both as State organizations, and as complexes of association in civil society, constitute for the art of politics as it were the 'trenches' and the permanent fortification of the front in the war of position."[2] It entails winning over the intellectuals of other classes, establishing its own hegemonic apparatus and win the consent of the allied classes. It is a long process and in the Western countries, when the ruling hegemony was disturbed by successive crises of structure, the need was to accelerate this struggle for hegemony in order to form alternate historic bloc. But some theorists could not perceive the differences and advocated war of movement at such times.

Rosa Luxemburg[3] was the chief proponent of war of movement. She believed that social contradictions, would among other things, also aggravate the class-relations and masses would spontaneously rise in insurrection against the exploitative state. She discounted the decisive role of organization and party in the process of revolution. For Rosa, then, the economic crises force revolutionary fervour among masses and induce spontaneous attempts of change. The bourgeois structure is cracked by economic crises and masses break through the structure via this breach. Rosa's theory postulated a direct relationship between politics and economics, and ignored the role of superstructures and prolonged political struggles. Gramsci conceded that the revolutionary uprisings in Europe after the First World War were no doubt manifestations of war of movement; but since the time was not ripe, they failed. The masses, he contended, can succeed in capturing state power but are unable to maintain their control in the face of the armour of civil society

---

1. Gramsci, Notebook. 8, 52, *Quaderni del Carcere*.
2 Gramsci, *Selections from Prison Notebooks*, p. 243.
3. See also Chapter II.

which is still in the hands of the bourgeoisie. In Soviet Union, as the institutions and apparatus of civil society were practically absent, the bourgeois revolution itself was not complete and the coercive aspect of political society was dominant. With a blow on this political society, Bolsheviks could capture the state. As they lacked personnel to establish their own hegemony, they established a dictatorship of proletariat to consolidate the gains of revolution against threats from bourgeoisie trying to entrench within the new system. Thus, the struggle for hegemony arose in Soviet Union after the revolution. But it was inappropriate to accept this pattern for developed countries where civil society is very strong. Rosa Luxemburg, Trotsky, et. al. made this fatal mistake of not grasping the need to direct the spontaneity of masses. The theory of 'permanent revolution' of Trotsky is a political aspect of war of movement. It can be acceptable only in some specific situations. Gramsci believes that if the "structures of national life are embryonic and loose and incapable of becoming 'trench' or fortress" only then can Trotsky's formulations succeed. The belief of Trotsky that world revolutions would succeed in this way, shows to Gramsci that Trotsky was "superficially national" as well as European whereas Lenin was both "profoundly national" and international on account of his understanding of specific national as well as international forces.

Gramsci perceived the need in the West to wage struggle for hegemony. This also helped Gramsci to carry out a critique of economist tendencies in Marxism, and to emphasise that Marxism is 'philosophy of praxis'. This in turm provided a philosophical dimension to the concept of hegemony. The Gramscian view was that by becoming the worldview of masses and by combating the great ideologies of the time, Marxism carried a struggle for hegemony. The economists like Bukharin reduce all struggle to the level of economic struggle and postulate a causal relationship between the base and the superstructure. They also ignore the Leninist formulation of primacy of politics over economics.

At this point an analysis of Americanism[1] and Fordism is in keeping in order to illustrate the role of production and its influence over culture. The study of these two phenomena has revealed the origin of hegemony in factories through the organic intellectuals. The attempt by Taylor to exploit the praductive forces to establish a hegemonic system conducive to capitalists was severely denounced by the Marxists, prominent among them Lenin, who realized that such a sys em would ultimately lead to take over of production processes by workers. Gramsci, pursuing the same line, denounced efforts to seek similarities between secialism and fascism. He also criticised Trotsky for advocating a military-coercive regime of work in order to bring about socialism. The hegemony of proletariat cannot be based on a work model in factories. It requires stress over cultural struggles as well. "It was through a critique of capitalist civilization that the unified consciousness of the proletariat was or is still being formed and a critique implies culture:"[2] The need is to propound an autonomous vision of the world and a mass philosophy. The attempts of Fordism to inculcate in workers a code of ethics, a model of living, is a distinguishing symptom of differences between development in Europe and America. In the latter 'base dominated the superstructure more directly, than in the former where superstructures are complex. The Fordist model attempts to create a consent by higher wage structure and ideology, as well as exercises force by destroying trade unions. 'Taylorism' tries to reduce worker to a machine with all responsibility residing in managers. This is the most recent method of monopoly capitalism to perpetuate its hegemony and to instil values that help to consolidate the system of work in the country. This is also an illustration of private

---

1. The impact of America on the rest of the world after First World War, led to a study of peculiar American characteristics—social as well as of production. Fordism is "an ultra-modern form of production and of working methods" offered by Ford's industry in America. See *Ibid* , pp. 279-81.
2. *Ibid* , p. 275.

initiative to advance the state ideology. This suggests that hegemony and hegemonic class apparatus are not simply determined by the superstructure. The relation between culture and production show that practical ideologies and behavioural pattern have their origin in the economic base. The degree of dominance between the two can be understood by studying the relation between economic and political moment. When the political phase develops characterizing the economic—corporate phase and attains the unity of class within the framework of the existing state, the struggle shifts from the structure to the terrain of superstructure for the attainment of hegemony or the state. The phenomenon of Americanism attempts to minimise the influence of ideological and professional political functionaries in order to secure consent through factories.

The resistance movement of Gandhi in far off India also caught Gramsci's attention. Dwelling on the 'passive' resistance of Gandhi, Gramsci explained that "this type of struggle is suitable for a country that is technically disarmed and militarily inferior, being dominated by technically developed and superior countries." As the protesting group is unable to match its antagonist, "the conciousness of material importance on the part of a great mass confronts a minority of oppressors."[1] However the Indian movement was not only one form of resistance. Gramsci perceived in it, "three forms of war : war of movement, war of position, and undergrouud warfare. Gandhi's passive resistance is a war of position, which at certain moments becomes a war of mevement, and at others underground warefare. Boycotts are a form of war of position, strikes of war of movent, the secret preparation of weapons and combat troops belongs to underground warfare."[2] The enemy forces also try to exhaust resistance and precipitate confrontation at appropriat times. He found the strength of British in India "in their ability to manoeuvre through control of the internal lines of communication,

---

1. Gramsci quoted in Glucksmann, *Gramsci and The State*, p. 252.
2. Gramsci, *Selections from Prison Notebooks*, pp. 229-30.

and to concentrate their forces at the 'sporadically' most dangerous spot."[1] Since the passive revolution of Gandhi also had religious overtones, there were various facets of the passive revolution—economic, political and religious.

The above analysis of various models and techniques of state control suggests that Gramsci's concept of state goes much beyond the concept of state as an exploitative tool. It is the site of class compromise, manifestation of the 'integral state.'

The road to the 'integral state' leads first to the reversal in the nature of hegemony and then to the construction of the regulated society. But "As long as the class State exists the regulated society cannot exist."[2] Therefore, the function of the state according to Gramsci, is "to raise the great mass of the population to a particular cultural and moral level, a level which corresponds to the needs of the productive forces for development."[3] Marxism or the philosophy of praxis poses itself as a process of contradictions and tries to resolve it. If that is so, Marxism is to be superceded as a worldview with the historical disappearance of the class struggle. Thus, withering away of state and of philosophy are two aspects of the same reality. The creation of Marxist state is the establishment of its worldview; and its supercession is the end of the philosophy of praxis.[4]

One of the important topics of Gramsci's prison writings thus centres upon the state—the origin, nature and destiny of the modern state. There is a departure from traditional theories in his concept of the State. His State includes both the civil and the political society. It is further expanded to include 'hegemony' as the function of integral state which also suggested tactics to overthrow the existing states. Not only this, Gramsci provided a new connotation to the 'civil society', and his conceptions are vital to understand various forms that try to perpetuate the exploitative order. And, it is

1. *Ibid.*, p. 230.
2. *Ibid.*, p. 257.
3. *Ibid.*, p. 258.
4. *Ibid.*, p. 168.

in relation to this aspect that the concept of the withering away of state was made to coincide with the disappearance of philosophy of praxis Moreover, as he explains: "It is possible to imagine the coercive element of the State withering away by degrees as ever more conscious elements of regulated society (or ethical state or civil society) make their appearance." The proletariat, after dictatorship of proletariat, "would lead to socialism; but it requires a long period of transition from capitalism to socialism"[1] as Lenin perceived it. In this long period of transition, the first stage, according to Gramsci, would necessarily be of economic transformation, which would ultimately lead to communist society. In an integral state, the preparation is not for its continuation but for its ultimate withering away, or for "the reabsorption of political society into civil society."[2]

1. Lenin, *Collected Works*, Vol. 28, p. 388.
2. Gramsci, *Selections from Prison Notebooks*, p. 253.

7

Conclusion

The logical implication that follows from the analysis of Gramsci's political philosophy in the foregoing pages is that Gramsci is the developer of the Marxist philosophy in the context of the changed and changing times. He is the developer of Marxist-Leninist ideas, even though his critics have branded him as a Hegelian and a social-democrat. This assertion calls for an account of criticism levelled against Gramsci as well as an examination of currents that claim to be his legatees.

Marx and Engels had received their schooling in the Hegelian tradition and had developed their theories against the backdrop of the Industrial Revolution. They carried a critique of past philosophies. However, the social and intellectual climate that spurred their novel thinking also limited their horizon and they could not foresee the forms of development (of their ideas) hidden in future. In fact, the immediate successors of Marx—such as Labriola (1843-1904) Mehring (1846-1919), Kautsky, (1854-1938) and Plekhanov (1856-1918) et. al.—were much concerned with the theoretical issues and tried to complete the texts of Marx. Thus, the Marxian analysis entered the specific study of arts, aesthetics literature, etc. It was only after the Russian Revolution that Marxism acquired a concrete and existential expression; and henceforth the Marxists tended to adopt Soviet system as a touchstone for testing their theories. The Russian Revolution also revealed the potential of 'revolution' hidden in other countries, and this factor forced the established governments to take cognizance of the threat posed by Marxism. It is against this scenario of active Marxist politics that Gramsci's philosophy flourished. Its relevance, therefore, has to be judged and its impact on different school has to be evoluated in the light of this scenario.

First, an analysis of the criticisms levelled against Gramsci. Various currents claiming independence from established Marxism of different countries, tried also to isolate the points of divergence in Gramsci and then to assimilate these in alternative models of communism. These currents belong to various hues; however, the main concern here is to evaluate these only insofar as they touch Gramscian political philosophy.[1]

Kolakowski takes up the issue of 'relativism' in Gramsci. For him Gramsci's rejection of 'absolute' truth for all times, rejection of Marxism as 'scientific philosophy' that 'reflected' 'reality as it was, regardless of whether we know it or not, and his emphasis on 'historicity'—all lead to relativism. Quoting Gramsci's warnings to avoid relativism, Kolakowski finds the very defect in Gramsci and reaches the conclusion that Gramsci's view of science as an element of superstructure clearly makes him a relativist and that there is in Gramsci a rejection of the view that superstructure is an expression of relations of production. There is also no suggestion in his writings of the primacy of the base or the superstructure. Kolakowski also analysis Gramsci's philosophy which makes "cognition an aspect of social development" on the same footing as economic changes, it (praxis) also suggests that "deliberate social behaviour" of men is their true attitude. As such, the theory of two kinds of *weltanschauung*—implicit and explicit—is unnecessary as it is a fact that social-classes often pursue interests contrary to accepted norms of culture

1. See chapter I.

to which they belong. Charging Gramsci with inconsistency Kolakowski finds that for Gramsci "a working man who took some action to defend his action was as much a theoretician as Marx" and this leads to nihilism. Moreover, Gramsci's supposition of 'humanly objective' and 'reality' as 'historical becoming', according to Kolakowski, marks him out totally in opposition to classical Marxism: and turns his Marxism into 'collective solipsism". Again, Gramsci's critique of materialism restored "historical immantism" or "collective subjectivism" as true philosophical content of Marxism. The struggle for hegemony, destroying the past, generates uncertainities. Thus, for Kolakowski, Gramsci's stand conflicts with Lenin's and provides an alternative communism—a communism that is more humane and democratic than any other Marxisits'.[1]

Femia,[2] Tamburrano[3] and McInnes also find Gramsci subjective realist'. McInnes[4] feels that Gramsci's attempts to get rid of Crocean transcendence leads him towards relativism. Femia regards Gramsci a Hegelian Marxist and asserts that in him 'subjectivity' is the core of Marxism, Piccone[5] finds in Gramsci's idealist Marxism an "informal and subjective method". He says, in Gramsci, "the subject never becomes completely absorbed in the logic of the objects thus, turning into a means for bureacratic manipulation. For Finocchioro,[6] Gramsci's "Crocean Marxism" first establishes Marxist foundations of Croce and then absorbs what is alive in Croce's theses of history and politics.

---

1. Kolakowski, *Main Currents of Marxism*, Vol. 3, (trans, by P.S. Falla), Oxford, Univ. Press, 1981, pp. 228-242.
2. Femia, *Gramsci's Political Thought*, also see, Femia, "Hegemony and consciousness in the thought to Antonio Gramsci, "*Political Studies*, 1975, pp. 29-47.
3. Tamburrano, quoted Femia "The Gramsci Phenomenon", *Political Studies,* 1974, p. 475.
4. McInnes, "Antonio Gramsci", *Survey*, 1964, p. 3-16.
5. Piccone, "Gramsci's Hegelian Marxism" *Political Theory* 1974 and in "Per Gramsci" *Telos*, 22, p. 74.
6. Finnocchian, "Gramsci's Crocean Marxism", *Telos,* 41, pp. 17-32.

In the light of these criticism, a return to Gramsci reveals that Marxism is "absolute historicism "and absolute humanism".[1] There is no absolute truth for all times to come; and to prove this, critique of vulgar materialism is required. Gramsci fulfills this requirement. He is emphatic that science cannot give "certainity of objective existence of the so-called external reality". He insists that it is wrong to seek such proof in science, as science "makes choice among sensations"; and in science "one establishes what is common to all men". Therefore, "we consider objective that reality that is ascertained by all men, that is, independent of every point of view, be it merely particular or that of a group". This postulates a critical approach; but this is lacking in a common sense view. The common sense view regards" "as objective a certian anachronistic subjectivity because it cannot even conceive that there could be a subjective view of the world." Realizing this limitation of science, Gramsci explains : "Science does not propose any form of metaphysical 'unknown' but it reduces what man does not know to an emirical 'non-knowledge' that does not exclude knowability but makes it dependent of development of physical and instrumental elements and of the historical intelligence of individual scientists."[2] Gramsci's fixed, causal, science is thus, a criticism of tendency to apply criticism of natural science methods to societal development as a "means of predicting and controlling human events".[3]

Gramsci's studies historical development and the development of philosophy on the basis of Marxian dictum that "mankind always sets itself such takes as it can resolve" : the task itself arises when the "material conditions for its development already exist or atleast are in the process of formation"; in other words, a "social order does not perish until all the productive forces for which it still has room have been developed and new higher relations of production have taken

---

1. See chapter III.
2. All quoted from Gramsci, "Science and Scientific Ideologies" (Trans. by Finnoechiari) *Telos*, No. 41. pp. 153-55.
3. Salamini, *Sociology of Political Praxis*, p. 68.

their place."[1] This leads to the Gramscian premise that Marxism is a theory of history and one cannot separate politics and economic from history.

In Gramsci's onalysis the "ensemble of material forces of production is the least variable element"[2] in historical development, and is to a great extent measurable. Thus the ensemble of the material forces of production is at the same time "a crystallisation of all past history and the basis of present and future history".[3] The humanly objective does not and cannot lead to nihilism. It is based on ensemble of relations that function to a large extent outside the volition of man and in which man enters albeit with a "concerte will" to chage them. The philosophies so far have been characterised by contradictions that are born of economic ensemble. With the disappearnace of contradictions, the philosophy of praxis, the very theory of capitalist contradiction, would disappear. The historicism for Gramsci is "total liberation from any form of abstract 'idealism', the real conquest of the historical world, the beginning of a new civilization".[4] The new civilization denotes a 'reign of freedom' in which morality would "become a search for the conditions necessary for the freedom of the will in a certain sense, aimed at a certain end, and the demonstration that these conditions exist. It should be a question also not of a hierarchy of ends but of a gradation of the ends to be attained, granted that what one wants to 'moralise' is not just each individual taken singly but also a whole society of individuals."[5]

Thus Gramsci's historicism, if taken arbitarily, may suggest relativism; but because it is conditioned by past and contains certain essentials, it has a goal of "transition from necessity into freedom through the society of men".[6] His historicism is dynamic and is inherent in the method of

---

1. Quoted by Gramsci, *Selections from Prison Notebooks*, p. 432
2. *Ibid.*, p. 466.
3. *Ibid.*
4. *Ibid.*, p. 399.
5. *Ibid.*, p. 410.
6. *Ibid.*, p. 407.

dialectic.[1] Any attempt to ignore dialectics lends to an insufficient understanding of Gramsci.

Gramsci accepts that a class may have an archaic conception of the World, and at the same time may occupy a highly progressive place in historical development; but he nowhere says that either the one or the other is more real. He provides the intellectuals, and particularly the collective intellectual (the party), with the task of making culture fit to the sphere of practice, and to make the worldview of that class coherent and critical. This can be done by making the class realize its historical place in the development process.

As regards materialism. Gramsci's reservaions about nomenclature has to be taken note of. He says: "Identity of terms does not mean identity of concepts".[2] The common usage of 'materialism' incudes "any practical attitude inspired by political realism;"[3] and hence he attempts to highlight 'historical' in historical materialism to separate it from traditional distortions. Gramsci's other criticisms regarding his 'idealist', 'Crocean' and 'Hegelian' connections have to be taken in this light, Moreover, as Gramsci was itent to 'combat modern ideologies in their most refined form' it required him to affirm the living forms of past philosophies. It is in this sense that the Crocean critique of positivism and mechanism was accepted by Gramsci as the "rational core of Marxism in a speculative form".[4]

Regarding base and superstructure the only point to be reiterated is Gramsci's stress on 'unity' given by 'dialectical development of contradictions' which is praxis in philosophy. The complex interplay between human will and economic structure excludes any causal relationship. But, nowhere has Gramsci deserted the Marxian notion that economics is determinant in the ultimate analysis.

---

1. See chapter III above.
2. Gramsci, *Selections from Prison Notebooks*, p. 456.
3. *Ibid.*, p. 454.
4. *Ibid.*

Althusser[1], Della Volpe and Tronti[2] are also critical of Gramsci's historicism. Tronti detects Hegelianism in Gramsci. Della Volpe is opposed to Gramsci's philosophical dialectics. The real dialectic, according to him, is a historically determinate scientific doctrine. Althusser accuses Gramsci for remaining enthralled to a Hegalian reading of Marx. Timpanaro[3] and Gruppi[4] too attack Gramsci's historicism. The main thesis of Althusser is that Marxism is not a historicism. Gramsci tends to make the theory of history and dialectical materialism coincide within historical materialism alone, although they form two distinct disciplines. After searching for philosophical problematic, Althusser also questions Gramsci's stress on ,historical materialism'. He accuses Gramsci of ignoring 'dialectical materialism' and even goes to the extent of suggesting that materialism in Gramsci sounds metaphysical. Gramsci's concept of science as an element of superstructure is also wrong according to Althusser. But all these points, if studied in the light of the analysis in previous chapters, are automatically annuled by quoting Althusser's own assessment of Gramsci. He says: "The authentically revolutionary character of Gramsci's historicism consists above all in his insistence on the political nature of philosophy in his thesis of the historical character of social formations and his correlative thesis of revolution in his demand for a unity of theory and practice"[5]

Gramsci's historicism and concept of intellectuals is often compared with Luckacs. Lukacs' reification theory is based on the concept of alienation in bourgeois civil society. Gramsci, Lukacs and Korsch, all the three stressed praxis.They affirmed it as the centre of Marxist theory in contrast to the previous marxist thinkers who had stressed on the primacy of

---

1. Althusser, *Reading Capital*, N.L.B. London, 1970.
2. Tronti and Della Volpe quoted in Gulcksmann, *Gramsci and The State*, p. 239.
3. *Ibid.*
4. Gruppi "The legacy of Gramsci", *World Marxist Review*, 1959.
5. Althusser, quoted in Glucksmann, *Gramsci and The State*, p. 342.

matter over mind. All the three[1] attacked the theory of positivism and the concept of direct causal relationship between base and superstructure. They all did not give much importance to pure economics, and thought that after the Great War, objective conditions were ripe for revolution in Western Europe, but the subjective factors were required to be mobilized. However an in depth study reveals that the problematic of Lukacs vastly differed from that of Gramsci; and hence the parting of ways.

The actual subjective consciousness of proleteriat, is not class consciousness for Lukacs. The 'ascribed' consciousness —the consciousness a class would have if it were fully aware of its own interests-is the consciousness which arises when the dialectical relationship between the subject and the object is secured. The 'fetish' character of commodities leads to reification' in which men become isolated beings with no intrinsic connection. That is why even when objective conditions for revolution are ripe there is no revolution. The need, according to Lukacs, is to make consciousness a 'deed'. In his own words: "In addtion to the mere contradiction the automatic product of capitalism—a new element is required; the consciousness of the prolatariat must become deed".[2] Elaborating the idea, he further conteds: "Only when the consciousness of the proletariat is able to point out the road along which the dialectic of history is objectively impelled . . . will the proletariat becomes the subject—object of history whose praxis will change reality.[3]

In Hegel also the unity of subject and object assumes a central place; but in him this unity is 'idealist'. In Luckacs, however, only the proletariat could embody this unity as its ascribed consciousness; and, thus, its objective role in hostory becomes consonent. He further contends that it is this unity

---

1. However, during the 30s, the three marxist thinkers took different roads Korsch left Marxist movement after his condemnation by Comintern; Lukacs toed Stalinist line.
2. Lukacs, *History and Class Consciousness* Merlic Press, London, 1971, p. 178.
3. *Ibid.*, p. 197.

the interaction between subject and object that is the "crucial determinant of dialectics."[1] As such, the whole, the totality; has primacy over parts; and all facts could be understood only in relation to the totality. But this totality of reality is destroyed due to reification. Only the class (proletariat) which "is itself a totality is crpable of penetration"[2] into totality. Thus proletariat as the subject of thought in society effects unity between cause and result of historical process in theory and practice.

The hallmarks of Luckacs[3] theory are his concept of totality, reification and 'ascribed' class consciousness. He is critical of Engels' dialectics of nature. His concept of philosophy as not about histoiy but the "*conceptual expression of history itself*" makes philosophy a critical and conscious expression of the present. The class consciousness is directly related to the class. At initial stages Lukacs felt no need of a party or intellectuals independent of the previous mode of production; rather, for him, intellectuals become continuers of bourgeois philosophy, because there is no difference between the social beings of the two classes in a reified society. Lukacs, thus, identified class in terms of ideological dominance; and not on mere (!) economic contradictions.[4]

In Lukacs' Hegelian framework the treatment of issues that also concern Gramsci is vastly different. His critique of economism is based on philosophy as 'present'; whereas for Gramsci the 'present' contains many tendencies and philosophy tends to resolve the contradictions. Not only this. In Gran sci, philosophy itself is a part of contradictions which it seeks to resolve leading to its ultimate dissolution. Moreover, there is no theory of superstructure in Lukacs, whereas class struggle and the role of superstructure is vital in Gramscian

---

1. *Ibid.*, n 6, p. 24.
2. *Ibid* , p. 49.
3. Lukacs quoted inG lucksmann, *Gramsci and The State*, p. 223.
4. Lukacs later on shifted his position many times. We are concerned with only such issues on relate to Gramsci.

philosophy. This also suggests multitudes of worldviews in fragmented societies, and the need to make masses' worldview critical to enable them to exercise hegemony. In Gramsci's scheme, then, intellectuals play a crucial role, being organized in a party and having autonomous views (from the previous mode of thinking); their aim being to infuse awareness of the struggle in the masses.

Gramsci's concepts of intellectuals, party, and state have also generated various controversies His stress on 'democratic centralism' and his theory of 'hegemonic struggle' are cited as examples of his being a reformist or a social democrat or even a neo-Marxist. The main currents that claim Gramsci to be their forerunner are-Eurocommunists, the PCI with its policy of *Via Italiana Al Socialismo* and New Left thinkers with Trotskyite leanings.

The PCI under Togliatti adopted an independent national policy under the concept of 'Third Road to Socialism'.[1] In this task of building the party, Togliatti claimed Gramscian moorings of his ideas. This led to a whole series of debate regarding Gramsci's place in the PCI. One commentator[2] went to the extent of accusing Gramsci of being active in "attempts to salvage bourgeois world". For Asor Rosa, Gramsci was an agrarian populist. Marcini and Galli saw Gramsci's adverse influence on PCI inasmuch as there was an excessive stress on rural masses in subsequent PCI programmes.[3] The claims of Togliatti to follow and continue Gramsci's views were inherent in PCI's efforts for alliance to prepare for revolution; but this needs be understood in the context of the specificity of Italian situation. Togliatti interpreted hegemony as equal to the dictatorship of the proletariat.

---

1. Togliatti advocating 'polycentrism' in communist movement decided to develop policies of PCI independent of C P.S.U. He also propunded policy of 'peaceful road to socialism' and equidistance from China and Soviet Union. All constitute 'third road' to socialism.
2. R. Orfei, quoted in Marcini and Galli, "Gramsci's presence" *Government and Opposition*, pp. 325.
3. *Ibld.*, pp. 325-337.

The contentions regarding differences between Togliatti and Gramsci are raised by Tarrow,[1] S. White,[2] Fiori[3] and Nemeth[4]. The issue of acceptance or rejection of particular institutions of state as reflected in Togliattis participation in successive governments, does not appear to be in conformity with Gramsci's stress that capitalist Institutions are geared for the good of their class and there is a need to evolve alternative hegemonic apparatus and institutions (the factory Council, being one such institution). Willians regards Togliatti's version of hegemony "a crude vulgarization with rival classes wearing their ideologies like uniforms."[5] The Togliattian view of class is also significant. For Gramsci classes are rooted in produ- tion even when formed through a dialectical process. For Togliatti classes are to be interpreted in additive terms and even petit-bourgeois are to be included in alliances. In fact the differences between the views of Gramsci and Togliatti can be traced back to the time of the Seventh Comintern Congress (1926) where Togliatti failed to convey to the Congress. Gramsci's reservations regarding treatment of dissidents (Trotsky, et al.) in C.P.S.U. Fiori[6] ventures that Gramsci appeared at that time ready to work outside the PCI and form a nuclei to perform among other tasks a critique of PCI. Togliatti's collaboration with forces not specifically proletarian (in various Governments) as an affirmation of Gramsci's slogan of Constituent Assembly' also appears as an effort to hide his reformist tendencies. The 'Third Road' produced glorious electoral results but gradually faded as its revolutionary content was watered down.

---

1. Tarrow, *Peasant Communism in Italy*, Yale Univ. Press, London, 1967, pp. 112-120.
2. S. White, "Gramsci and Italian Communist Party" *Government and Opposition*, 7,2, 1972, pp. 188 205.
3. See Fiori, *Antonio Gramsci—Life of A Revolutionary* NLB, London, 1970.
4. See Nemeth, *Gramsci's Philosophy*, Harvesta Press, Sussex, 1980.
5. William, "Concept of Egemonia in Gramsci", *Journal of History of Ideas*, 1960, xxi, 4, p. 587.
6. Fiori, *Antonio Gramsci—Life of a Revolutionary* pp. 292-93.

This experience later on gave birth to Eurocommunism. Thus Eurocommunism, inherent in the Third Road and highlighting local conditions was characterised by attempts to ignore the question of the natuie of the state, stress on democracy, and electoral policies. It had no common theoretical matrix; it was rather marked by a distance from orthodoxy, with its stress on specific conditions and different tacties. It denounced bureaucratism of sstablished communist regimes and emphasised on decentralization.

The Eurocommunists claim Gramsci as their precursor on specific issues such as "a rejection of theoretical rigidity and the authoritanism of the Comintern and an emphasis on national cultures, on democracy within the party, on freedom speech and research for intellectuals"[1] Moreover, it is held that Gramsci's strategies for seizure of state and provision for hegemonic struggles also lead to the Eurcommunist concept of "peaceful transition".[2]

These views are disputed by the New Left who regard Gramsci's 'war of position'[3] as a preparatory step to insurrection. Born as a reaction against American Vietnames War, the New Left had emerged as a voice of minorities and of the working class. The New Left regarded early writings of Marx as more relevant for their stress on 'alienation'. It regards Gramsci's imperative need to win the working class most vital to the success of revolution. "It is in this time that Anderson says: "The means of achieving this conquest not of the institutions of the state, but of the conviction of workers although in the end there will be no separation between the two-are the prime agenda of any real socialist stragegy today."[4]

Needless to say that all the above views highlight partial aspects of Gramsci's thought. In fact, their adherence to one or the other tenet of his (Gramsci's) Marxism reveals that what

---

1. Marzoni, *The Promise of Eurocommunism* Lawerence, Hill & Co. Connecticut 1980, p. 35.
2. *Ibid.*, p. 36.
3. See above Chapter VI.
4. Anderson, "The Antinomies of Antonio Gramsci", *New Left Review*, No. 100 p. 78.

they are searching is not their ideational moorings but justification for their specific stances. None of the currents above have any dialectical relationship with Gramsci's thought.

Gramsci's differences with Stalin's views are to be placed in historical perspective. Gramsci emphasized on Lennist line of achieving the unity of the party which consists "in there not being within party two political lines which are completely different on all questions."[1]

As the communist movement itself later proved Stalinist aberrations were contrary to Leninism which was supported by the active Gramsci till his impriosnment. It is a moot question whether Gramsci would have continued in the PCI during Ltalinist period had be been free, with no bearing on his political philosophy as illustrated in his writings.

The above discussion or Gramsci's so-called connections with different hues of Marxism in a tabloid form suggests certain basic issues of his political philosophy. In fact, the cardinal points of one's philosophy could be brought into relief only when its raw material is scanned throughly; and, that is exactly what has been attempted in the preceding chapters. Gramsci himself endorses this method when he says: "A work can never be identified with the raw materials collected for its compilation. It is the definitive choice, the way the component elements are arranged, the greater or lesser importance given to this or that element of those collected in the preparatory phase which are precisely what constitutes effective work".[2]

In short, the contention is that the main points of Gramscis' political philosophy, that have been suggested in the preceding pages by way of analysing Gramsci's connections with various hues of Marxism, have already been brought forth in the preceding chapters by way of an elaborate (as far as possible) analysis of the "raw matterials" that Gramsci left behind.

---

1. Gramsci, *Selections from Political Writings*, Vol 2, p. 426.
2. Gramsci, *Selections from Prison Notebooks*, p. 385.

The deductions drawn in those chapters are recapitulated here, mainly in the words of Gramsci himself. To start "an introduction to the study of philosophy must expound in synthetic form the problems that have grown up in the process of the development of culture as a whole and which are partially reflected in history of philosophy".[1] Hence the first chapter, explaining philosophy and the historical development. As it is "not a question of introducing from scratch a scientific from of thought...but of renovating and making critical an existing activity".[2] The need is to carry a criticism "of the philosophy of the intellectuals out of which the history of philosophy developed and which can be considered as marking the highpoints of the progress made by the common sense."[3] Thus, the second chapter deals with the ideational currents that influenced Gramsci. Out of this fertile terrain the worldview of Gramsci was formed; and, the "choice and the criticism of the world is also a political matter."[4] The systematic exposition of the world is characteristic of human nature. As such, "man is essentially 'political' since it is through the activity of transforming and consciously directing other men that man realises his 'humanity', his human nature".[5] The political activity of men, if made coherent and critical by the philosophy of praxis, is rooted in the historical reality of mode of production. The philosophy of praxis—dialectical unity between theory and conscious practice has two tasks to perform; first, "to combat modern ideologies in their most refined form", and second, to "educate the popular masses."[6] To perform the first task the need is to carry out a study of intellectuals who give the class of their origin a "homogeneity, and an awareness of its own function not only in economic but also in the social and political fields."[7] Both

1. *Ibid.*, p. 330.
2. *Ibid.*
3. *Ibid.*, p. 331.
4. *Ibid.*, p. 327.
5. *Ibid.*, p. 360.
6. *Ibid.*
7. *Ibid.*, p. 15.

the tasks are largely performed on the terrain of superstructure. The intellectuals try to make commonsense of masses critical. "The relation between commonsense and the upper level of philosophy is assured by 'politics'".[1] Politics is an autonomous science, and its aim is the founding of a new State. A state is generally thought of as a coercive authority; but in actual practice it is "hegemony+dictatorship".[2] To overthrow such a state, different strategies in different countries are required. If it is true that no life of State can avoid passing through a phase of economic-corporate primitivism, it may be deduced that the context of the political hegemony of the new type of State must be "predominantly of an economic order". The end-stage of the coercive element of the state withering away by degrees, leads to the emergence of ever more conspicuous elements of regulated society."[3]

Marx initiated discussions about 'praxis' and 'ideological' level of consciousness, These were given shape by Lenin. However, Lenin's praxis-the concretization of these in the Soviet Union also led to their canonization and ossification by his successors. The Western Marxists, either mechanistically applied Marx and Lenin; or searched for theoretical matrix in other schools that resulted in the diffusion of the revolutionary fervour of Marxism. Gramsci is one political philosopher and activist (and philosophy for him is praxis) who posed a real threat to the Fascists in his time. Imprisonment failed to prevent him from outlining his dialectical development. As a politician, grounded in Marxist tenets, he sought to analyse specific condtions of development of society in both 'old' technologically advanced and 'newly' emergent nations. He, thus, provided a link between the Eastern and Western varieties of Marxism by highlighting the cardinal points of dialectical-historical-materialism and praxis. There may be ambiguities in his political philosophy that may have given rise to some partial, sectaian currents,[4] but in the historical

1. *Ibid.*
2. *Ibid.*, p. 230.
3. *Ibid.*, p. 263.
4. See same chapter above.

context, Gramsci remained a Marxist armed with theoretical arsenal, steeped in Leninist practices, who showed the way for revolution in the modern-day complex societies. The base-superstructure analogy, role of party based on democratic centralism as well as the transient nature of philosophy etc. are highly original themes developed dialectically independent of any direct contact with Leninist texts and grounded in specific Italian variety of Marxism.

But, from this vantage point he created a worldview of Marxism, and reasserted its international character and relevance. Indeed, he can be credited with being the real successor of Marx and Lenin. Gramsci's political philosophy stirred hopes of world revolution because 'philosophy' for him is 'praxis' is contained in 'politics'.

The philosophy of praxis bases itself as a part of contradiction and tries to resolve it by actively intervening in the conjuncture. It world be superceded as a worldview, with the historical disappearance of the class-struggle. Thus, withering away of the state and of philosophy are two aspects of the same reality. Through the phase of economic transformation of society and subsequent appearance of the class-less society, the stage of 'integral state' would be reached, leading to the process of the ultimate away of the state too the "reabsorption of political society into civil society."

This is Revolution. Gramsci's Political Philosophy rekindled hopes of a world revolution.

Bibliography

PRIMARY SOURCES

Books

Modern Prince and other Writings (Ed. L. Marks) Lawrence and Wishart, London, 1937.

Selections from Prison Notebooks, (edited and translated by Q. Hoare and N. Smith) Lawrence and Wishart, London, 1971.

History, Philosophy and Culture in the Young Gramsci (Ed. by Piccone and Cavalcanti) Telos Press, St. Louis, 1975.

Letters from Prison (Selected, translated introduced by Lowner) Quartet Books, London, 1975.

Selections from Political Writings 1910-1920 (Translated by Mathews, Edited by Hoare) Lawrence and Wishart, London, 1977.

Selections from Political Writings 1921-1926 (Edited and translated by Hoare and Smith)) Lawrence and Wishart, London 1978.

Gramsci's Cultural Writings (Ed. by Forgas and Smith) Haward Univ. Press, Cambridge, 1985.

Articles

"In Search of Educational Principles" *New Left Review*, 32, pp. 53-62.

"Notes from Gramsci", *Promethean Review*, 4, 1959.

"Selection from Gramsci", *New Reasoner*, 9, 10, 1959.

The New Ediaburgh Review, (Ed. C.K. Maisels) 1974, 3 special Gramsci issues.

"Science and Scientific Ideologies", (translated by Finocchiaro) *Telos*, 41.

"Marxism and Culture in Italy", *Times Litrary Supplement* 28.8.48.

"More About Gramsci, *Times Litrary Supplement*, 5-12-52.

The following are the standard Italian editions of Gramsci's works, all published by Einaudi:

Scritti Giovanili, Turin, 1958.

L'Ordine Nuovo, Turin, 1955.

Socialismo e Fascismo, Turin, 1966.

La Costruzione del partito comunista, Turin, 1971.

II materialismo storico e la Filosofia di Benedetto Croce, Turin, 1966.

Note sul Machiavelli, sulla Politica e sullo Stato moderno, Turin. 1955.

Gli Intellettuali e L'Organizazione della Culture, Turin, 1966.

Passato e Presente, Turin, 1966.

Il Risorgimento, Turin, 1966.

Letteratura e Vita nazionale, Turin, 1966.

Quaderni del carcere, (edited by Valentino Gerratana), Turin, 1975.

SECONDARY SOURCES

Books

Adamson, W.L. *Hegemony and Revolution—A Study of Gramsci's Political and cultural Theory*, Univ. of California Press, Berkeley, 1980.

Afanasyev, V *Scientific Communism*, Progress Publishers, Moscow, 1967.

Althusser, L., *For Marx*, Penguin Press, London, 1969.

Althusser, L., *Reading Capital*, N.L.B., London, 1970.

Althusser, L., *Lenin and Philosophy and other Essays*, N.L B., London, 1971.

Avineri S., *The Social and Political Though of Karl Marx*, University Press Cambridge, 1971.

Barkenau, Franz, *World Communism—A History of Communist International*, University of Michigan Press, Ann. Arbor, 1960.

Boggs Carl, *Gramsci's Marxism*, Pluto Press, London, 1976.

Lichtheim *Marxism—A Historical and Critical Studies* Routledge and Kegan Paul, London, 1961.

Lipset and Reinhart (Ed.) *Class Status and Power* Free Press, Glencoe, 1953.

Lipset, *Political Man*, Anchor book, New York, 1963.

Mandel, *from Stalinism to Eurocommunism*, NLB, London, 1977.

Marx, Engels, Lenin, *On Historical Materialism*, Progress Publishers Moscow 1978.

Marx, *Early Writings*, Penguin Books in association with New Left Review, Harmonds Worths, 1977.

Marzonic, *The Open Marxism of Antonio Gramsci*, Cameroom Associates, New York, 1951.

Marzonic, *The Promise of Eurocommunism*, Lawrence Hill and Co., Connecticut, 1980.

McLellan, D., *Marx*, Fontana, London, 1975.

McLellan D., *Marxism After Marx* Macmillan, London, 1975.

MaLellan, D., *Marx Grundrisse* Macmillan, London, 1977.

McInnes, N., *The Communist Pary of Europe*, Oxford Univ. Press, London, 1976.

Michel, *Political Parties* The Free Press Glencoe, Illinois 1949.

Mill, C.W. *The Marxist* The Dell Publishing Co. New York, 1962.

Mouffe and Shoustock, *Gramsci and Marxist Theory* Rougledge and K. Paul, London, 1979.

Nadels, *Contemporary Capitalism and Middle Classes*, Progress publishers, Moscow, 1983.

Nemeth, Thomas, *Gramsci's Philosophy—a Critical Philosophy*, Harvester Press, Sussex, 1980.

Newfield, *Italy—School for Awakening Countries* Carnell Univ., Ithaca, 1961.

Pareto V., *The Mind and Society* (Arthur Livington Ed.) Harcoat Brac, New York, 1939.

Parsons T., *On Intellectuals*, Doubleday, New York, 1969.

Piccone, P., *Italian Marxism*, Callifornia Press, 1983.

Plekhnov, *Frundamental Problem of Marxism* (trans J. Kalzer), Lawrence and Wishart, London, 1969.

Plotke and Boggs, *The Politics of Eurocommunism* NLB, London.

Pozzolini, *Antonio Gramsci—An Introduction To His Thought*, Pluto Press, London, 1967.

Proccacci, *History of the Italian People*, Penguin, Harwordsworth, 1973.

Salamini, *The Sociology of Political Praxis*, Routledge and Kagan Paul, London, 1981.

Sorel G., *Reflection on Violence*, Collian, New York, 1961.

Sassoon, A.S., *Gramsci's Politics*, Croomhelms Ltd., London, 1980.

Sasoon Donald, *The Strategy of Italian Communist Party*, Frances Printer Ltd., London, 1983.

Seton Watson, *Italy from Liberation to Fascism*, Methium and Co., London, 1967.

Sforza, Count Carld, *The Living Thought of Machiavelli*, Cassel and Co. Ltd., London, 1942.

Sforza C., *Contemporary Italy—Its Intellectual and Moral Origins*, F. Muller Ltd., London, 1940.

Shaw, W.H., *Marxis Theory of History*, Hutchinson Press, London, 1975.

Silk, Robert Kilroy, *Socialism Since Marx*, Allenlane and Penguin Press, London, 1972.

Simon R., *Gramsci's Political Thought*, Lawrence and Wishart, London, 1982.

Smith, *Italy—A Modern History*, Univ. of Michigen, An Arbour, 1959.

Tarrow and Blackmer, *Italian Communism*, University Press, Princeton, 1975.

Tarrow, *Peasant Communism in Southern Italy*, Yale University Press, London, 1967.

Timpanary, *On Materialism*, Princeton University Press, 1968.

Togliatti *Lectures on Fascism*, Lawrence and Wishart, London, 1976.

Togliatti, *On Gramsi and other Essays*, Lawrence and Wishart, London, 1979.

Thompson, *Europe since Napoleon*, Penguin, Harmondsworth, 1966.

Trotsky, *The Permanent Revolution—Results and Prospects*, Pathfinder, New York, 1969.

Urry, *The Anatomy of Capitalist Societies—The Economy, Civil Society and the State*, MacMillan Press, London, 1981.

Vazquez, *The Philosophy of Praxis*, Merlin Press, London, 1977.

William G.A., *The Proletarian Order*, Pluto Press, London, 1975.

Young, H., *The Italian Left—A Short History of Political Socialism in Italy*, Longmann and Green, London, 1949.

Articles and Journals

Adler, "Factory Councils, Gramsci and the Industrialist.' *Telos*, no. 31, 1977.

Amendola, "The Italian road to socialism-an interview" *New Left Review* no. 32.

Anderson, "Introduction to Gramsci "*New Left Review*, no. 51.

Anderson, The Antinomies of António Gramsci *New Left Review*, no. 100, 1976.

Andreucci, Sylvers, "The Italian Communist write their history" *Science and Society*, no. 40, 1976.

Arismendi, "On interpretations of Marx's Philosophy" *World Marxist Review*, no. 4, 1983.

Bates, "Gramsci and the theory of Hegemony" *Journal of History of Ideas*, 1975.

Baldan, "Gramsci as an Historian of 30s" *Telos*, no. 31, 1977.

Bonncy, "Gramsci on law, morality and power", *International Journal of Sociology of Law*, Vol. II, May, 1983.

Boggs, Gramsci's Prison Notebooks" *Socialist Revolution* II, 12, 1972.

Bonacchi, "The Council Communist" *Telos*, 30, 1976.

Cammeti, "Two Recent polemics on the character of Italian Risorgimento "*Science and Society*. no. 27, 1963.

Davidson, "Varying seasons of Gramscian studies", *Political Studies*, no. XX, 1972.

Davidson, "Gramsci and Lenin", *Socialist Register*, 1974.

Davidson, "Gramsci and Reading Machiavelli" *Science and Society*, 37, 1, 1973.

Debray R. "Schema for a Study of Gramsci", *Political Studies* XX, 4.

Edmund, Jacobitti, "Labriola, Croce and Italian Marxism, "*Journal of History of Ideas* Vol. 36, 1975.

Femia J,V., "The Gramsci Phenomenon" *Political Studies*, 1974.

Femia J.V., "Gramsci and Via Italian" *Government and Opposition*, 1979.

Femia J.V., "Hemegony and Consciousness in the Thought of Gramsci" *Political Studies*, XXIII, 1975.

Femia, "Review article" Gramsci's Patrimony" *Journal of Political Science*, Vol. 1, 13, 1983.

Finocchioro, "Gramsci's Crocean Marxism, *Telos*, no. 41.

Gruppi, "The Legacy of Gramsci"' *World Marxist Review*, 12, vol. 2, 1951.

Hallett, "Antonio Gramsci" *Political Affairs* no. 40, April 1958, pp. 55-59.

Harvey James, "Antonio Gramsci," *Marxism Today* no. 4, 1967.

Harwley, J.P. "Antonio Gramsci's Marxism", Class, State and Work" *Social Problem* Vol. 27, June 1980.

Karabel "Revolutionary Contradictions—Antonio Gramsci and The Problem of Intellectuals" *Politics and Society* Vol. 6(2) 1976 Okiernan, "Gramsci and Marxism". *The Socialist Register*, 1972.

Girling, "Thailand in Gramscian Perspective" *Politic Affairs* Vol. 57, 1984.

Marcini & Galli "Gramsci's presence, "*Government and Opposition*" no. III., 1968.

Markovic, "Gramsci on Unity of Politics and Philosophy" *Praxis* no. 3, 1967, pp. 333-339.

Martinelli. "In Defence of Dialetics" *Berkley Journal of Sociology*, no. 13, 1968, pp. 1-27.

McInnes, "Antonio Gramsci", *Survey*, 1964.

McInnes Neil, "From Marx to Marcuse" *Survey* 1971.

Mrrtin Clark, "The patron saint of the Left" *Times Literary Supplemen*, 31, Oct. 1975.

Maks, "Antonio Gramsci" *Marxist Quarterly*, no. 4, 1956.

Margi, "Antonio Gramsci" *New Left Review*, no. 60.

Merrington, "Theory and practice in Gramsci's Marxism *Socialist Register*, 1968.

Mouffe, Sassoon, "On Gramsci", *Economy and Society*, no. 6, 1977.

Pagri. L. "Gramsci's General theory of Marxism" *Telos*, no. 33, 1977.

Piccone, P., "Gramsci's Hegelian Marxism", *Political Theory*, Vol. 2, 1974.

Piccone, P., "Per Gramsci" *Telos*, no. 22, 1974-75.

Piccone. P., "Gramsci's Marxism-Beyond Lenin and Togliatti "*Theory and Society* 1976.

Rossi-Doria, "The Land Tenure System and class in Southern Italy "*American Historical Review*, LXIV, 1958.

Sen. Mohit. "Leninism of Gramsci" *Marxist Miscellany* no. 5, 1974.

Salamone, "The Risorgimento between Ideology and History" *American Historical.*

Todd, "Ideological similarities in Gramsci and Mao", *Journal of History of ideas*, Vol. 35, no. 1, 1975.

White, S., "Gramsci and the Italian Communist Party", *Government and Opposition* 7(2), 1972.

Williams, "Concept of Egemonia in the though of Antonio Gramsci, "*Journal of History of Ideas*, 1975.

Kaviraj, S. "The Subtler side of Domination", *Teaching Politics*, 1977.

Webster, R.A., "Autarchy, Expansion, and the underlying continuity of the Lalian State "*Italian Quarterly*, 1964.

Special Gramsci Numbers

Economic and Political Weekly, Vol. XXIII, no. 5, Jan. 30, 1988.

New Edinburgh Review, 1974, Vol. 23-4, 25, 26, 27 Ed. by C.K. Maisal.

New Reasoner, no. 89, 10, 1959.

Promethean Review, no. 4, 1959.
Radical America, May-June, 1980.

Encyclopaedia and Dictionaries

Carr. Coulson, Eagle, Hutchinson (Ed.) *The Oxford Illustrated Dictionary*, Clarendon Press, Oxford, 1984.

Edwards, Tyron (revised and enlarged by Catervas; J, Edwards, Ralnh Emerson, Brown),

New *Dictionary of Thought*, Standard Book Company, New York 1966.

Frilov, I., (Ed.), *Dictionary of Philosophy*, Progress Publishers, Moscow, 1980.

Hastings, J (Ed.) *Encyclopaedia of Religion and Ethics*, Vol, X, T & T. Clark, Edinburg, 1963.

Kirkpatrick, E.M. (Ed.) *Chambers 20th Century Dictionary*, Allied Publishers, Bombay, 1984.

Runes, (Ed.), *Dictionary of Philosophy*, Vision Press, London, 1982.

Scruton, R., *A Dictionary of Political Thought*, Pan books in association with MacMillan Press, London, 1982.

Index